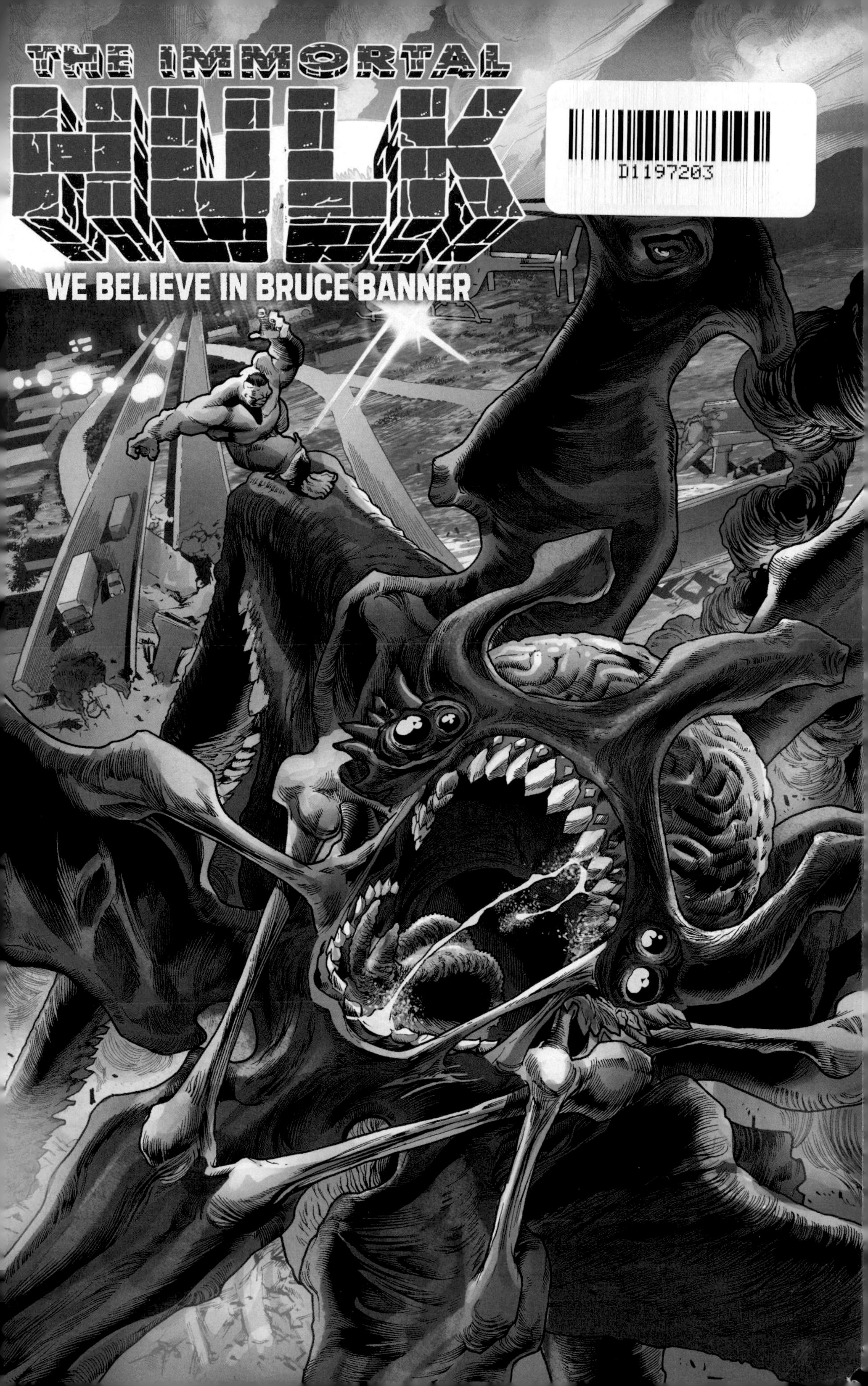
THE IMMORTAL
HULK
WE BELIEVE IN BRUCE BANNER

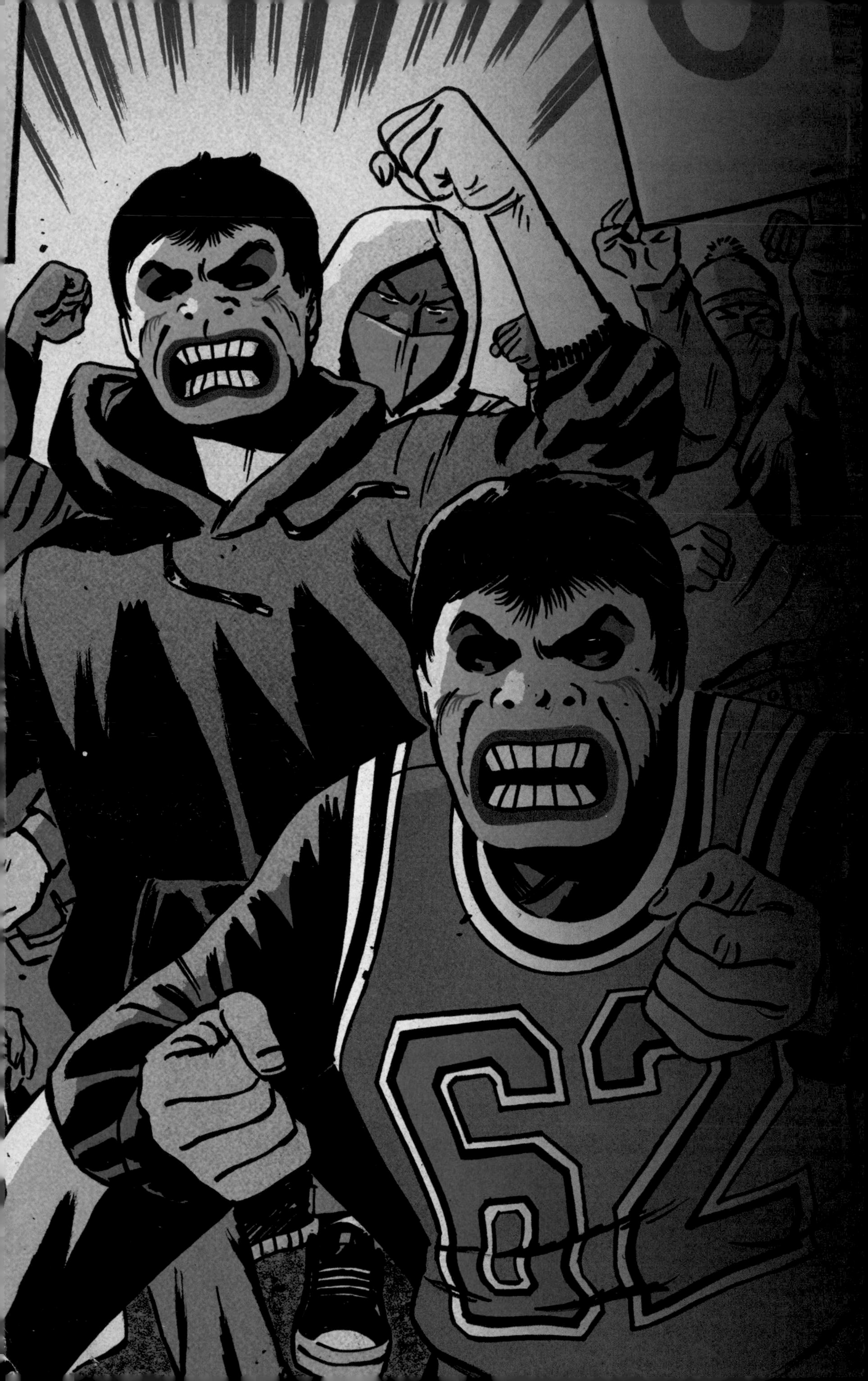

THE IMMORTAL HULK

WE BELIEVE IN BRUCE BANNER

AL EWING
WRITER

JOE BENNETT [#26-27, #29-30] AND
TOM REILLY & **MATÍAS BERGARA** [#28]
PENCILERS

RUY JOSÉ [#26-27, #29-30], **BELARDINO BRABO** [#27, #29-30],
MARC DEERING [#27], **SEAN PARSONS** [#27], **TOM REILLY** [#28],
MATÍAS BERGARA [#28] AND **CAM SMITH** [#29-30]
INKERS

PAUL MOUNTS [#26-27, #29-30] & **CHRIS O'HALLORAN** [#28]
COLOR ARTISTS

VC'S CORY PETIT
LETTERER

ALEX ROSS
COVER ARTIST

SARAH BRUNSTAD
ASSOCIATE EDITOR

WIL MOSS
EDITOR

TOM BREVOORT
EXECUTIVE EDITOR

COLLECTION EDITOR: MARK D. BEAZLEY
ASSISTANT MANAGING EDITOR: MAIA LOY
ASSISTANT MANAGING EDITOR: LISA MONTALBANO
SENIOR EDITOR, SPECIAL PROJECTS: JENNIFER GRÜNWALD

VP PRODUCTION & SPECIAL PROJECTS: JEFF YOUNGQUIST
BOOK DESIGNER: ADAM DEL RE
SVP PRINT, SALES & MARKETING: DAVID GABRIEL
EDITOR IN CHIEF: C.B. CEBULSKI

HULK
CREATED BY
STAN LEE &
JACK KIRBY

IMMORTAL HULK VOL. 6: WE BELIEVE IN BRUCE BANNER. Contains material originally published in magazine form as IMMORTAL HULK (2018) #26-30. First printing 2020. ISBN 978-1-302-92050-0. Published by MARVEL WORLDWIDE, INC., a subsidiary of MARVEL ENTERTAINMENT, LLC. OFFICE OF PUBLICATION: 1290 Avenue of the Americas, New York, NY 10104.

Printed in Canada. KEVIN FEIGE, Chief Creative Officer; DAN BUCKLEY, President, Marvel Entertainment; JOHN NEE, Publisher; JOE QUESADA, EVP & Creative Director; TOM BREVOORT, SVP of Publishing; DAVID BOGART, Associate Publisher & SVP of Talent Affairs; Publishing & Partnership; DAVID GABRIEL, VP of Print & Digital Publishing; JEFF YOUNGQUIST, VP of Production & Special Projects; DAN CARR, Executive Director of Publishing Technology; ALEX MORALES, Director of Publishing Operations; DAN EDINGTON, Managing Editor; SUSAN CRESPI, Production Manager; STAN LEE, Chairman Emeritus. For information regarding advertising in Marvel Comics or on Marvel.com, please contact Vit DeBellis, Custom Solutions & Integrated Advertising Manager, at vdebellis@marvel.com. For Marvel subscription inquiries, please call 888-511-5480. **Manufactured between 1/24/2020 and 2/25/2020 by SOLISCO PRINTERS, SCOTT, QC, CANADA.**

10 9 8 7 6 5 4 3 2 1

26

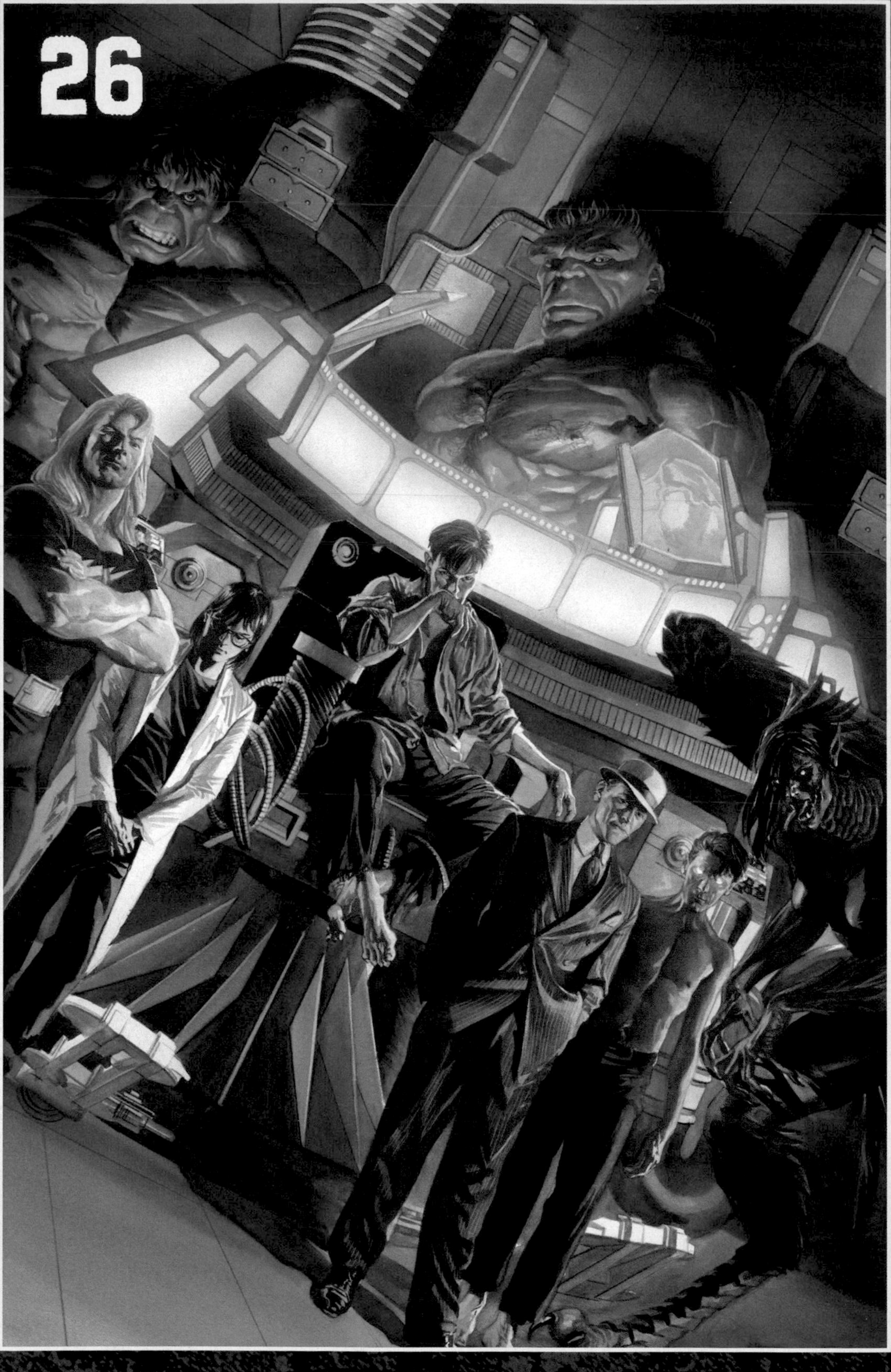

"THAT STONY LAW I STAMP TO DUST; AND SCATTER RELIGION ABROAD
TO THE FOUR WINDS AS A TORN BOOK, & NONE SHALL GATHER THE LEAVES..."

— WILLIAM BLAKE, *AMERICA: A PROPHECY*

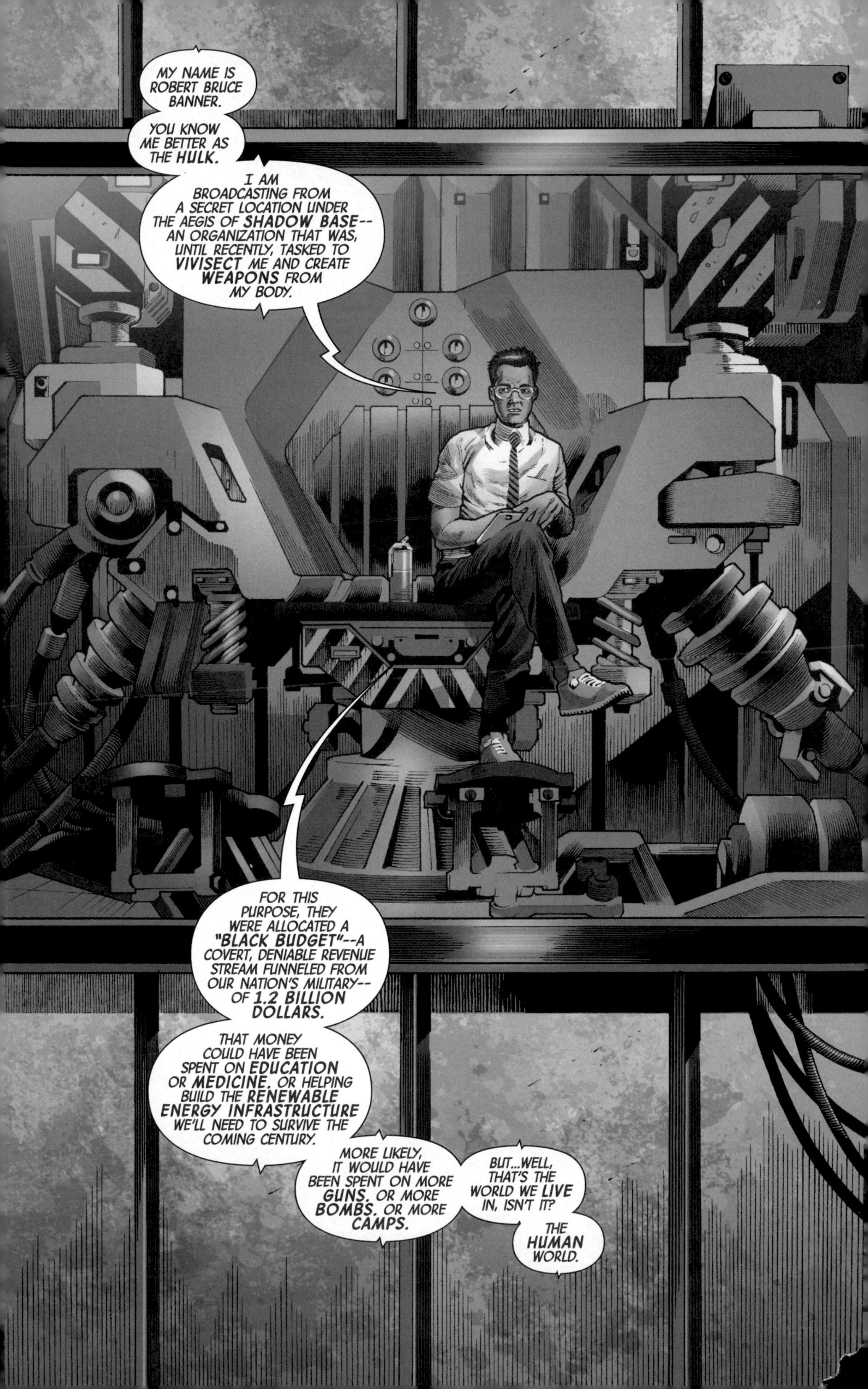
MY NAME IS ROBERT BRUCE BANNER.
YOU KNOW ME BETTER AS THE HULK.
I AM BROADCASTING FROM A SECRET LOCATION UNDER THE AEGIS OF SHADOW BASE-- AN ORGANIZATION THAT WAS, UNTIL RECENTLY, TASKED TO VIVISECT ME AND CREATE WEAPONS FROM MY BODY.
FOR THIS PURPOSE, THEY WERE ALLOCATED A "BLACK BUDGET"--A COVERT, DENIABLE REVENUE STREAM FUNNELED FROM OUR NATION'S MILITARY-- OF 1.2 BILLION DOLLARS.
THAT MONEY COULD HAVE BEEN SPENT ON EDUCATION OR MEDICINE. OR HELPING BUILD THE RENEWABLE ENERGY INFRASTRUCTURE WE'LL NEED TO SURVIVE THE COMING CENTURY.
MORE LIKELY, IT WOULD HAVE BEEN SPENT ON MORE GUNS. OR MORE BOMBS. OR MORE CAMPS.
BUT...WELL, THAT'S THE WORLD WE LIVE IN, ISN'T IT?
THE HUMAN WORLD.

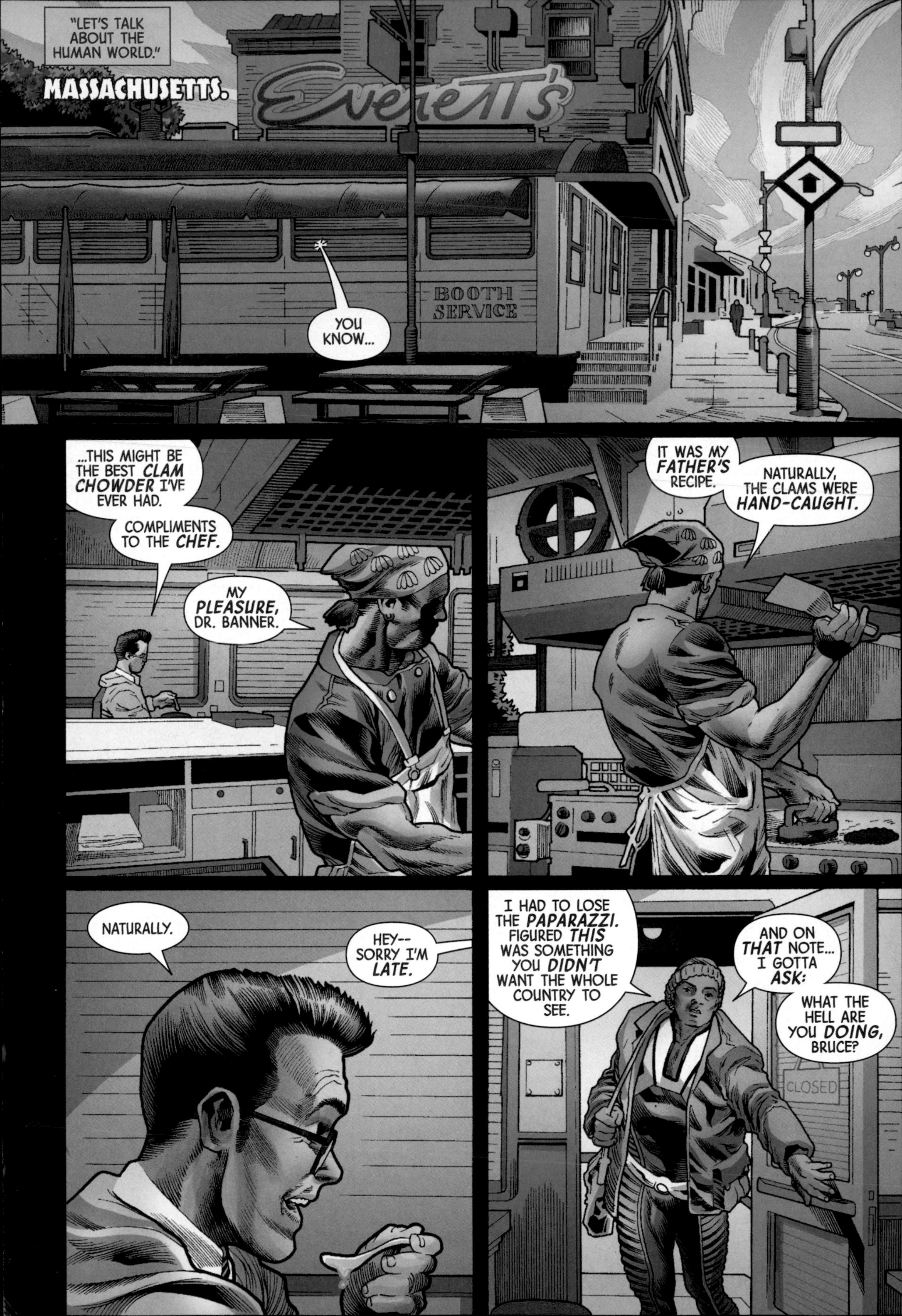
"LET'S TALK ABOUT THE HUMAN WORLD."
MASSACHUSETTS.
Everett's
BOOTH SERVICE
YOU KNOW...
...THIS MIGHT BE THE BEST CLAM CHOWDER I'VE EVER HAD.
COMPLIMENTS TO THE CHEF.
MY PLEASURE, DR. BANNER.
IT WAS MY FATHER'S RECIPE.
NATURALLY, THE CLAMS WERE HAND-CAUGHT.
NATURALLY.
HEY-- SORRY I'M LATE.
I HAD TO LOSE THE PAPARAZZI. FIGURED THIS WAS SOMETHING YOU DIDN'T WANT THE WHOLE COUNTRY TO SEE.
AND ON THAT NOTE... I GOTTA ASK:
WHAT THE HELL ARE YOU DOING, BRUCE?
CLOSED

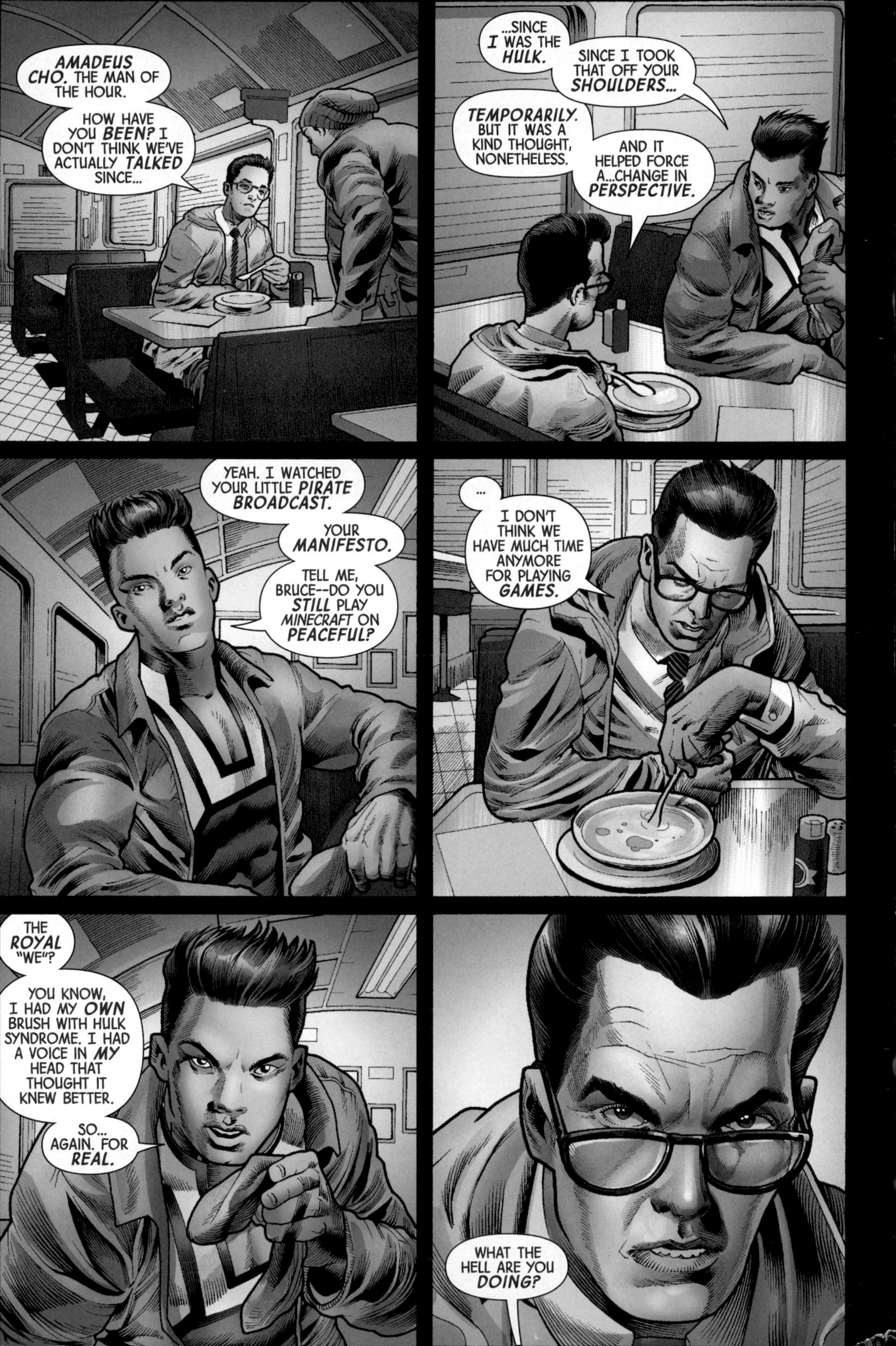
AMADEUS CHO. THE MAN OF THE HOUR.
HOW HAVE YOU BEEN? I DON'T THINK WE'VE ACTUALLY TALKED SINCE...
...SINCE I WAS THE HULK.
SINCE I TOOK THAT OFF YOUR SHOULDERS...
TEMPORARILY. BUT IT WAS A KIND THOUGHT, NONETHELESS.
AND IT HELPED FORCE A...CHANGE IN PERSPECTIVE.
YEAH. I WATCHED YOUR LITTLE PIRATE BROADCAST.
YOUR MANIFESTO.
TELL ME, BRUCE--DO YOU STILL PLAY MINECRAFT ON PEACEFUL?
...
I DON'T THINK WE HAVE MUCH TIME ANYMORE FOR PLAYING GAMES.
THE ROYAL "WE"?
YOU KNOW, I HAD MY OWN BRUSH WITH HULK SYNDROME. I HAD A VOICE IN MY HEAD THAT THOUGHT IT KNEW BETTER.
SO... AGAIN. FOR REAL.
WHAT THE HELL ARE YOU DOING?

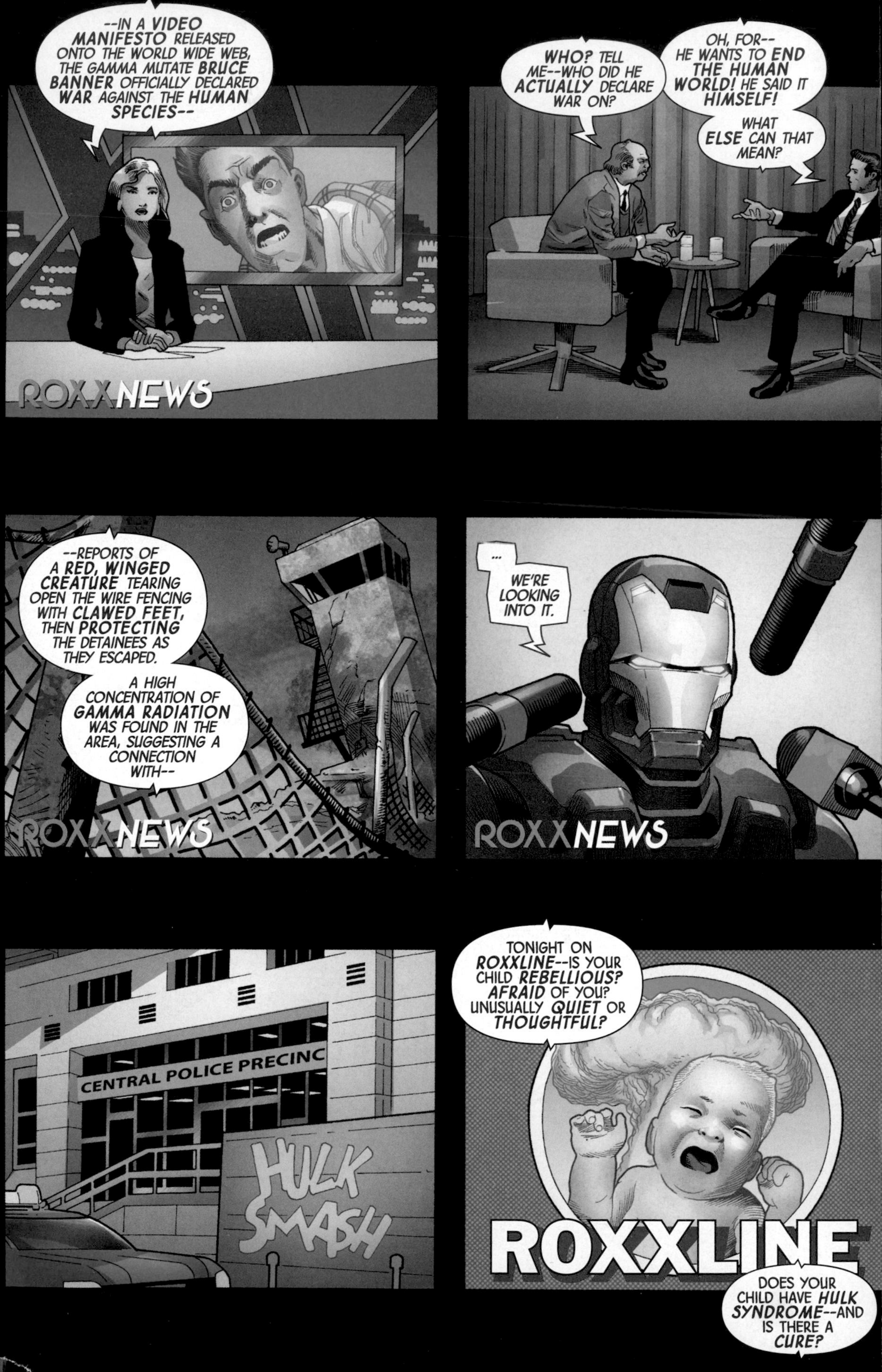
--IN A VIDEO MANIFESTO RELEASED ONTO THE WORLD WIDE WEB, THE GAMMA MUTATE BRUCE BANNER OFFICIALLY DECLARED WAR AGAINST THE HUMAN SPECIES--
ROXXNEWS
WHO? TELL ME--WHO DID HE ACTUALLY DECLARE WAR ON?
OH, FOR-- HE WANTS TO END THE HUMAN WORLD! HE SAID IT HIMSELF!
WHAT ELSE CAN THAT MEAN?
--REPORTS OF A RED, WINGED CREATURE TEARING OPEN THE WIRE FENCING WITH CLAWED FEET, THEN PROTECTING THE DETAINEES AS THEY ESCAPED.
A HIGH CONCENTRATION OF GAMMA RADIATION WAS FOUND IN THE AREA, SUGGESTING A CONNECTION WITH--
ROXXNEWS
... WE'RE LOOKING INTO IT.
ROXXNEWS
CENTRAL POLICE PRECINC
HULK SMASH
TONIGHT ON ROXXLINE--IS YOUR CHILD REBELLIOUS? AFRAID OF YOU? UNUSUALLY QUIET OR THOUGHTFUL?
ROXXLINE
DOES YOUR CHILD HAVE HULK SYNDROME--AND IS THERE A CURE?

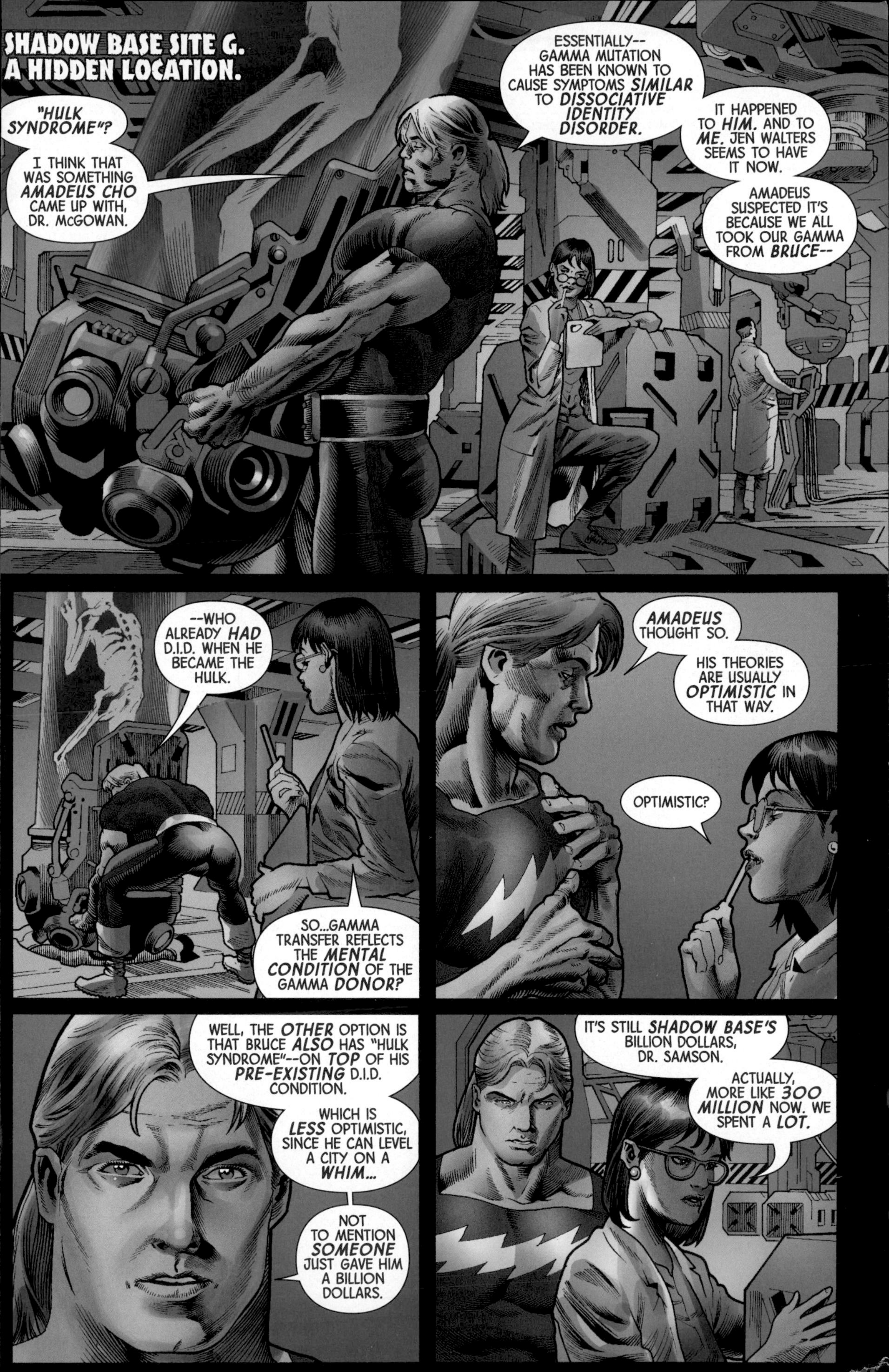
SHADOW BASE SITE G. A HIDDEN LOCATION.
"HULK SYNDROME"?
I THINK THAT WAS SOMETHING AMADEUS CHO CAME UP WITH, DR. McGOWAN.
ESSENTIALLY-- GAMMA MUTATION HAS BEEN KNOWN TO CAUSE SYMPTOMS SIMILAR TO DISSOCIATIVE IDENTITY DISORDER.
IT HAPPENED TO HIM. AND TO ME. JEN WALTERS SEEMS TO HAVE IT NOW.
AMADEUS SUSPECTED IT'S BECAUSE WE ALL TOOK OUR GAMMA FROM BRUCE--
--WHO ALREADY HAD D.I.D. WHEN HE BECAME THE HULK.
SO...GAMMA TRANSFER REFLECTS THE MENTAL CONDITION OF THE GAMMA DONOR?
AMADEUS THOUGHT SO.
HIS THEORIES ARE USUALLY OPTIMISTIC IN THAT WAY.
OPTIMISTIC?
WELL, THE OTHER OPTION IS THAT BRUCE ALSO HAS "HULK SYNDROME"--ON TOP OF HIS PRE-EXISTING D.I.D. CONDITION.
WHICH IS LESS OPTIMISTIC, SINCE HE CAN LEVEL A CITY ON A WHIM...
NOT TO MENTION SOMEONE JUST GAVE HIM A BILLION DOLLARS.
IT'S STILL SHADOW BASE'S BILLION DOLLARS, DR. SAMSON.
ACTUALLY, MORE LIKE 300 MILLION NOW. WE SPENT A LOT.

A LOT OF THE REST IS *EARMARKED*-- MAINTENANCE COSTS, SALARIES FOR THOSE WHO DIDN'T DEFECT TO *OTHER* BLACK-BUDGET GROUPS LIKE *ORCHIS* OR TO THE *PRIVATE SECTOR.*

WE LOST OUR *MERCENARY FORCE* THAT WAY, UNFORTUNATELY--THE ONES WHO *SURVIVED.* PLUS HALF THE *MONITORS*...MOST OF *ADMIN...*

YOU'RE NOT WORRIED ABOUT WHAT THEY *KNOW?*

THEY DON'T KNOW ABOUT *THIS* PLACE. SITE G WAS A *PURE SCIENCE* FACILITY-- AND SCIENCE TEAM STAYED *LOYAL.*

ANYONE WITH *CLEARANCE* TO KNOW ABOUT THIS PLACE IS WITH *US.*

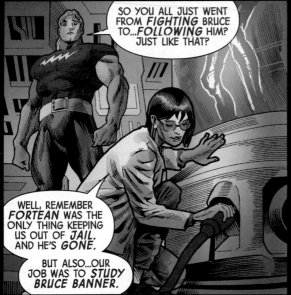

SO YOU ALL JUST WENT FROM *FIGHTING* BRUCE TO...*FOLLOWING* HIM? JUST LIKE THAT?

WELL, REMEMBER *FORTEAN* WAS THE ONLY THING KEEPING US OUT OF *JAIL.* AND HE'S *GONE.*

BUT ALSO...OUR JOB WAS TO *STUDY BRUCE BANNER.*

NOW HE *LIVES* HERE. AND WITH WHAT WE'RE *LEARNING* FROM HIM...WE CAN DO SO MUCH *GOOD.*

DEL HERE-- WE COULD GIVE HIM HIS *LIFE* BACK. GIVE RICK JONES HIS *FACE* BACK...

HOW MUCH OF THIS IS *GUILT* TALKING, DOCTOR?

...HE'S *RIGHT,* LEONARD.

WHAT HE'S *SAYING*...THOSE *BROADCASTS* HE'S MAKING...I HONESTLY THINK HE'S RIGHT.

I BELIEVE IN BRUCE BANNER.

DO *YOU?*

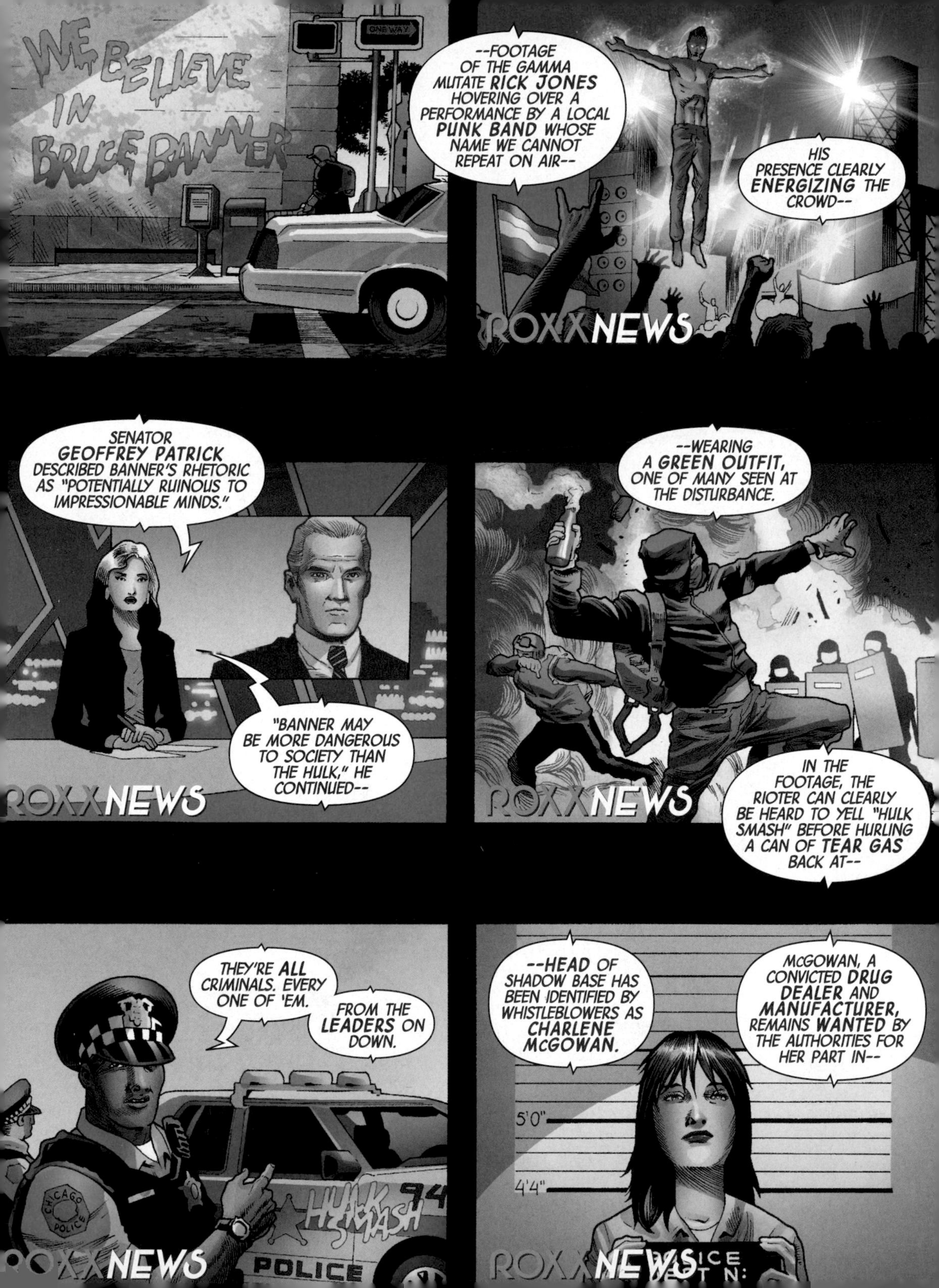
WE BELIEVE IN BRUCE BANNER
ONE WAY
--FOOTAGE OF THE GAMMA MUTATE RICK JONES HOVERING OVER A PERFORMANCE BY A LOCAL PUNK BAND WHOSE NAME WE CANNOT REPEAT ON AIR--
HIS PRESENCE CLEARLY ENERGIZING THE CROWD--
ROXXNEWS
SENATOR GEOFFREY PATRICK DESCRIBED BANNER'S RHETORIC AS "POTENTIALLY RUINOUS TO IMPRESSIONABLE MINDS."
"BANNER MAY BE MORE DANGEROUS TO SOCIETY THAN THE HULK," HE CONTINUED--
ROXXNEWS
--WEARING A GREEN OUTFIT, ONE OF MANY SEEN AT THE DISTURBANCE.
IN THE FOOTAGE, THE RIOTER CAN CLEARLY BE HEARD TO YELL "HULK SMASH" BEFORE HURLING A CAN OF TEAR GAS BACK AT--
ROXXNEWS
THEY'RE ALL CRIMINALS. EVERY ONE OF 'EM.
FROM THE LEADERS ON DOWN.
CHICAGO POLICE
HULK SMASH
94
POLICE
ROXXNEWS
--HEAD OF SHADOW BASE HAS BEEN IDENTIFIED BY WHISTLEBLOWERS AS CHARLENE McGOWAN.
McGOWAN, A CONVICTED DRUG DEALER AND MANUFACTURER, REMAINS WANTED BY THE AUTHORITIES FOR HER PART IN--
5'0"
4'4"
ROXXNEWS

THE NEW *SHADOW BASE COMMANDER.* SHE'S THE KEY. SHE ALWAYS *WAS.*

RICK *TOLD* ME HOW SHE PUT HER LIFE ON THE LINE FOR HER *TEAM.* THOSE WHO *STAYED* WITH THE BASE--WITH *HER*-- SHE HAS THEIR *ABSOLUTE LOYALTY.*

AND SHE'S CHOSEN TO WORK WITH *ME.*

SO *I* HAVE THEIR ABSOLUTE LOYALTY.

...WHAT HAPPENED TO THE *OLD* SHADOW BASE COMMANDER?

OKAY. I HAVE *ANOTHER* QUESTION. I'M A *GAMMA GUY,* BRUCE.

IF I *DIE...* DO I *STAY DEAD?*

PERSONALLY, I WOULDN'T RISK IT. I DON'T THINK THERE ARE HARD AND FAST *RULES.*

GENERAL *ROSS* IS STILL DEAD...SO IS *WALTER...*

YEAH, BUT I READ THAT HE CAME BACK THE *FIRST TIME.*

WHICH REMINDS ME--YOU KNOW YOUR REPORTER FRIEND WANTED TO *INTERVIEW* ME ABOUT YOU?

SHE'S MORE THE *HULK'S* FRIEND...

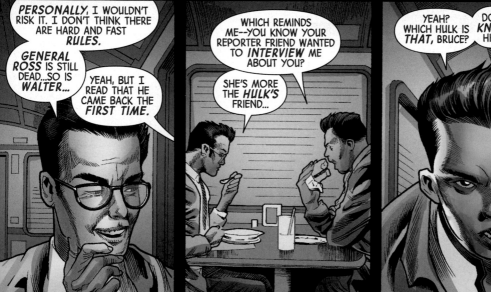

YEAH? WHICH HULK IS *THAT,* BRUCE?

DO I *KNOW* HIM?

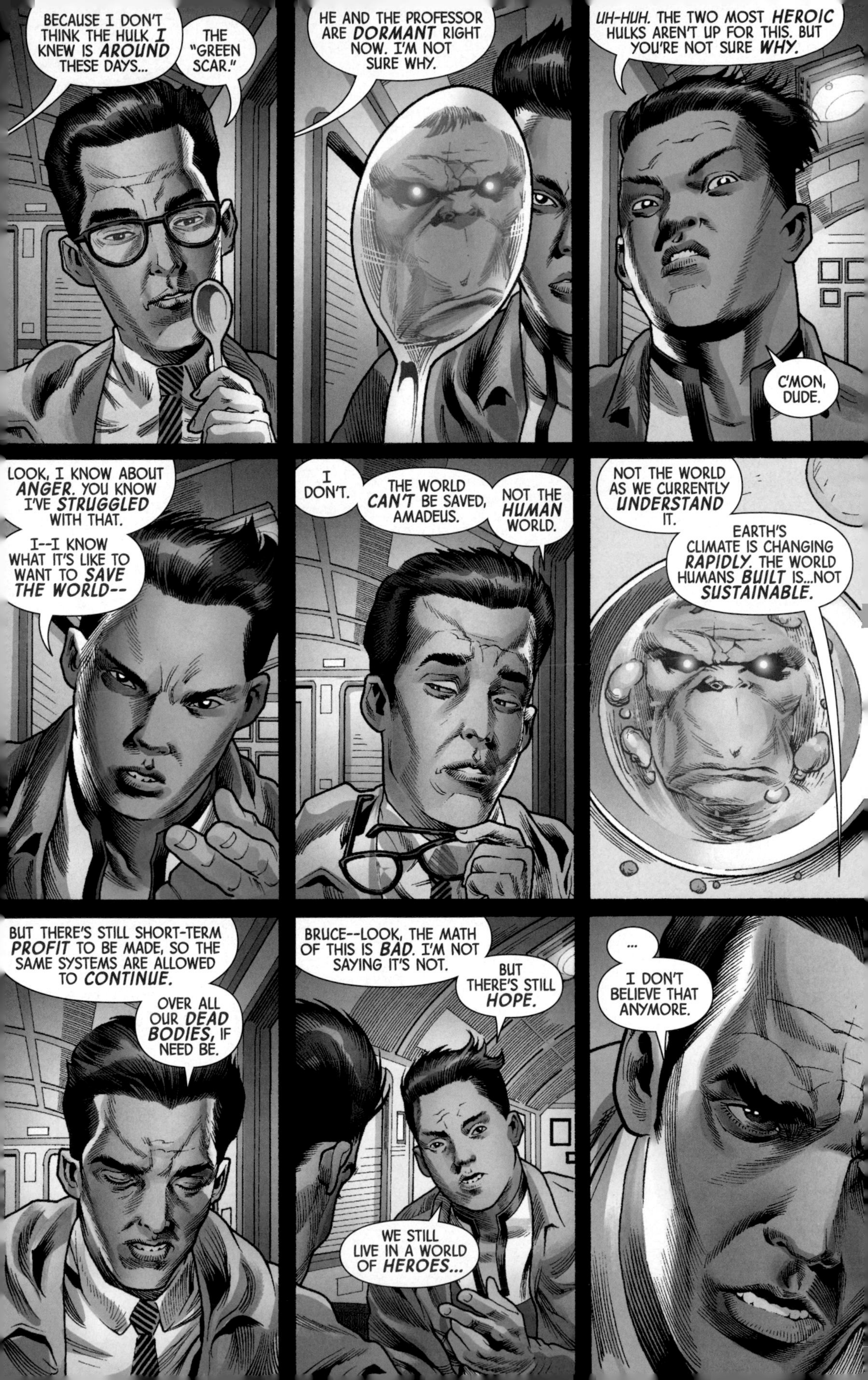
BECAUSE I DON'T THINK THE HULK I KNEW IS AROUND THESE DAYS...
THE "GREEN SCAR."
HE AND THE PROFESSOR ARE DORMANT RIGHT NOW. I'M NOT SURE WHY.
UH-HUH. THE TWO MOST HEROIC HULKS AREN'T UP FOR THIS. BUT YOU'RE NOT SURE WHY.
C'MON, DUDE.
LOOK, I KNOW ABOUT ANGER. YOU KNOW I'VE STRUGGLED WITH THAT.
I--I KNOW WHAT IT'S LIKE TO WANT TO SAVE THE WORLD--
I DON'T.
THE WORLD CAN'T BE SAVED, AMADEUS.
NOT THE HUMAN WORLD.
NOT THE WORLD AS WE CURRENTLY UNDERSTAND IT.
EARTH'S CLIMATE IS CHANGING RAPIDLY. THE WORLD HUMANS BUILT IS...NOT SUSTAINABLE.
BUT THERE'S STILL SHORT-TERM PROFIT TO BE MADE, SO THE SAME SYSTEMS ARE ALLOWED TO CONTINUE.
OVER ALL OUR DEAD BODIES, IF NEED BE.
BRUCE--LOOK, THE MATH OF THIS IS BAD. I'M NOT SAYING IT'S NOT.
BUT THERE'S STILL HOPE.
WE STILL LIVE IN A WORLD OF HEROES...
...
I DON'T BELIEVE THAT ANYMORE.

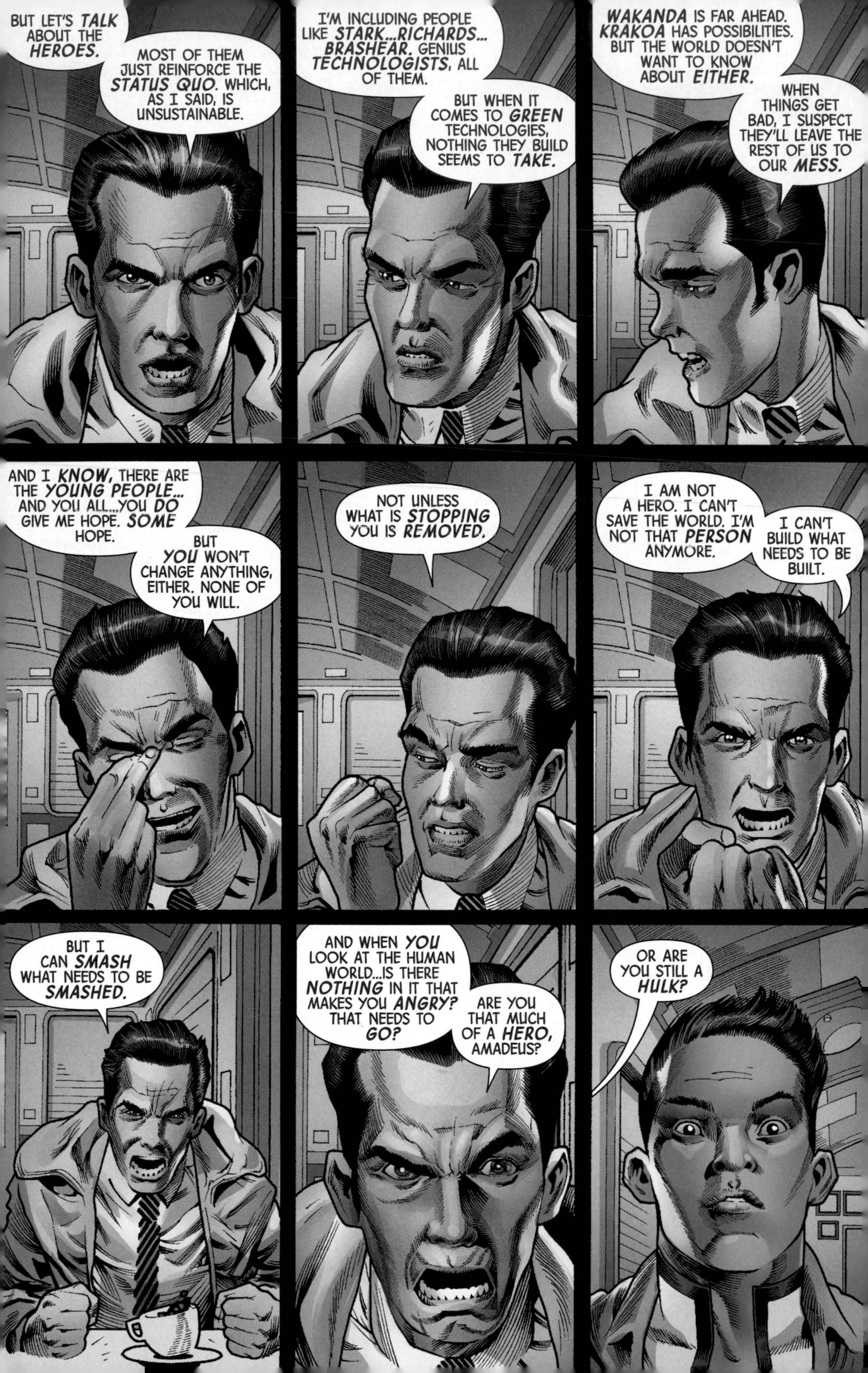

BUT LET'S TALK ABOUT THE HEROES.
MOST OF THEM JUST REINFORCE THE STATUS QUO. WHICH, AS I SAID, IS UNSUSTAINABLE.
I'M INCLUDING PEOPLE LIKE STARK...RICHARDS... BRASHEAR. GENIUS TECHNOLOGISTS, ALL OF THEM.
BUT WHEN IT COMES TO GREEN TECHNOLOGIES, NOTHING THEY BUILD SEEMS TO TAKE.
WAKANDA IS FAR AHEAD. KRAKOA HAS POSSIBILITIES. BUT THE WORLD DOESN'T WANT TO KNOW ABOUT EITHER.
WHEN THINGS GET BAD, I SUSPECT THEY'LL LEAVE THE REST OF US TO OUR MESS.
AND I KNOW, THERE ARE THE YOUNG PEOPLE... AND YOU ALL...YOU DO GIVE ME HOPE. SOME HOPE.
BUT YOU WON'T CHANGE ANYTHING, EITHER. NONE OF YOU WILL.
NOT UNLESS WHAT IS STOPPING YOU IS REMOVED.
I AM NOT A HERO. I CAN'T SAVE THE WORLD. I'M NOT THAT PERSON ANYMORE.
I CAN'T BUILD WHAT NEEDS TO BE BUILT.
BUT I CAN SMASH WHAT NEEDS TO BE SMASHED.
AND WHEN YOU LOOK AT THE HUMAN WORLD...IS THERE NOTHING IN IT THAT MAKES YOU ANGRY? THAT NEEDS TO GO?
ARE YOU THAT MUCH OF A HERO, AMADEUS?
OR ARE YOU STILL A HULK?

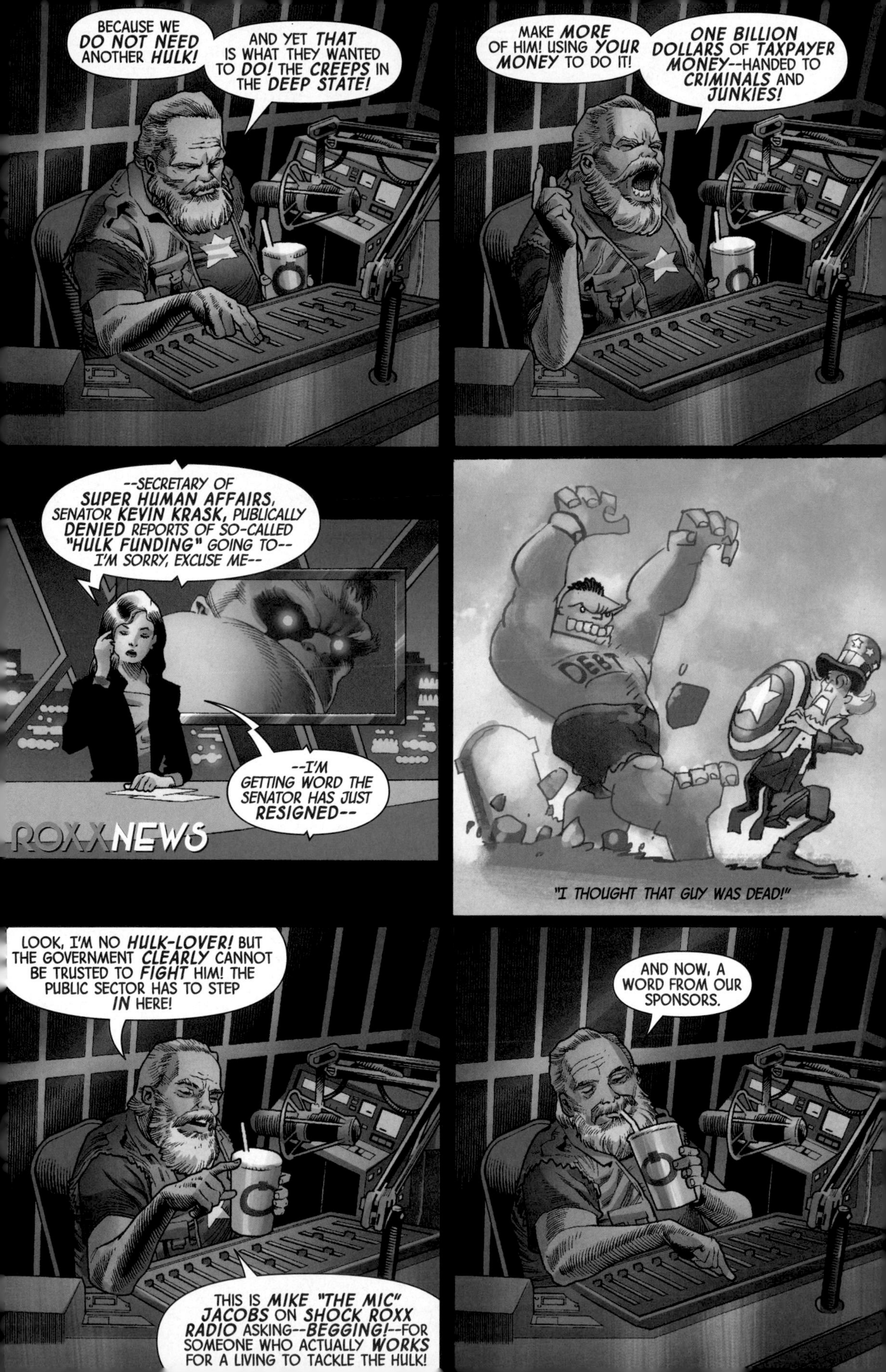
BECAUSE WE DO NOT NEED ANOTHER HULK!
AND YET THAT IS WHAT THEY WANTED TO DO! THE CREEPS IN THE DEEP STATE!
MAKE MORE OF HIM! USING YOUR MONEY TO DO IT!
ONE BILLION DOLLARS OF TAXPAYER MONEY--HANDED TO CRIMINALS AND JUNKIES!
--SECRETARY OF SUPER HUMAN AFFAIRS, SENATOR KEVIN KRASK, PUBLICALLY DENIED REPORTS OF SO-CALLED "HULK FUNDING" GOING TO-- I'M SORRY, EXCUSE ME--
--I'M GETTING WORD THE SENATOR HAS JUST RESIGNED--
ROXX NEWS
DEBT
"I THOUGHT THAT GUY WAS DEAD!"
LOOK, I'M NO HULK-LOVER! BUT THE GOVERNMENT CLEARLY CANNOT BE TRUSTED TO FIGHT HIM! THE PUBLIC SECTOR HAS TO STEP IN HERE!
THIS IS MIKE "THE MIC" JACOBS ON SHOCK ROXX RADIO ASKING--BEGGING!--FOR SOMEONE WHO ACTUALLY WORKS FOR A LIVING TO TACKLE THE HULK!
AND NOW, A WORD FROM OUR SPONSORS.

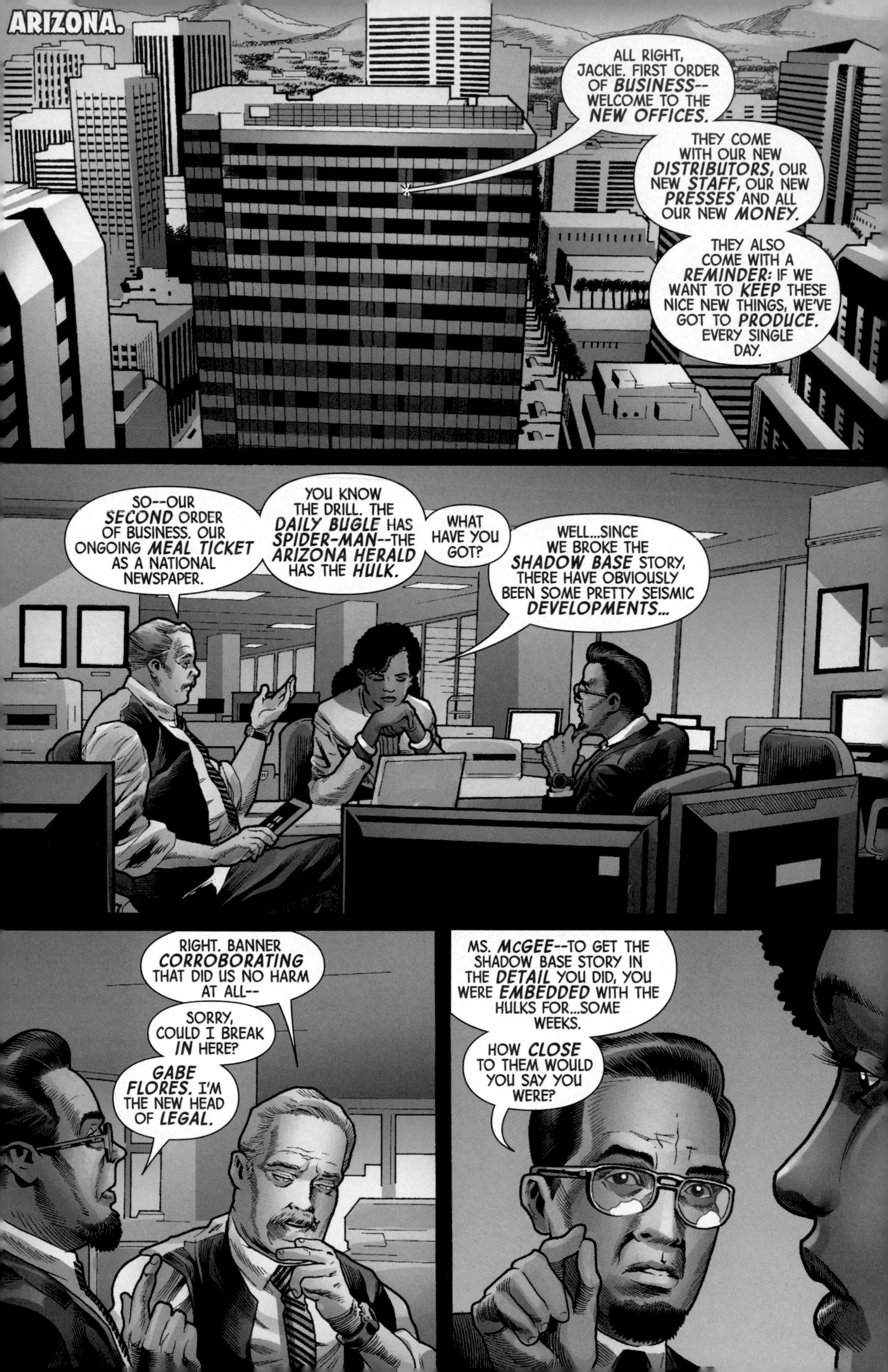
ARIZONA.
ALL RIGHT, JACKIE. FIRST ORDER OF BUSINESS-- WELCOME TO THE NEW OFFICES.
THEY COME WITH OUR NEW DISTRIBUTORS, OUR NEW STAFF, OUR NEW PRESSES AND ALL OUR NEW MONEY.
THEY ALSO COME WITH A REMINDER: IF WE WANT TO KEEP THESE NICE NEW THINGS, WE'VE GOT TO PRODUCE. EVERY SINGLE DAY.
SO--OUR SECOND ORDER OF BUSINESS. OUR ONGOING MEAL TICKET AS A NATIONAL NEWSPAPER.
YOU KNOW THE DRILL. THE DAILY BUGLE HAS SPIDER-MAN--THE ARIZONA HERALD HAS THE HULK.
WHAT HAVE YOU GOT?
WELL...SINCE WE BROKE THE SHADOW BASE STORY, THERE HAVE OBVIOUSLY BEEN SOME PRETTY SEISMIC DEVELOPMENTS...
RIGHT. BANNER CORROBORATING THAT DID US NO HARM AT ALL--
SORRY, COULD I BREAK IN HERE?
GABE FLORES. I'M THE NEW HEAD OF LEGAL.
MS. McGEE--TO GET THE SHADOW BASE STORY IN THE DETAIL YOU DID, YOU WERE EMBEDDED WITH THE HULKS FOR...SOME WEEKS.
HOW CLOSE TO THEM WOULD YOU SAY YOU WERE?

...I WASN'T JUST AN *EYEWITNESS* FOR THE SHADOW BASE RAID.

I HELPED PLAN IT.

TALKING TO *McGOWAN,* PERSUADING HER TO TURN ON *FORTEAN*-- THAT WAS MY IDEA.

I DIDN'T KNOW IT'D WORK OUT LIKE... IT *HAS*...BUT FORTEAN WAS GOING TO HAVE ME *KILLED.*

I'M NOT SORRY.

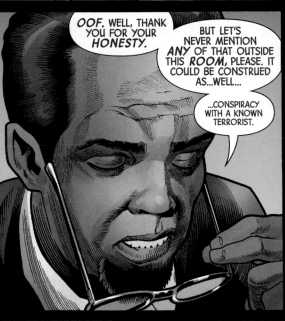

OOF. WELL, THANK YOU FOR YOUR *HONESTY.*

BUT LET'S NEVER MENTION *ANY* OF THAT OUTSIDE THIS *ROOM,* PLEASE. IT COULD BE CONSTRUED AS...WELL...

...CONSPIRACY WITH A KNOWN TERRORIST.

NOT TO MENTION THE POTENTIAL IMPLICATION THAT WE *MANUFACTURED THE NEWS* ON THIS ONE.

"YOU PROVIDE THE *PICTURES,* WE'LL PROVIDE THE *HULK.*"

WE'RE ALREADY BEING ACCUSED OF *MONETIZING* BANNER...

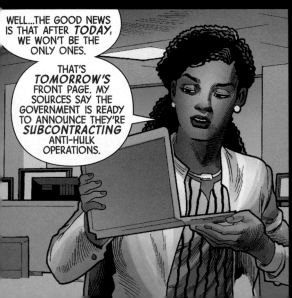

WELL...THE GOOD NEWS IS THAT AFTER *TODAY,* WE WON'T BE THE ONLY ONES.

THAT'S *TOMORROW'S* FRONT PAGE. MY SOURCES SAY THE GOVERNMENT IS READY TO ANNOUNCE THEY'RE *SUBCONTRACTING* ANTI-HULK OPERATIONS.

ROXXNEWS.COM
Brought to you by ROXXON

HULK PROMISES NEW WAVE OF TERROR

GUESS WHO THE *WINNING BIDDER* WAS?

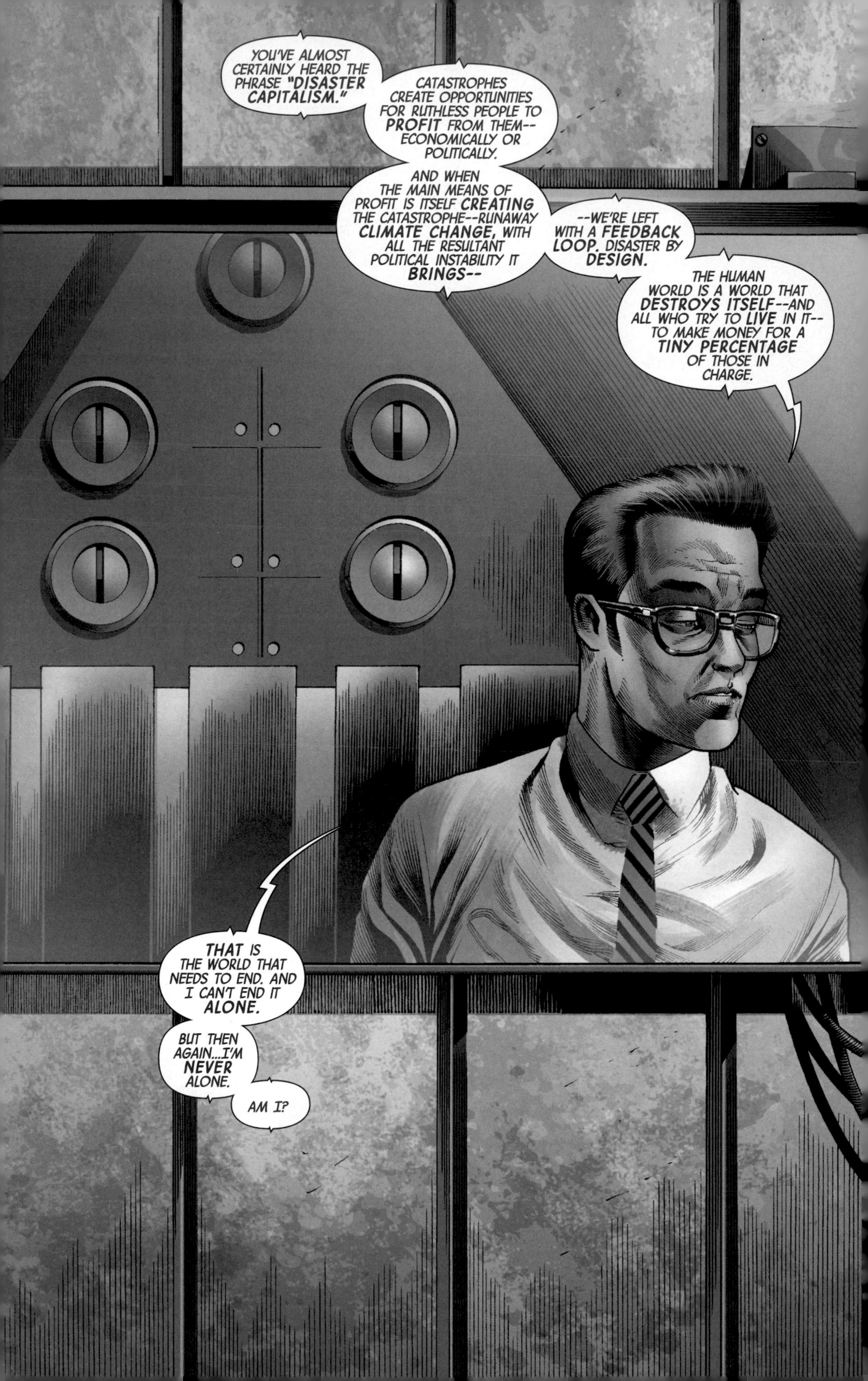
YOU'VE ALMOST CERTAINLY HEARD THE PHRASE "DISASTER CAPITALISM."
CATASTROPHES CREATE OPPORTUNITIES FOR RUTHLESS PEOPLE TO PROFIT FROM THEM-- ECONOMICALLY OR POLITICALLY.
AND WHEN THE MAIN MEANS OF PROFIT IS ITSELF CREATING THE CATASTROPHE--RUNAWAY CLIMATE CHANGE, WITH ALL THE RESULTANT POLITICAL INSTABILITY IT BRINGS--
--WE'RE LEFT WITH A FEEDBACK LOOP. DISASTER BY DESIGN.
THE HUMAN WORLD IS A WORLD THAT DESTROYS ITSELF--AND ALL WHO TRY TO LIVE IN IT-- TO MAKE MONEY FOR A TINY PERCENTAGE OF THOSE IN CHARGE.
THAT IS THE WORLD THAT NEEDS TO END. AND I CAN'T END IT ALONE.
BUT THEN AGAIN...I'M NEVER ALONE.
AM I?

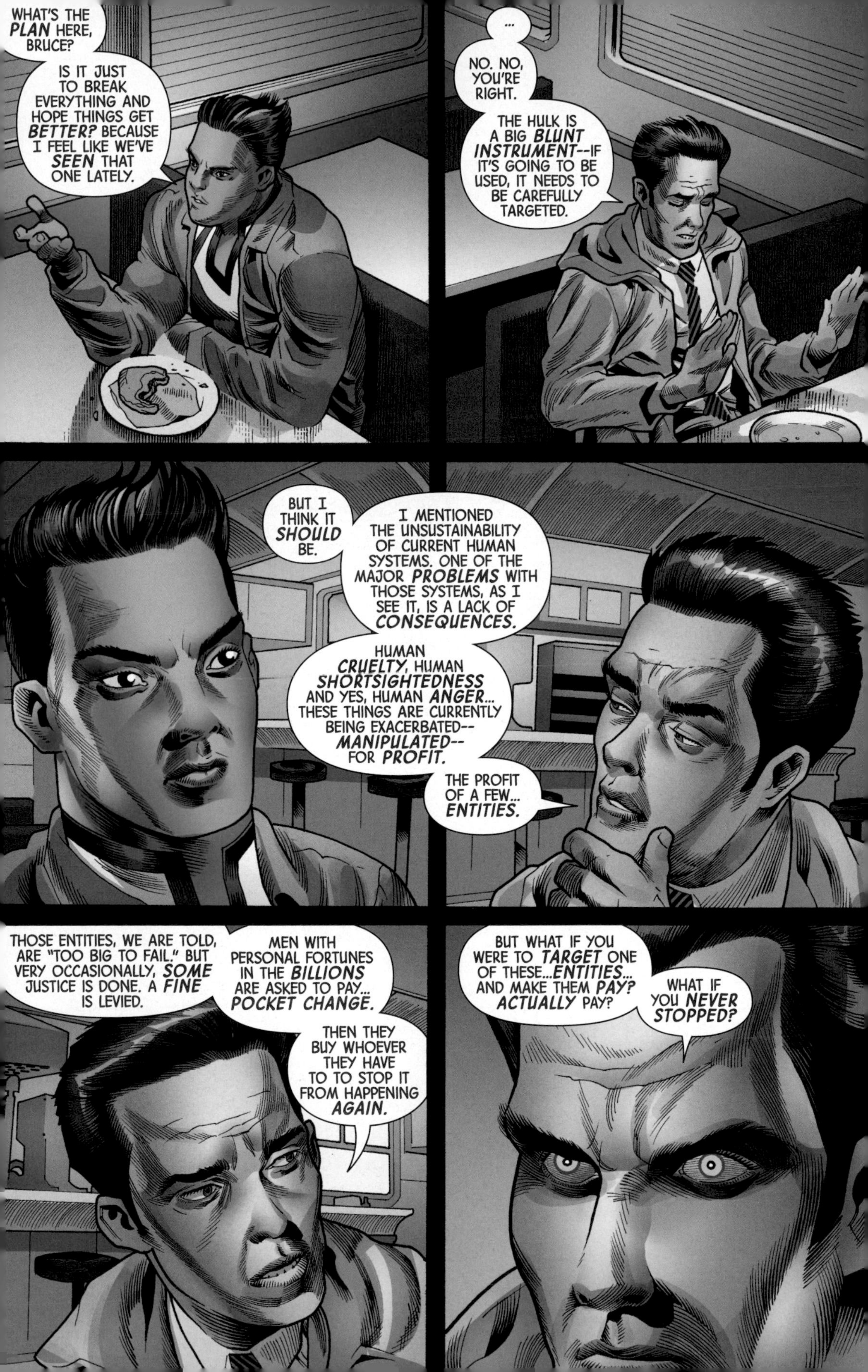
WHAT'S THE PLAN HERE, BRUCE?
IS IT JUST TO BREAK EVERYTHING AND HOPE THINGS GET BETTER? BECAUSE I FEEL LIKE WE'VE SEEN THAT ONE LATELY.
...
NO. NO, YOU'RE RIGHT.
THE HULK IS A BIG BLUNT INSTRUMENT--IF IT'S GOING TO BE USED, IT NEEDS TO BE CAREFULLY TARGETED.
BUT I THINK IT SHOULD BE.
I MENTIONED THE UNSUSTAINABILITY OF CURRENT HUMAN SYSTEMS. ONE OF THE MAJOR PROBLEMS WITH THOSE SYSTEMS, AS I SEE IT, IS A LACK OF CONSEQUENCES.
HUMAN CRUELTY, HUMAN SHORTSIGHTEDNESS AND YES, HUMAN ANGER... THESE THINGS ARE CURRENTLY BEING EXACERBATED-- MANIPULATED-- FOR PROFIT.
THE PROFIT OF A FEW... ENTITIES.
THOSE ENTITIES, WE ARE TOLD, ARE "TOO BIG TO FAIL." BUT VERY OCCASIONALLY, SOME JUSTICE IS DONE. A FINE IS LEVIED.
MEN WITH PERSONAL FORTUNES IN THE BILLIONS ARE ASKED TO PAY... POCKET CHANGE.
THEN THEY BUY WHOEVER THEY HAVE TO TO STOP IT FROM HAPPENING AGAIN.
BUT WHAT IF YOU WERE TO TARGET ONE OF THESE...ENTITIES... AND MAKE THEM PAY? ACTUALLY PAY?
WHAT IF YOU NEVER STOPPED?

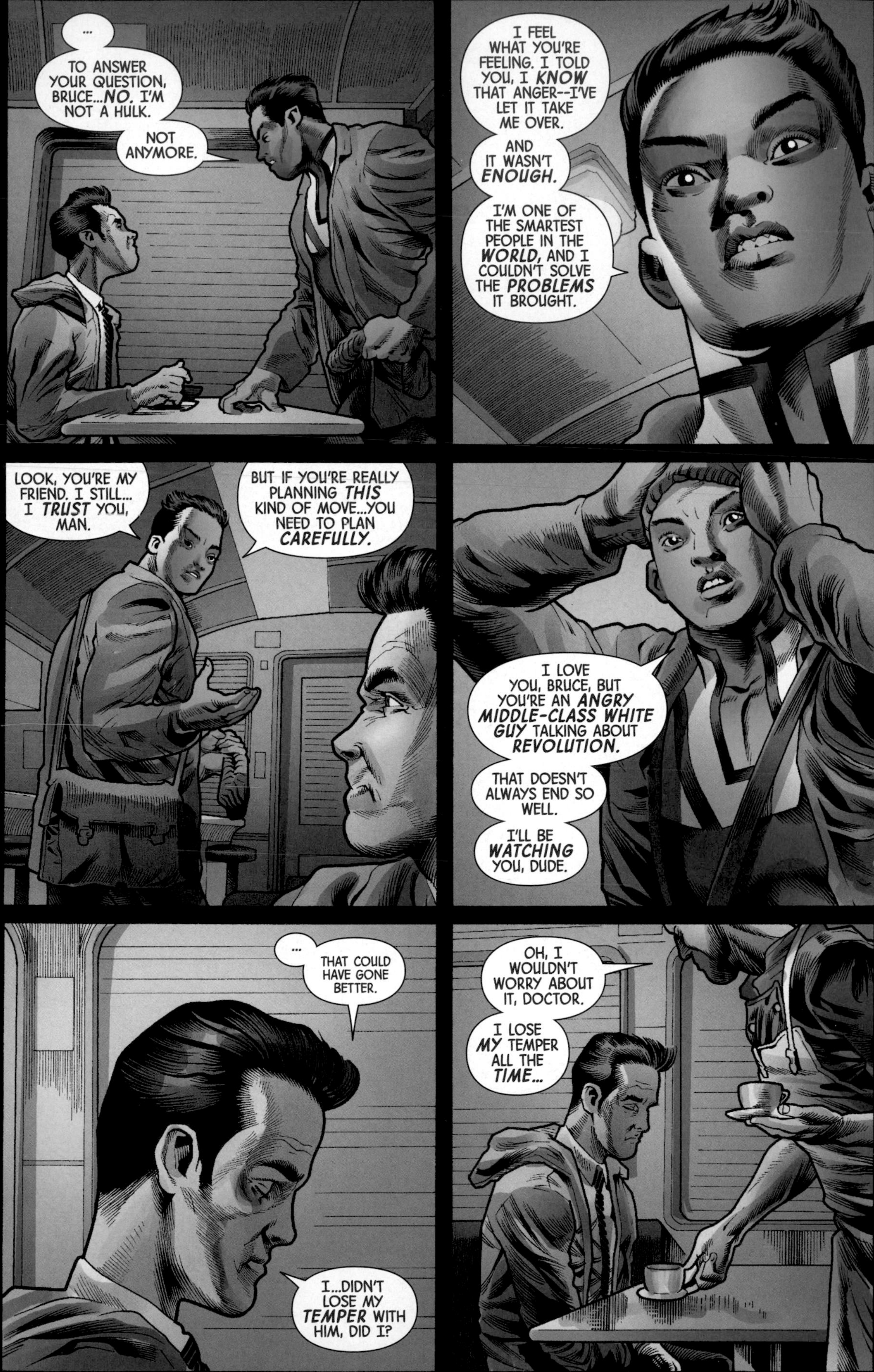
...
TO ANSWER YOUR QUESTION, BRUCE...NO. I'M NOT A HULK.
NOT ANYMORE.
I FEEL WHAT YOU'RE FEELING. I TOLD YOU, I KNOW THAT ANGER--I'VE LET IT TAKE ME OVER.
AND IT WASN'T ENOUGH.
I'M ONE OF THE SMARTEST PEOPLE IN THE WORLD, AND I COULDN'T SOLVE THE PROBLEMS IT BROUGHT.
LOOK, YOU'RE MY FRIEND. I STILL... I TRUST YOU, MAN.
BUT IF YOU'RE REALLY PLANNING THIS KIND OF MOVE...YOU NEED TO PLAN CAREFULLY.
I LOVE YOU, BRUCE, BUT YOU'RE AN ANGRY MIDDLE-CLASS WHITE GUY TALKING ABOUT REVOLUTION.
THAT DOESN'T ALWAYS END SO WELL.
I'LL BE WATCHING YOU, DUDE.
...
THAT COULD HAVE GONE BETTER.
I...DIDN'T LOSE MY TEMPER WITH HIM, DID I?
OH, I WOULDN'T WORRY ABOUT IT, DOCTOR.
I LOSE MY TEMPER ALL THE TIME...

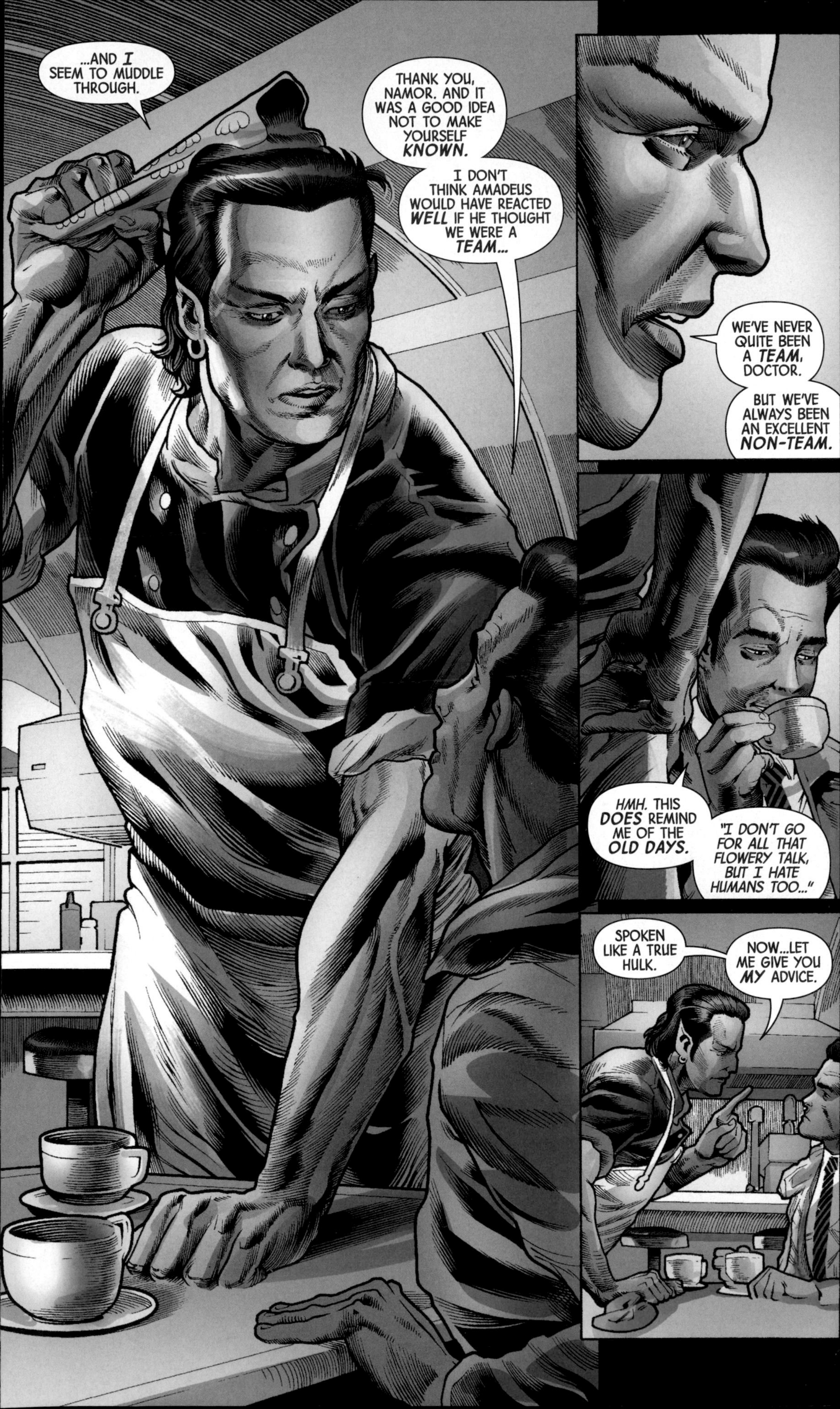

...AND *I* SEEM TO MUDDLE THROUGH.
THANK YOU, NAMOR. AND IT WAS A GOOD IDEA NOT TO MAKE YOURSELF **KNOWN.**
I DON'T THINK AMADEUS WOULD HAVE REACTED **WELL** IF HE THOUGHT WE WERE A *TEAM...*
WE'VE NEVER QUITE BEEN A *TEAM*, DOCTOR.
BUT WE'VE ALWAYS BEEN AN EXCELLENT **NON-TEAM.**
HMH. THIS **DOES** REMIND ME OF THE **OLD DAYS.**
"I DON'T GO FOR ALL THAT FLOWERY TALK, BUT I HATE HUMANS TOO..."
SPOKEN LIKE A TRUE HULK.
NOW...LET ME GIVE YOU **MY** ADVICE.

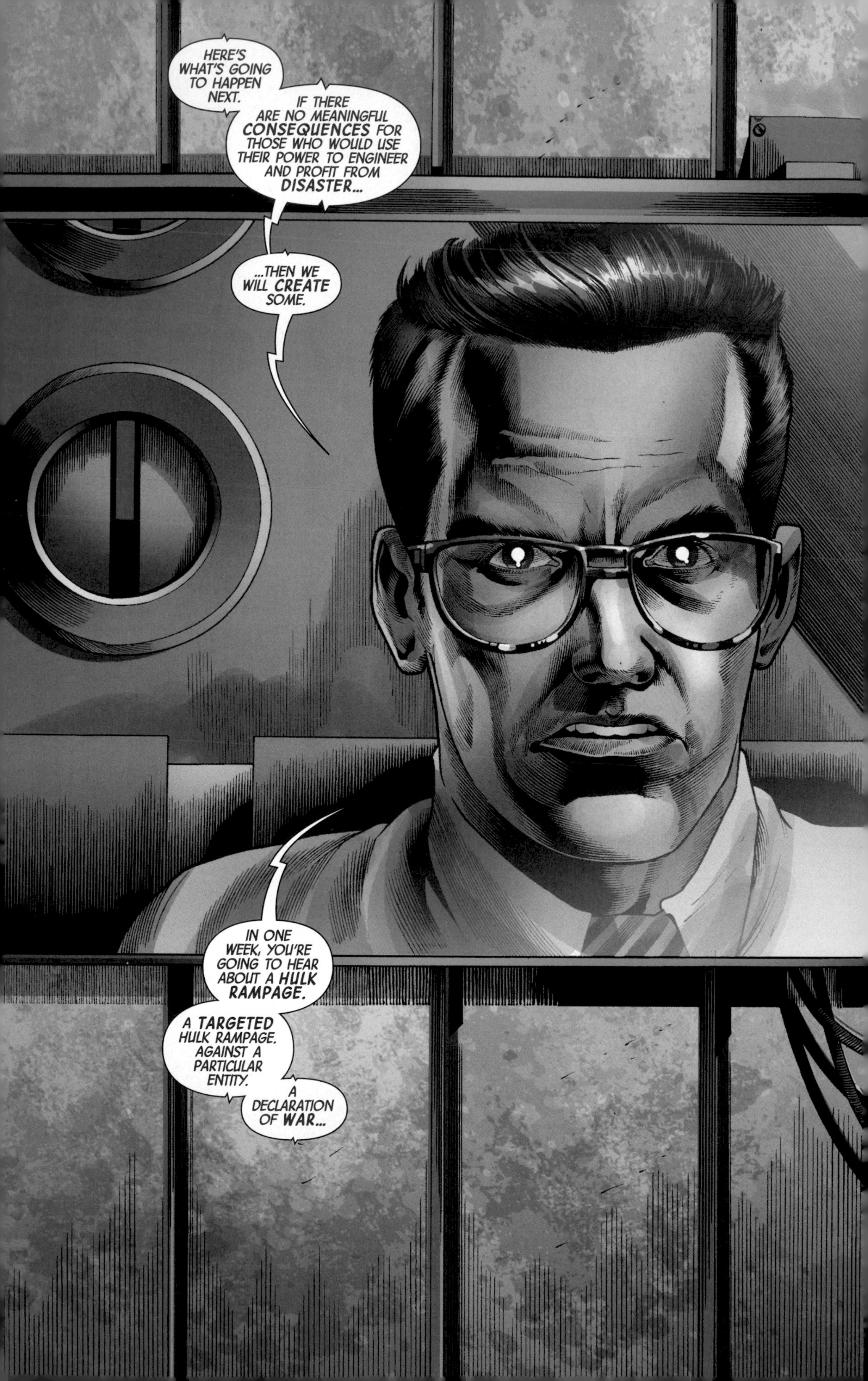
HERE'S WHAT'S GOING TO HAPPEN NEXT.
IF THERE ARE NO MEANINGFUL CONSEQUENCES FOR THOSE WHO WOULD USE THEIR POWER TO ENGINEER AND PROFIT FROM DISASTER...
...THEN WE WILL CREATE SOME.
IN ONE WEEK, YOU'RE GOING TO HEAR ABOUT A HULK RAMPAGE.
A TARGETED HULK RAMPAGE. AGAINST A PARTICULAR ENTITY.
A DECLARATION OF WAR...

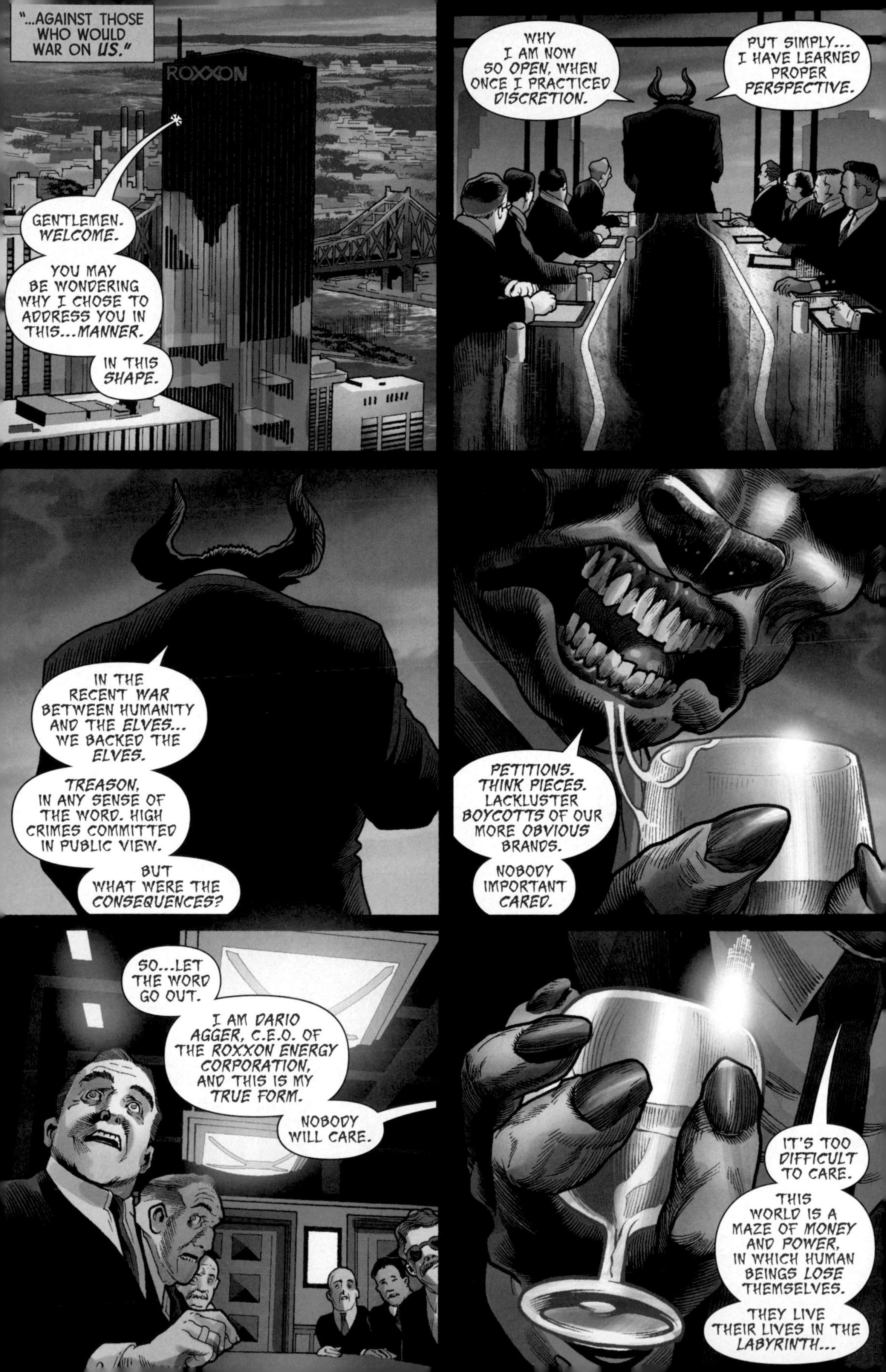
"...AGAINST THOSE WHO WOULD WAR ON US."
ROXXON
GENTLEMEN. WELCOME.
YOU MAY BE WONDERING WHY I CHOSE TO ADDRESS YOU IN THIS...MANNER.
IN THIS SHAPE.
WHY I AM NOW SO OPEN, WHEN ONCE I PRACTICED DISCRETION.
PUT SIMPLY... I HAVE LEARNED PROPER PERSPECTIVE.
IN THE RECENT WAR BETWEEN HUMANITY AND THE ELVES... WE BACKED THE ELVES.
TREASON. IN ANY SENSE OF THE WORD. HIGH CRIMES COMMITTED IN PUBLIC VIEW.
BUT WHAT WERE THE CONSEQUENCES?
PETITIONS. THINK PIECES. LACKLUSTER BOYCOTTS OF OUR MORE OBVIOUS BRANDS.
NOBODY IMPORTANT CARED.
SO...LET THE WORD GO OUT.
I AM DARIO AGGER, C.E.O. OF THE ROXXON ENERGY CORPORATION, AND THIS IS MY TRUE FORM.
NOBODY WILL CARE.
IT'S TOO DIFFICULT TO CARE.
THIS WORLD IS A MAZE OF MONEY AND POWER, IN WHICH HUMAN BEINGS LOSE THEMSELVES.
THEY LIVE THEIR LIVES IN THE LABYRINTH...

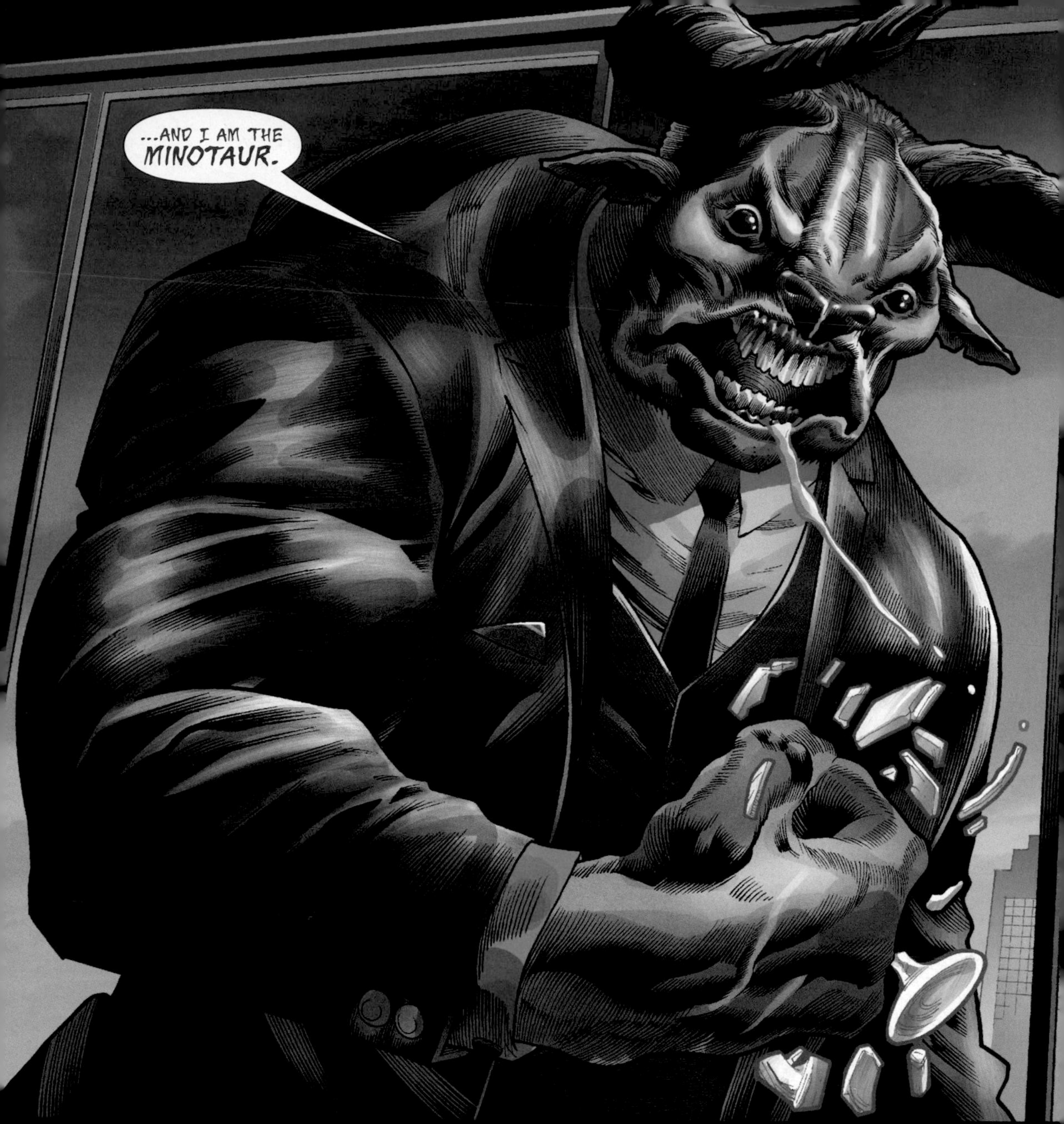
...AND I AM THE MINOTAUR.

STATUS QUO ANTE

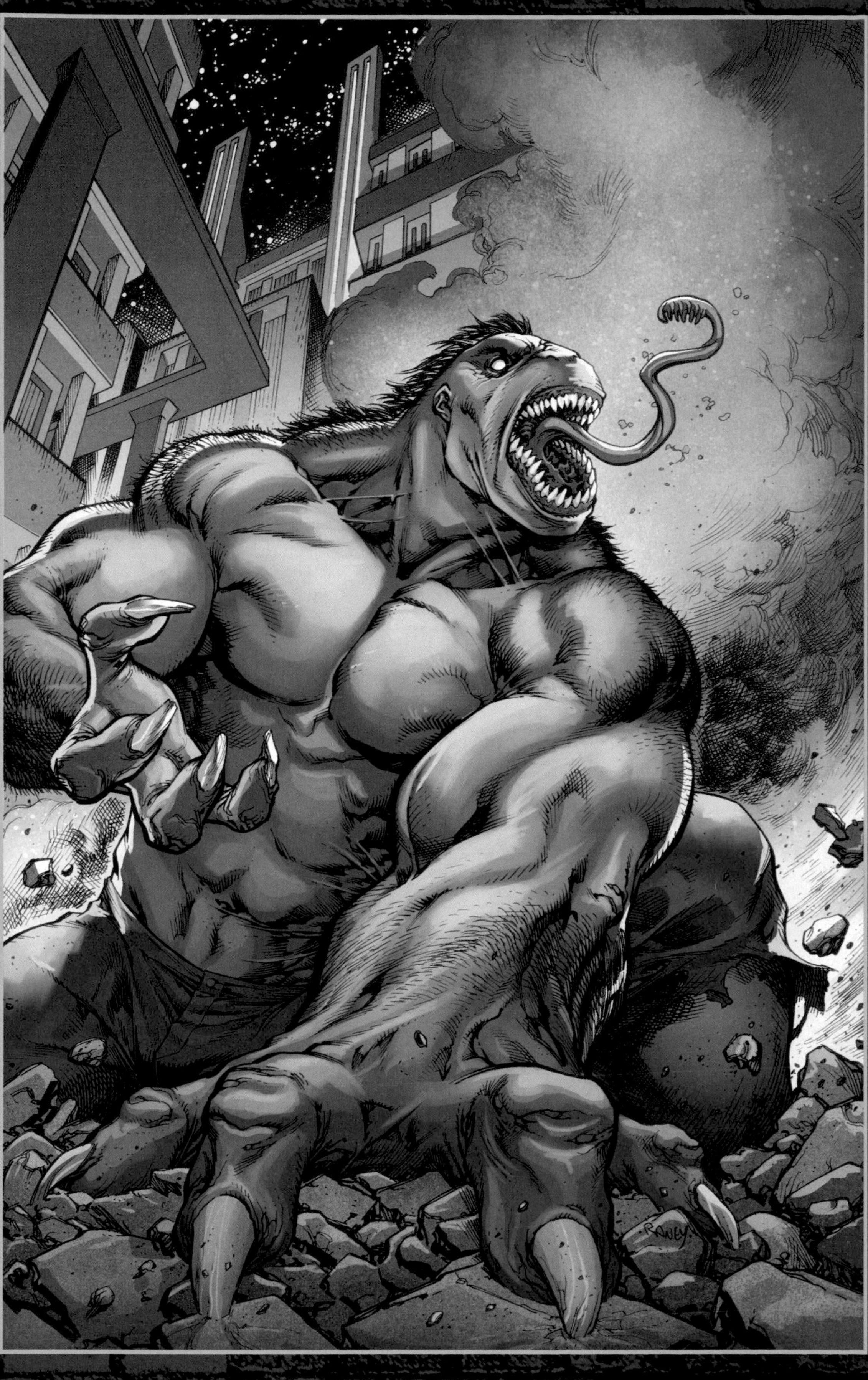
RANEY

TOM RANEY & RACHELLE ROSENBERG
#27 2099 VARIANT

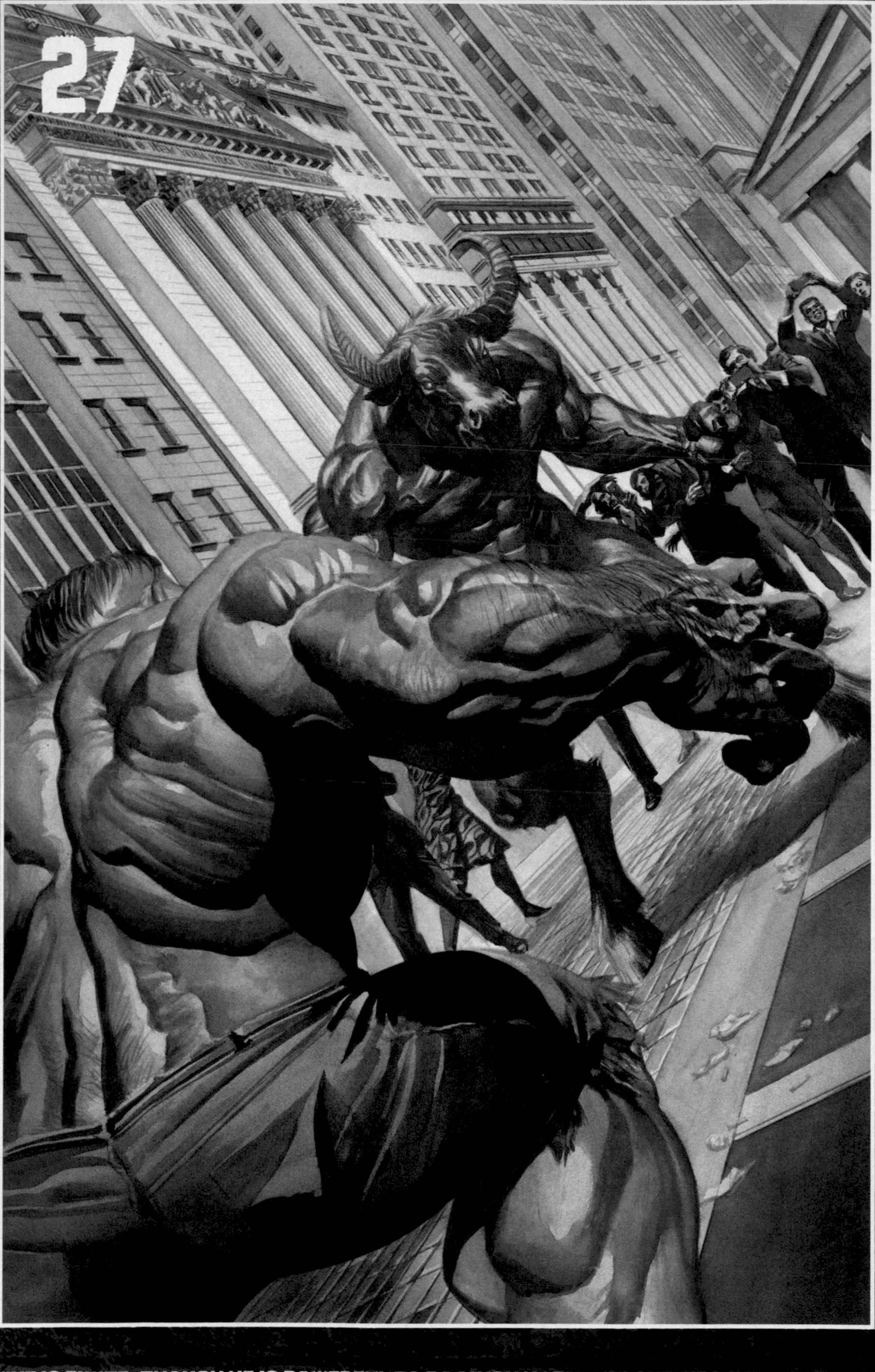

"HE IS FINITE, THOUGH HE IS POWERFUL TO DO MUCH HARM AND SUFFERS NOT AS WE DO. BUT WE ARE STRONG, EACH IN OUR PURPOSE; AND WE ARE ALL MORE STRONG TOGETHER."

— BRAM STOKER, *DRACULA*

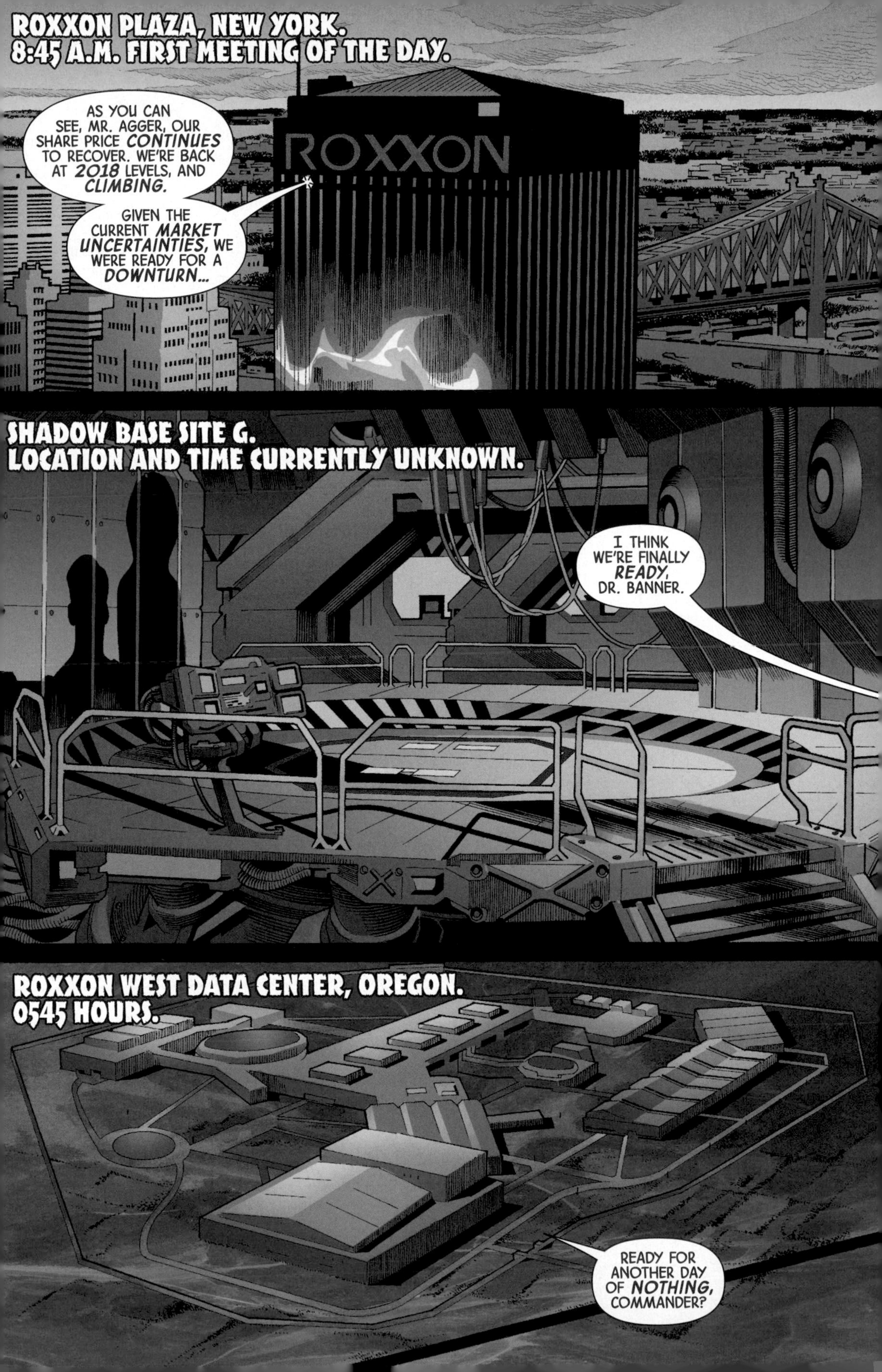
ROXXON PLAZA, NEW YORK.
8:45 A.M. FIRST MEETING OF THE DAY.
ROXXON
AS YOU CAN SEE, MR. AGGER, OUR SHARE PRICE CONTINUES TO RECOVER. WE'RE BACK AT 2018 LEVELS, AND CLIMBING.
GIVEN THE CURRENT MARKET UNCERTAINTIES, WE WERE READY FOR A DOWNTURN...
SHADOW BASE SITE G.
LOCATION AND TIME CURRENTLY UNKNOWN.
I THINK WE'RE FINALLY READY, DR. BANNER.
ROXXON WEST DATA CENTER, OREGON.
0545 HOURS.
READY FOR ANOTHER DAY OF NOTHING, COMMANDER?

...BUT NOTHING TO REPORT ON *THAT* FRONT AS YET. STILL, I'D SUGGEST AVOIDING *RISKY VENTURES*--

DON'T BE A *COWARD*, HIGGINS.

ROXXON

SHARE PRICE

THE MINOTAUR.

WE'RE NOT SOME MOM-AND-POP STORE THAT CLOSES DOWN IN A *STRONG* WIND. WE...ARE THE *HURRICANE*.

UNCERTAINTY IS WHAT WE *WANT*.

I'M *STILL* NOT CERTAIN ABOUT THIS.

I DON'T CARE *HOW* EASY *REED RICHARDS* MAKES IT LOOK-- TRANSLOCATION IS *BEYOND* DANGEROUS.

THE HULK.

IF IT WERE UP TO *ME*, YOU WOULDN'T BE DOING THIS AT *ALL*.

BUT AT LEAST *YOU* GIVE ME TIME TO RUN THE NECESSARY *CHECKS*...

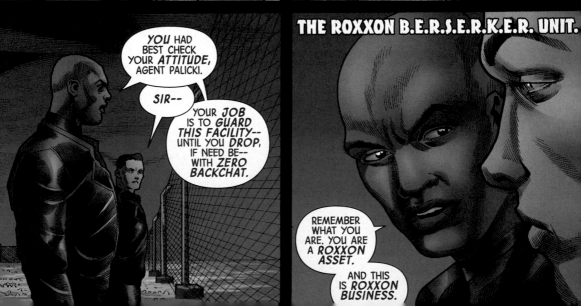

YOU HAD BEST CHECK YOUR *ATTITUDE*, AGENT PALICKI.

SIR--

YOUR *JOB* IS TO *GUARD* THIS FACILITY-- UNTIL YOU *DROP*, IF NEED BE-- WITH *ZERO* BACKCHAT.

THE ROXXON B.E.R.S.E.R.K.E.R. UNIT.

REMEMBER WHAT YOU ARE. YOU ARE A *ROXXON ASSET*.

AND THIS IS *ROXXON BUSINESS*.

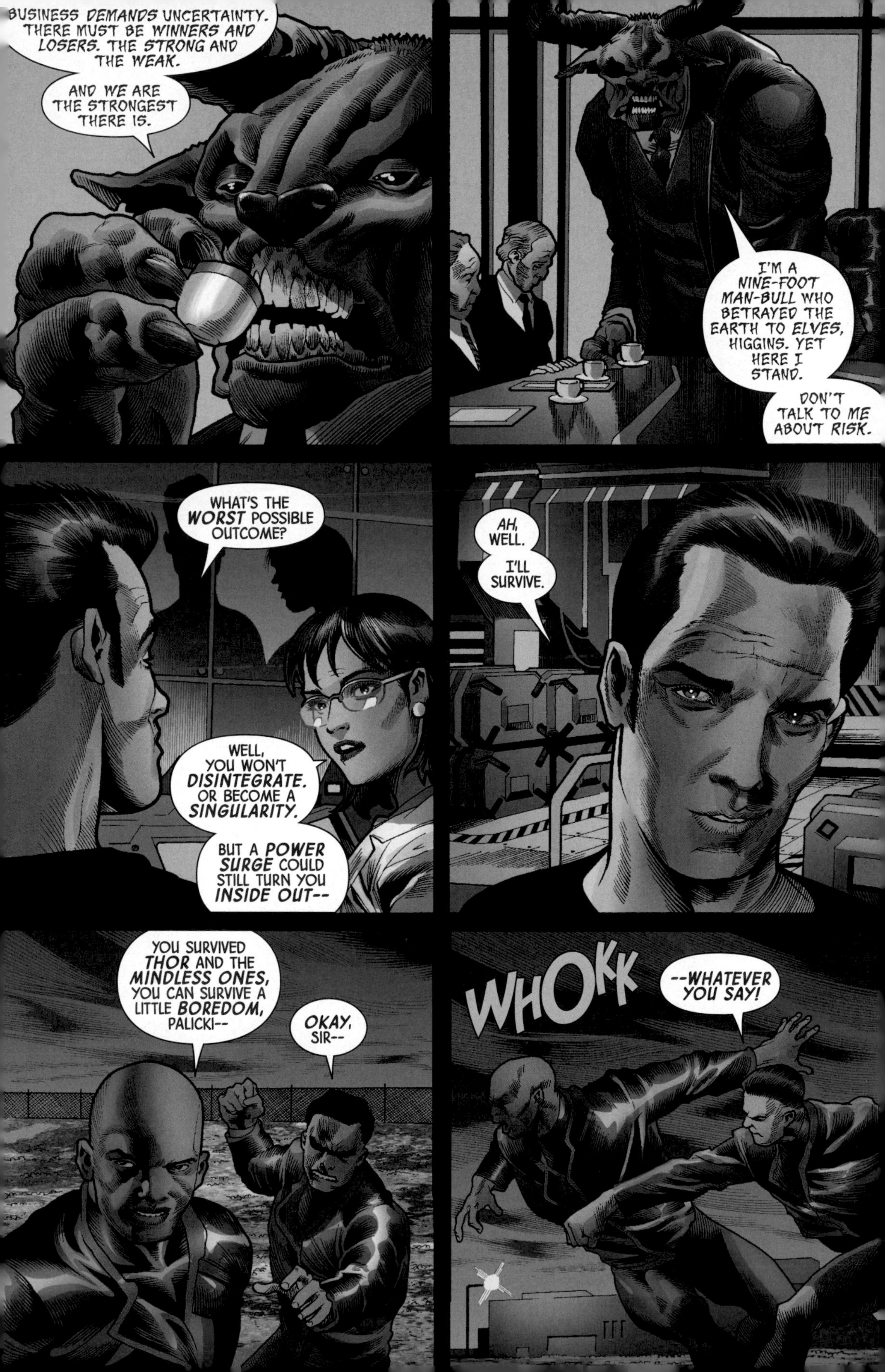
BUSINESS DEMANDS UNCERTAINTY. THERE MUST BE WINNERS AND LOSERS. THE STRONG AND THE WEAK.
AND WE ARE THE STRONGEST THERE IS.
I'M A NINE-FOOT MAN-BULL WHO BETRAYED THE EARTH TO ELVES, HIGGINS. YET HERE I STAND.
DON'T TALK TO ME ABOUT RISK.
WHAT'S THE WORST POSSIBLE OUTCOME?
WELL, YOU WON'T DISINTEGRATE. OR BECOME A SINGULARITY.
BUT A POWER SURGE COULD STILL TURN YOU INSIDE OUT--
AH, WELL.
I'LL SURVIVE.
YOU SURVIVED THOR AND THE MINDLESS ONES, YOU CAN SURVIVE A LITTLE BOREDOM, PALICKI--
OKAY, SIR--
WHOKK
--WHATEVER YOU SAY!

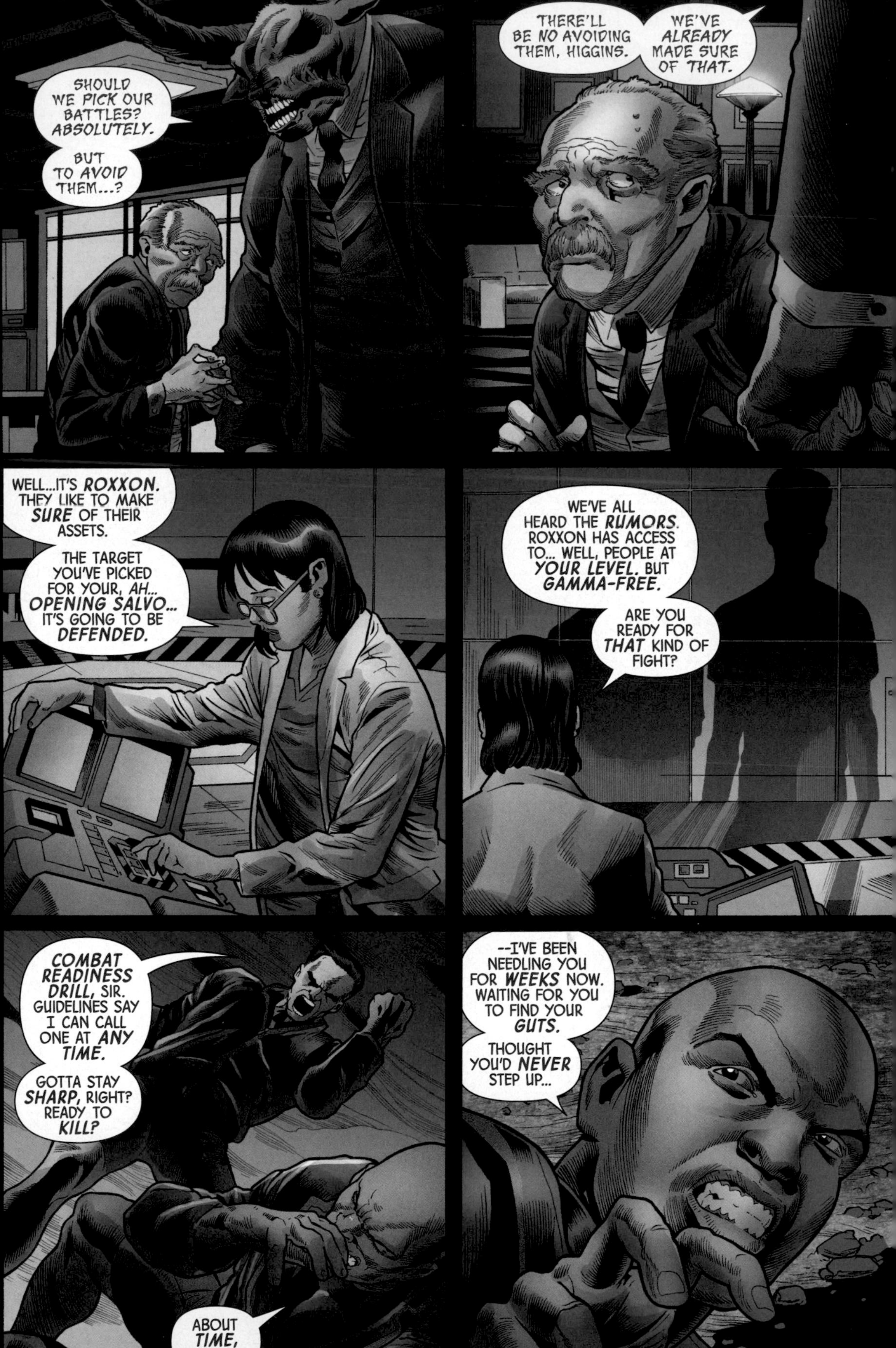

SHOULD WE PICK OUR BATTLES? ABSOLUTELY.
BUT TO AVOID THEM...?
THERE'LL BE NO AVOIDING THEM, HIGGINS.
WE'VE ALREADY MADE SURE OF THAT.
WELL...IT'S ROXXON. THEY LIKE TO MAKE SURE OF THEIR ASSETS.
THE TARGET YOU'VE PICKED FOR YOUR, AH... OPENING SALVO... IT'S GOING TO BE DEFENDED.
WE'VE ALL HEARD THE RUMORS. ROXXON HAS ACCESS TO... WELL, PEOPLE AT YOUR LEVEL. BUT GAMMA-FREE.
ARE YOU READY FOR THAT KIND OF FIGHT?
COMBAT READINESS DRILL, SIR. GUIDELINES SAY I CAN CALL ONE AT ANY TIME.
GOTTA STAY SHARP, RIGHT? READY TO KILL?
ABOUT TIME, PRIVATE--
--I'VE BEEN NEEDLING YOU FOR WEEKS NOW. WAITING FOR YOU TO FIND YOUR GUTS.
THOUGHT YOU'D NEVER STEP UP...

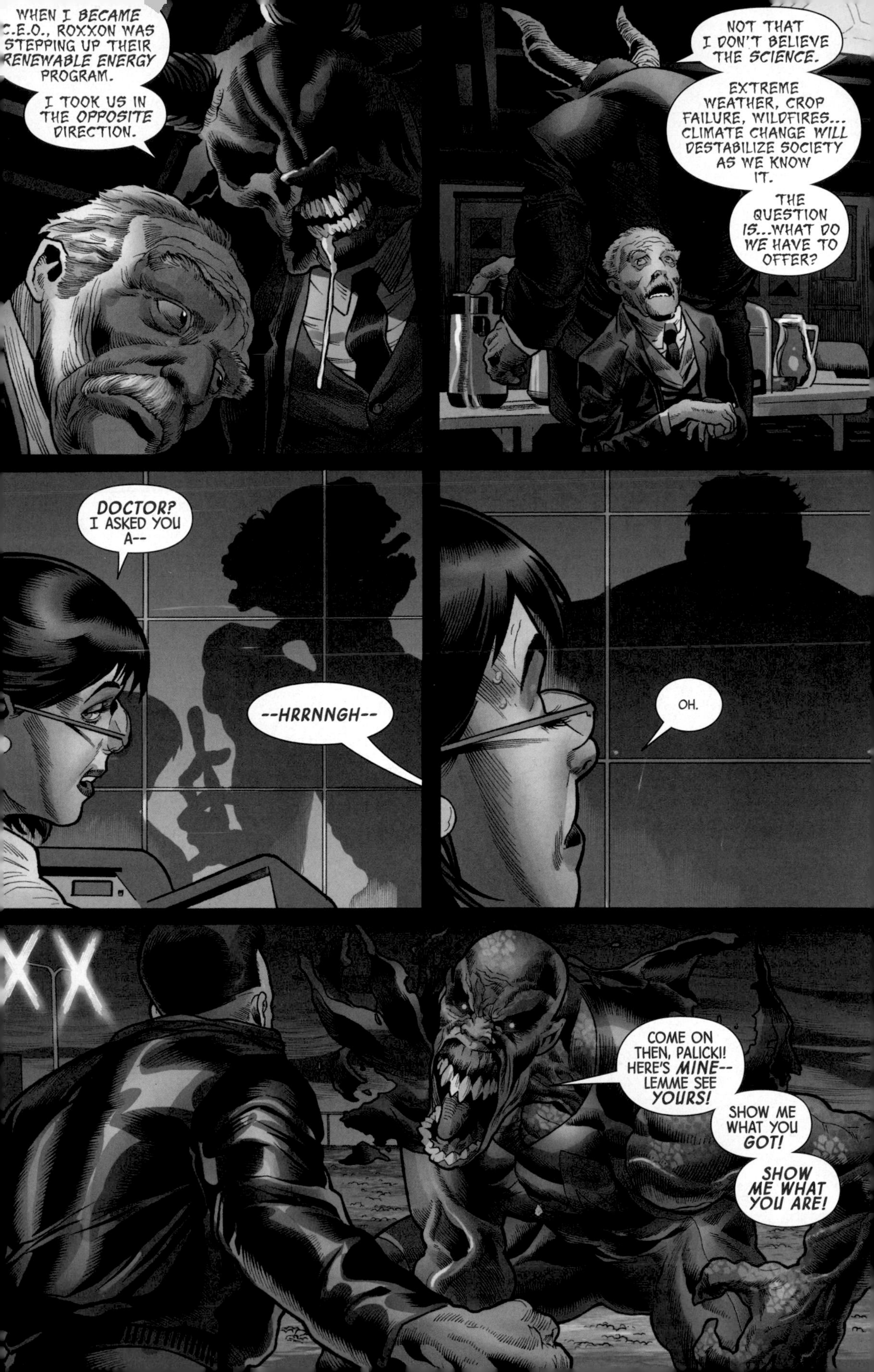
WHEN I BECAME C.E.O., ROXXON WAS STEPPING UP THEIR RENEWABLE ENERGY PROGRAM.
I TOOK US IN THE OPPOSITE DIRECTION.
NOT THAT I DON'T BELIEVE THE SCIENCE.
EXTREME WEATHER, CROP FAILURE, WILDFIRES... CLIMATE CHANGE WILL DESTABILIZE SOCIETY AS WE KNOW IT.
THE QUESTION IS...WHAT DO WE HAVE TO OFFER?
DOCTOR? I ASKED YOU A--
--HRRNNGH--
OH.
COME ON THEN, PALICKI! HERE'S MINE-- LEMME SEE YOURS!
SHOW ME WHAT YOU GOT!
SHOW ME WHAT YOU ARE!

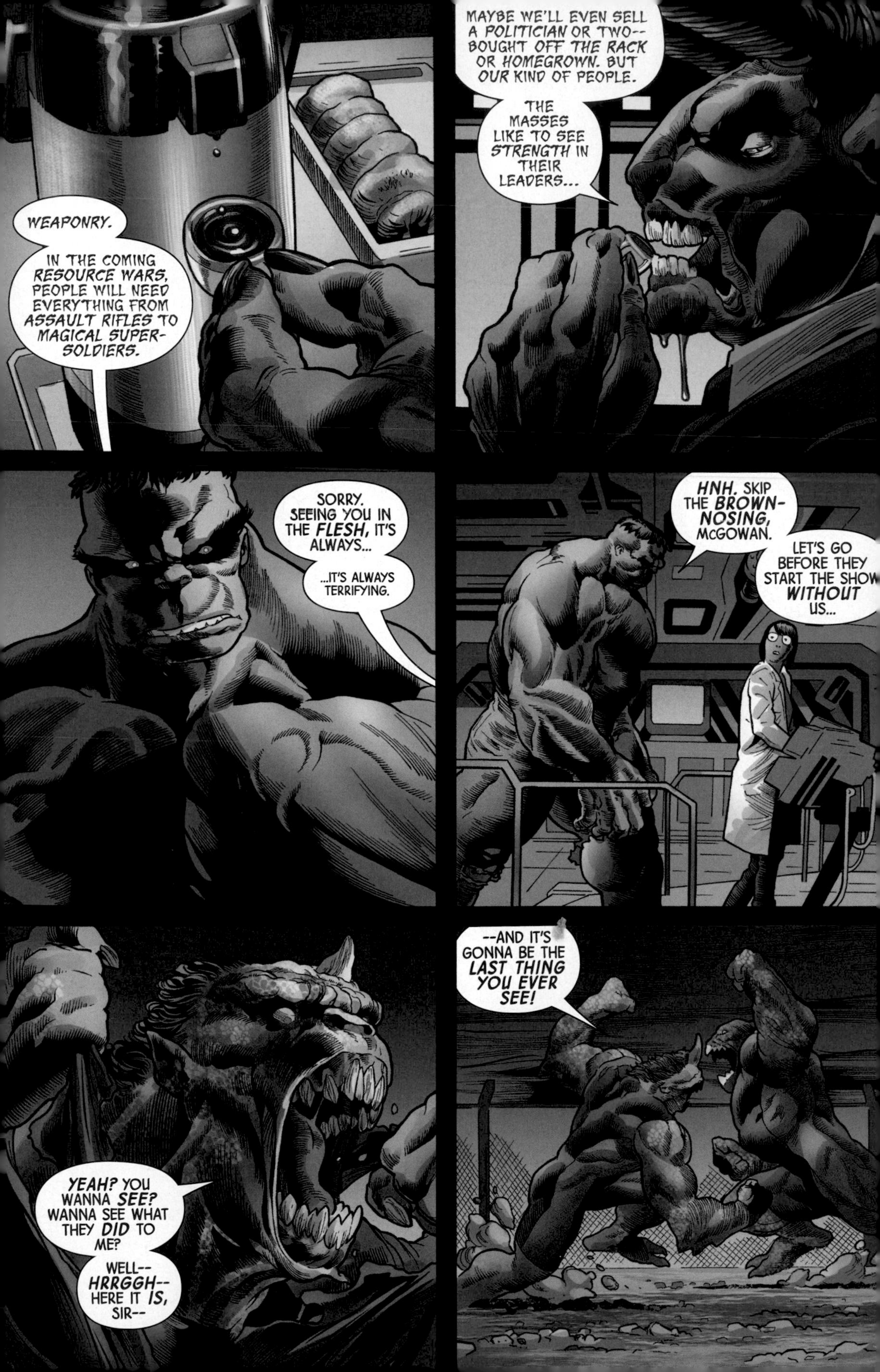
WEAPONRY.
IN THE COMING RESOURCE WARS, PEOPLE WILL NEED EVERYTHING FROM ASSAULT RIFLES TO MAGICAL SUPER-SOLDIERS.
MAYBE WE'LL EVEN SELL A POLITICIAN OR TWO-- BOUGHT OFF THE RACK OR HOMEGROWN. BUT OUR KIND OF PEOPLE.
THE MASSES LIKE TO SEE STRENGTH IN THEIR LEADERS...
SORRY. SEEING YOU IN THE FLESH, IT'S ALWAYS...
...IT'S ALWAYS TERRIFYING.
HNH. SKIP THE BROWN-NOSING, McGOWAN.
LET'S GO BEFORE THEY START THE SHOW WITHOUT US...
YEAH? YOU WANNA SEE? WANNA SEE WHAT THEY DID TO ME?
WELL-- HRRGGH-- HERE IT IS, SIR--
--AND IT'S GONNA BE THE LAST THING YOU EVER SEE!

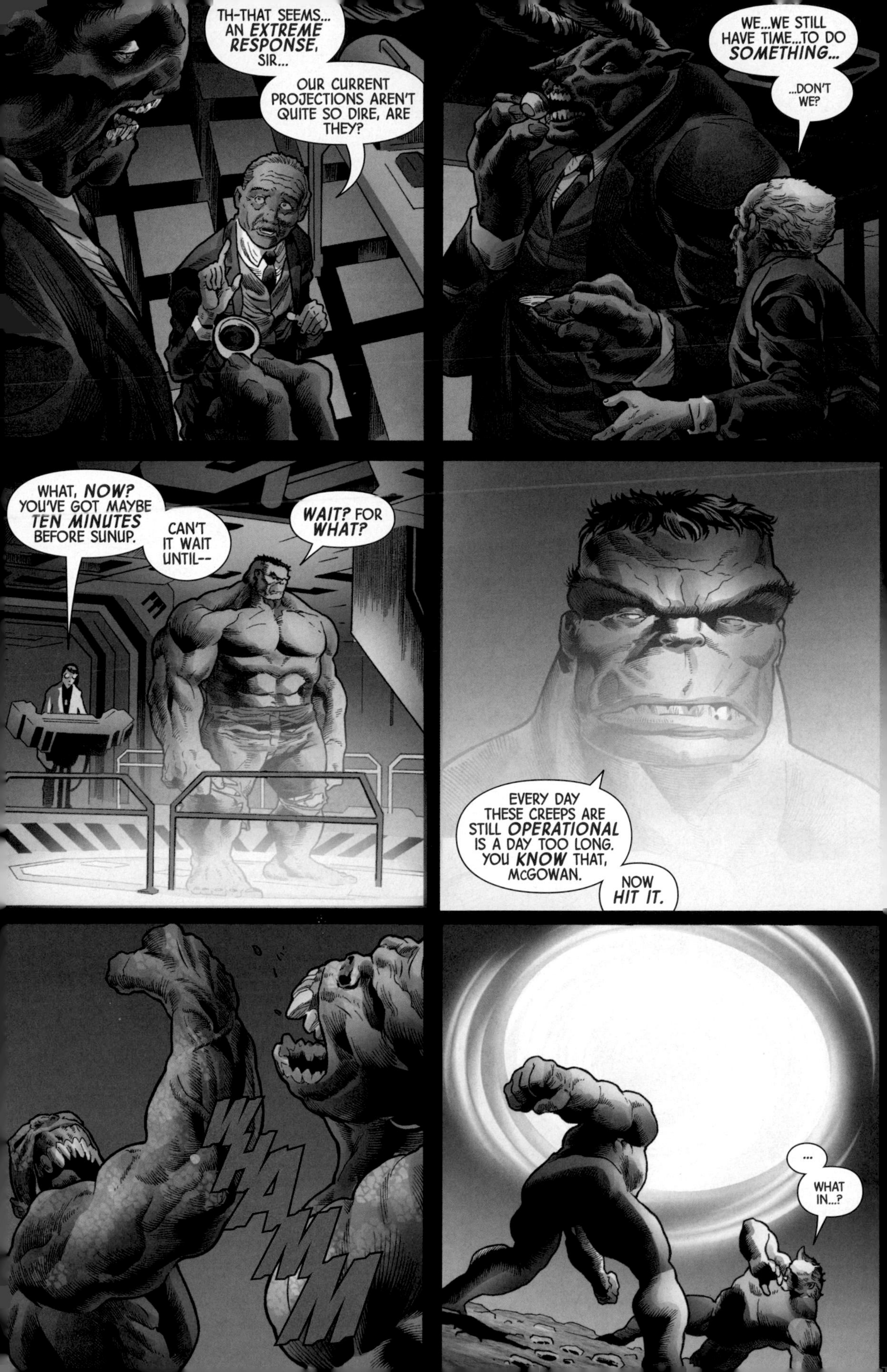

TH-THAT SEEMS... AN EXTREME RESPONSE, SIR...
OUR CURRENT PROJECTIONS AREN'T QUITE SO DIRE, ARE THEY?
WE...WE STILL HAVE TIME...TO DO SOMETHING...
...DON'T WE?
WHAT, NOW? YOU'VE GOT MAYBE TEN MINUTES BEFORE SUNUP.
CAN'T IT WAIT UNTIL--
WAIT? FOR WHAT?
EVERY DAY THESE CREEPS ARE STILL OPERATIONAL IS A DAY TOO LONG. YOU KNOW THAT, McGOWAN.
NOW HIT IT.
WHAM
...
WHAT IN...?

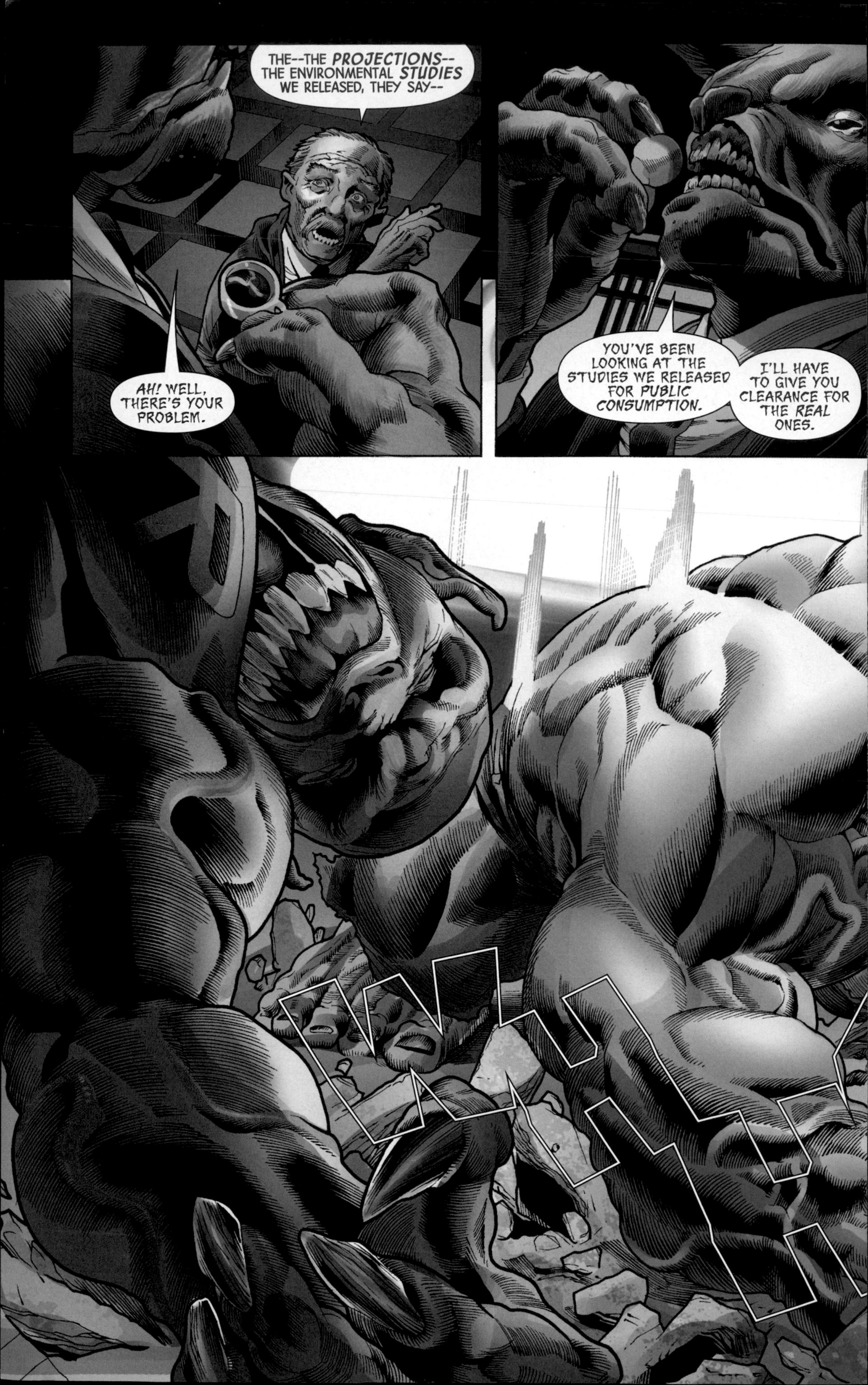
THE--THE PROJECTIONS-- THE ENVIRONMENTAL STUDIES WE RELEASED, THEY SAY--
AH! WELL, THERE'S YOUR PROBLEM.
YOU'VE BEEN LOOKING AT THE STUDIES WE RELEASED FOR PUBLIC CONSUMPTION.
I'LL HAVE TO GIVE YOU CLEARANCE FOR THE REAL ONES.

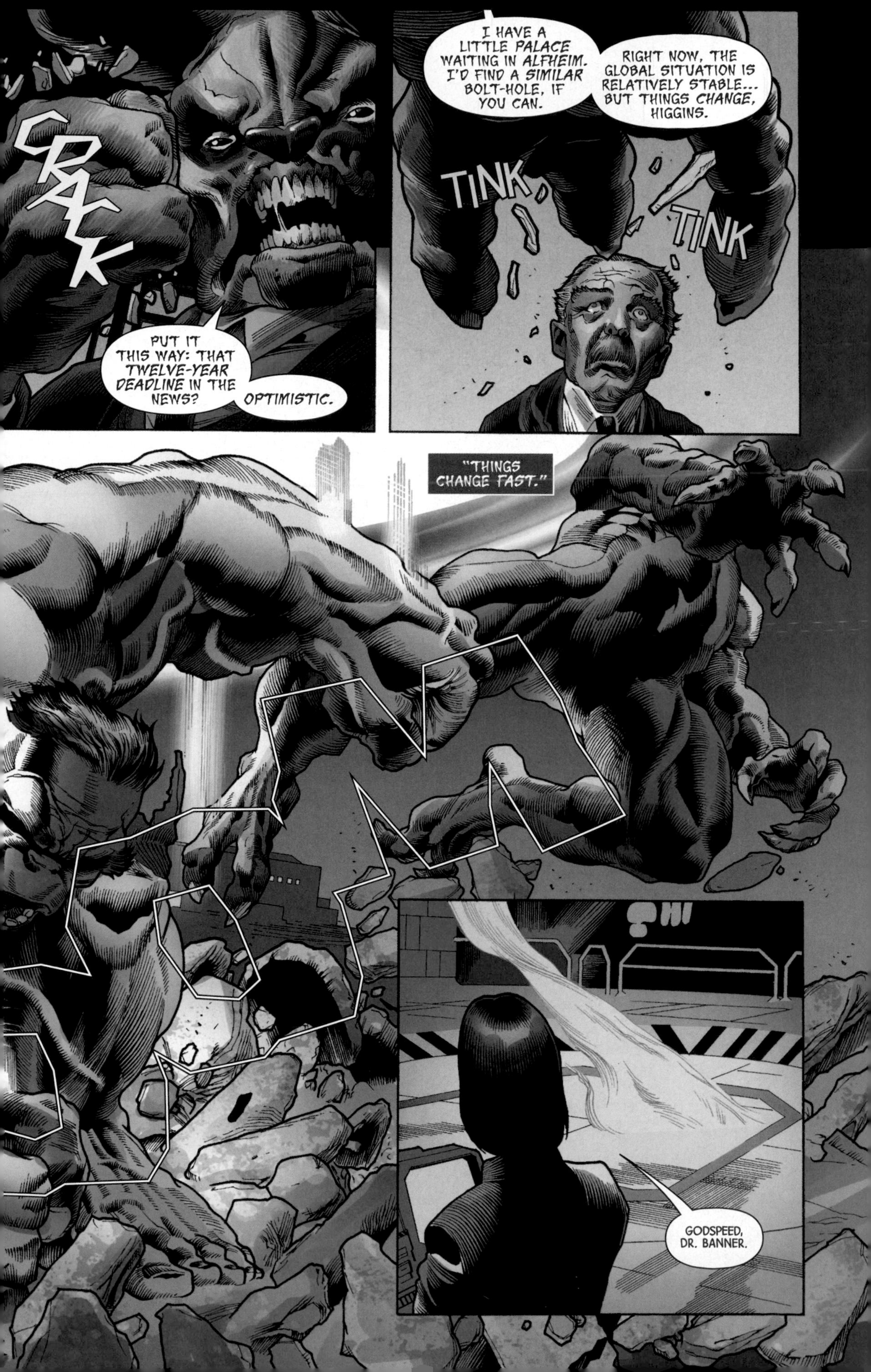
CRACK
PUT IT THIS WAY: THAT TWELVE-YEAR DEADLINE IN THE NEWS?
OPTIMISTIC.
I HAVE A LITTLE PALACE WAITING IN ALFHEIM. I'D FIND A SIMILAR BOLT-HOLE, IF YOU CAN.
RIGHT NOW, THE GLOBAL SITUATION IS RELATIVELY STABLE... BUT THINGS CHANGE, HIGGINS.
TINK
TINK
"THINGS CHANGE FAST."
GODSPEED, DR. BANNER.

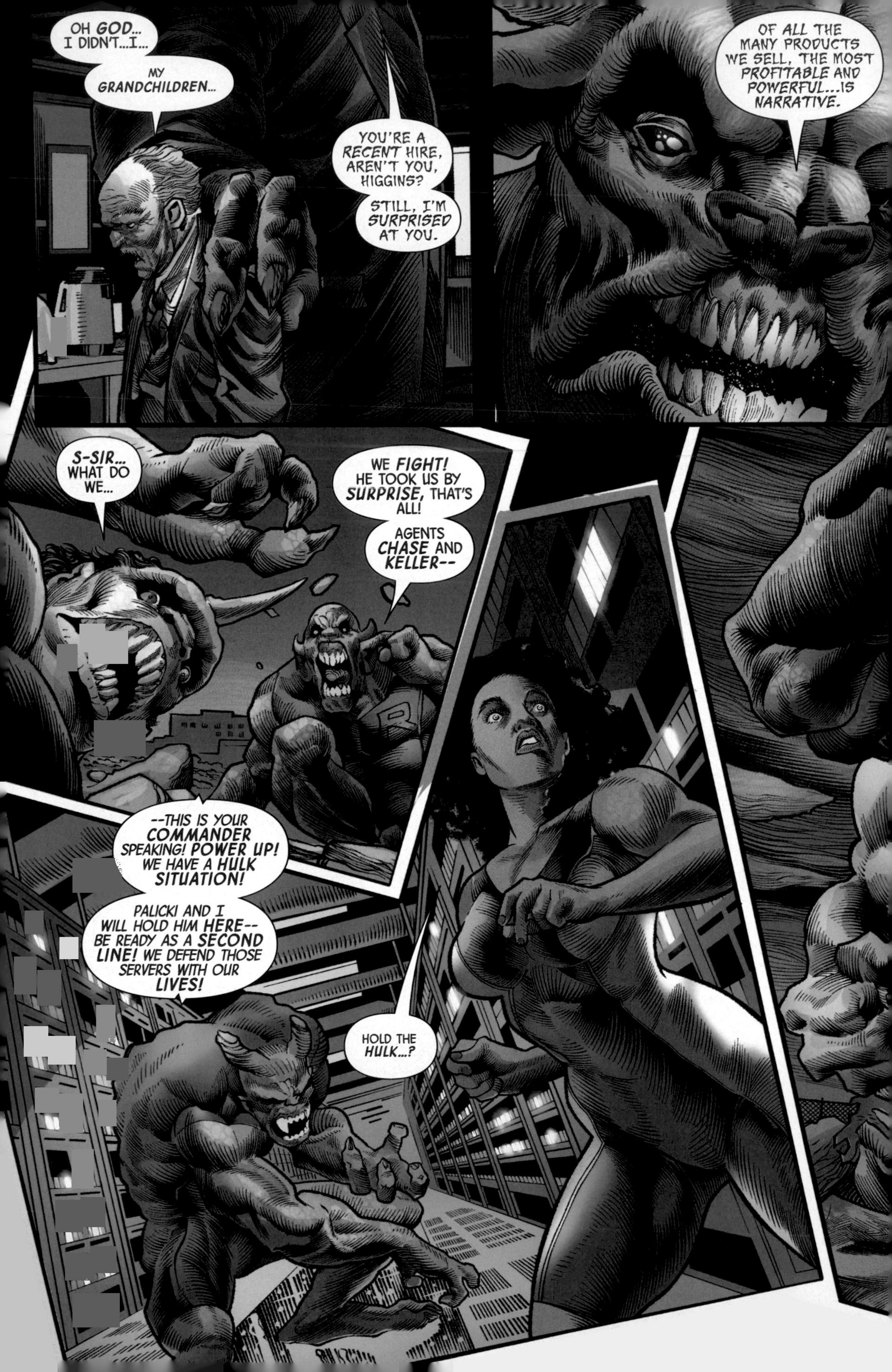
OH GOD... I DIDN'T...I...
MY GRANDCHILDREN...
YOU'RE A RECENT HIRE, AREN'T YOU, HIGGINS?
STILL, I'M SURPRISED AT YOU.
OF ALL THE MANY PRODUCTS WE SELL, THE MOST PROFITABLE AND POWERFUL...IS NARRATIVE.
S-SIR... WHAT DO WE...
WE FIGHT! HE TOOK US BY SURPRISE, THAT'S ALL!
AGENTS CHASE AND KELLER--
--THIS IS YOUR COMMANDER SPEAKING! POWER UP! WE HAVE A HULK SITUATION!
PALICKI AND I WILL HOLD HIM HERE-- BE READY AS A SECOND LINE! WE DEFEND THOSE SERVERS WITH OUR LIVES!
HOLD THE HULK...?

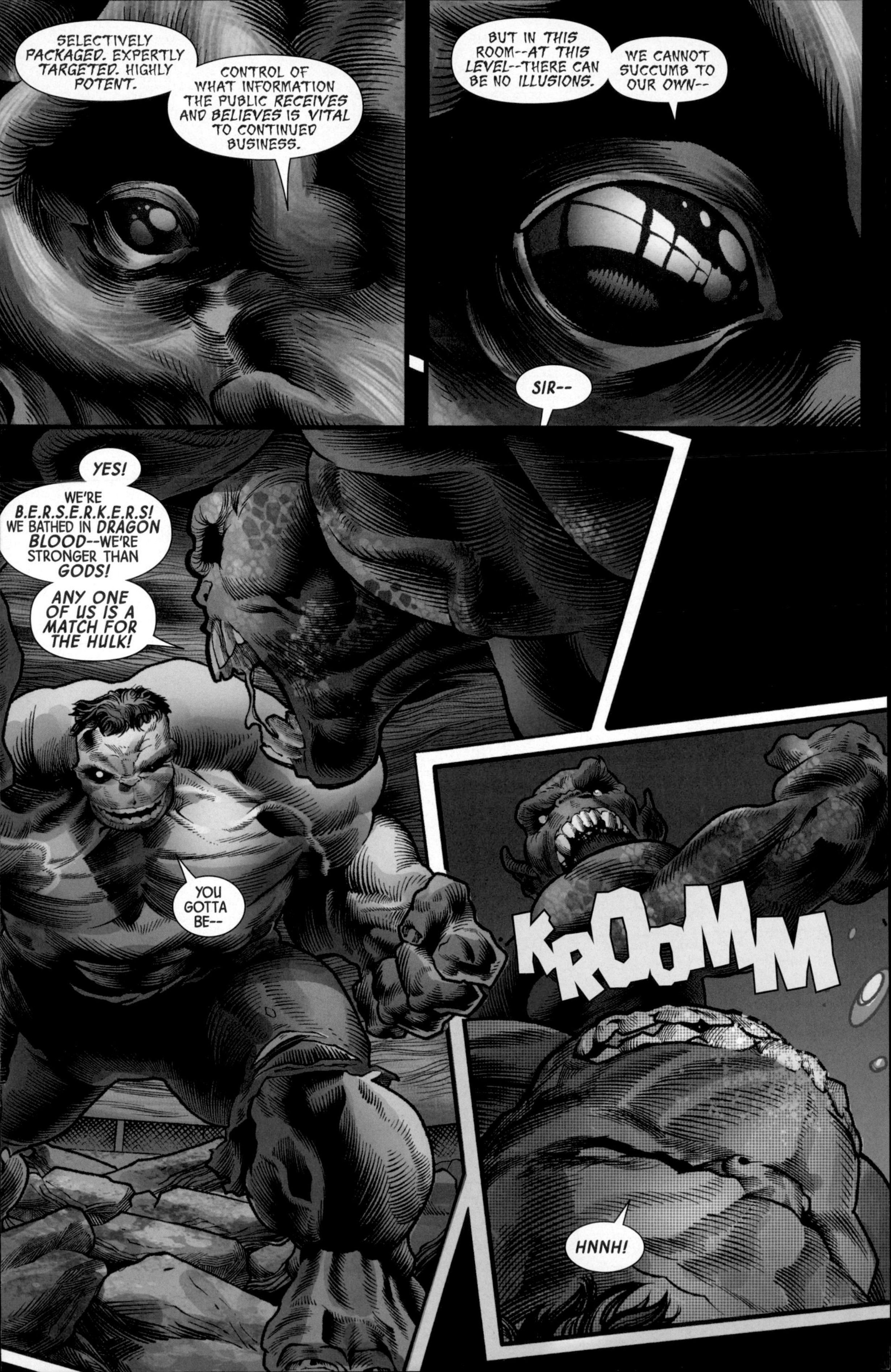
SELECTIVELY PACKAGED. EXPERTLY TARGETED. HIGHLY POTENT.
CONTROL OF WHAT INFORMATION THE PUBLIC RECEIVES AND BELIEVES IS VITAL TO CONTINUED BUSINESS.
BUT IN THIS ROOM--AT THIS LEVEL--THERE CAN BE NO ILLUSIONS.
WE CANNOT SUCCUMB TO OUR OWN--
SIR--
YES!
WE'RE B.E.R.S.E.R.K.E.R.S! WE BATHED IN DRAGON BLOOD--WE'RE STRONGER THAN GODS!
ANY ONE OF US IS A MATCH FOR THE HULK!
YOU GOTTA BE--
KROOMMM
HNNH!

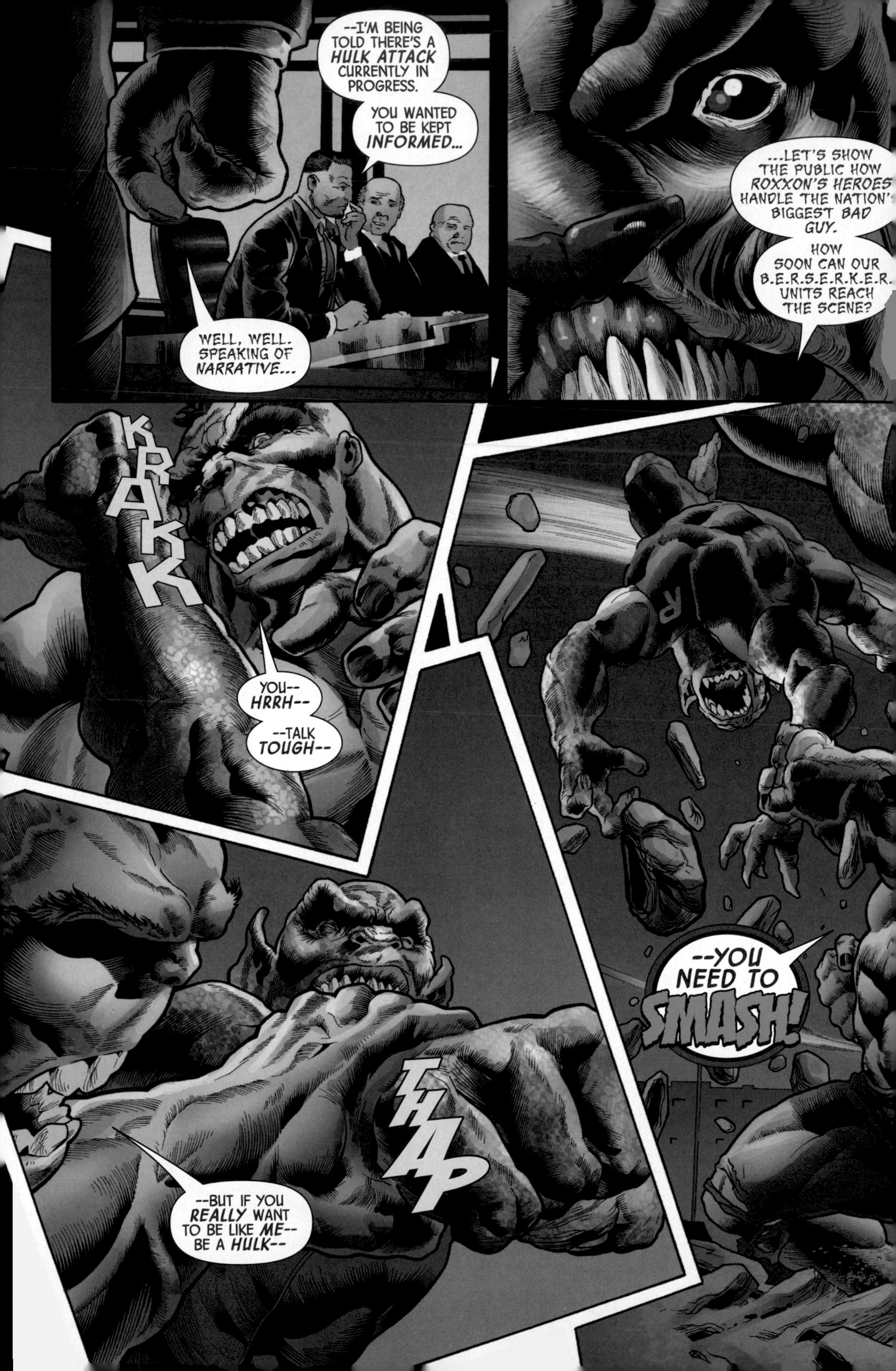
--I'M BEING TOLD THERE'S A HULK ATTACK CURRENTLY IN PROGRESS.
YOU WANTED TO BE KEPT INFORMED...
WELL, WELL. SPEAKING OF NARRATIVE...
...LET'S SHOW THE PUBLIC HOW ROXXON'S HEROES HANDLE THE NATION'S BIGGEST BAD GUY.
HOW SOON CAN OUR B.E.R.S.E.R.K.E.R. UNITS REACH THE SCENE?
KRAKK
YOU-- HRRH--
--TALK TOUGH--
--BUT IF YOU REALLY WANT TO BE LIKE ME-- BE A HULK--
THAP
--YOU NEED TO SMASH!

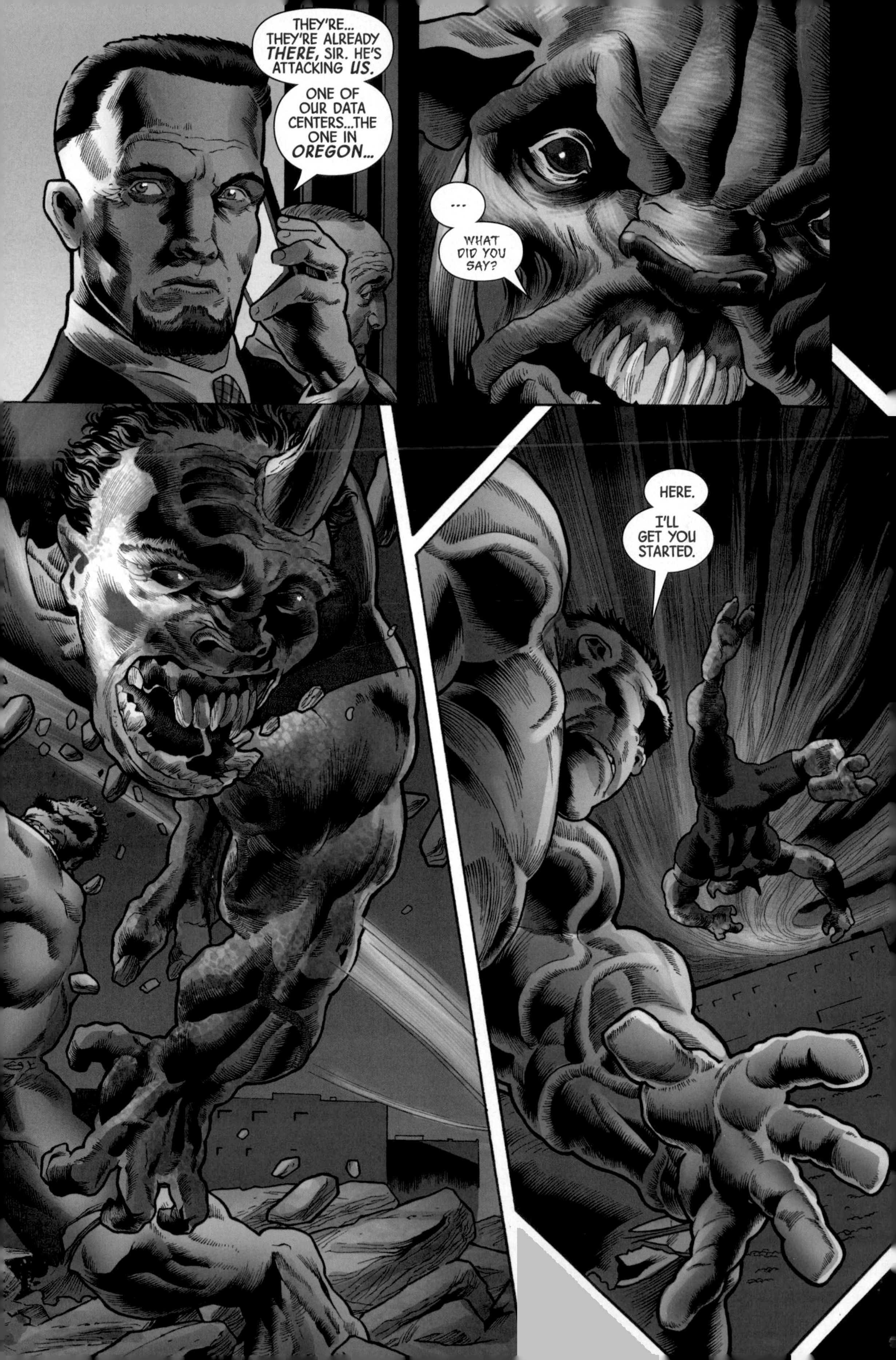
THEY'RE... THEY'RE ALREADY THERE, SIR. HE'S ATTACKING US.
ONE OF OUR DATA CENTERS...THE ONE IN OREGON...
...
WHAT DID YOU SAY?
HERE.
I'LL GET YOU STARTED.

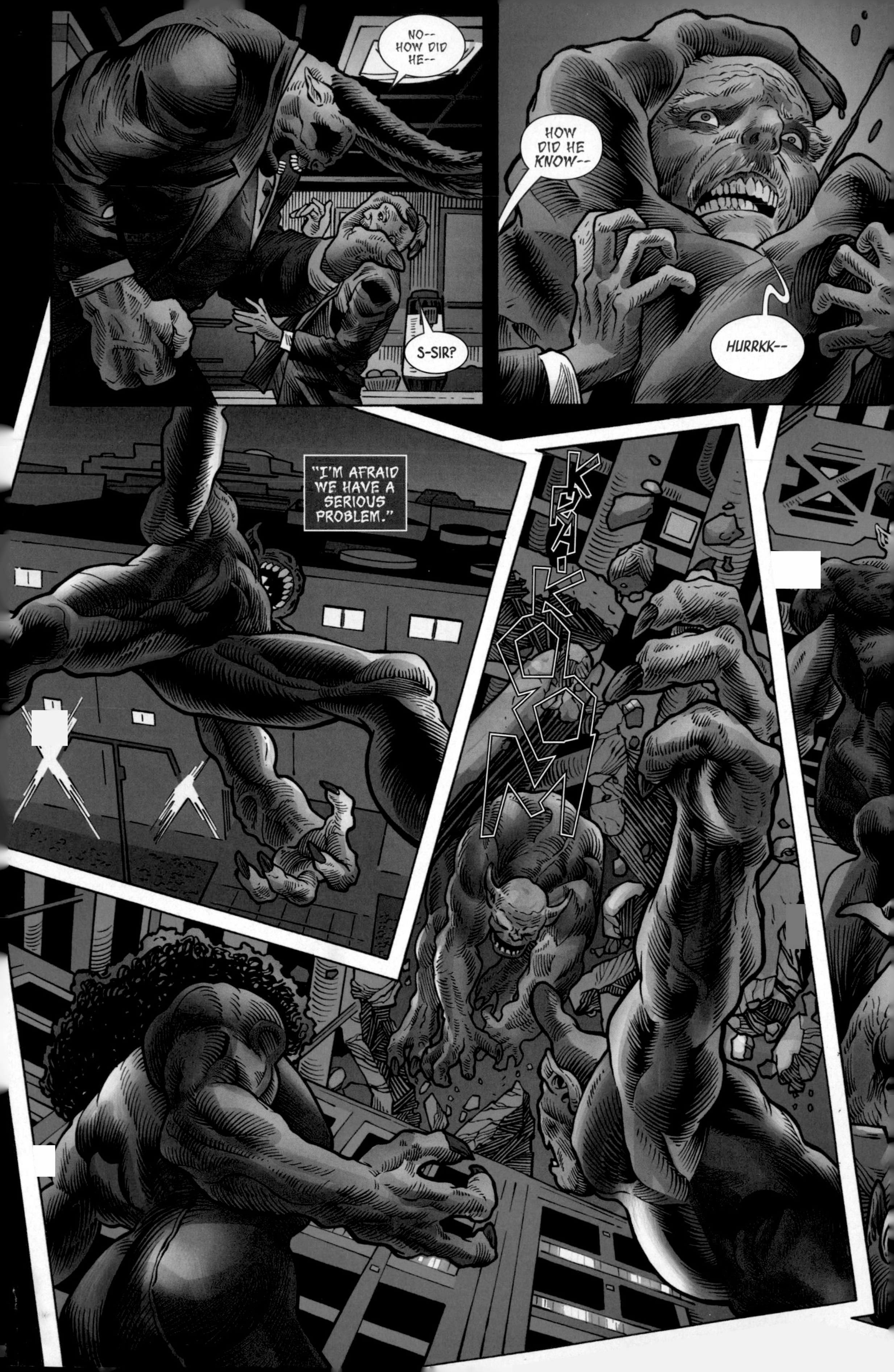
NO--
HOW DID
HE--
S-SIR?
HOW
DID HE
KNOW--
HURRKK--
"I'M AFRAID
WE HAVE A
SERIOUS
PROBLEM."
KRA-KOOOM

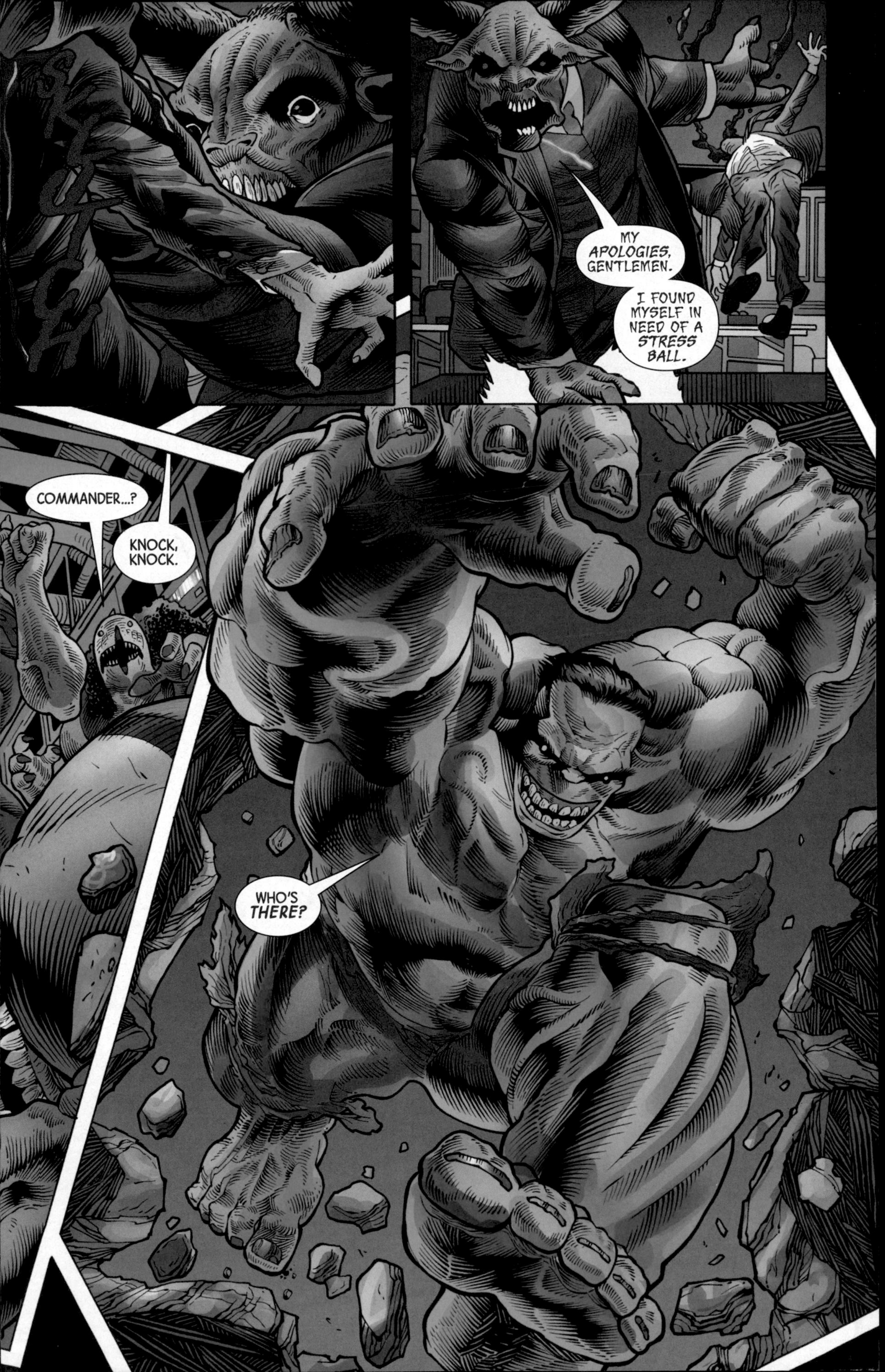

MY APOLOGIES, GENTLEMEN.
I FOUND MYSELF IN NEED OF A STRESS BALL.
COMMANDER...?
KNOCK, KNOCK.
WHO'S THERE?

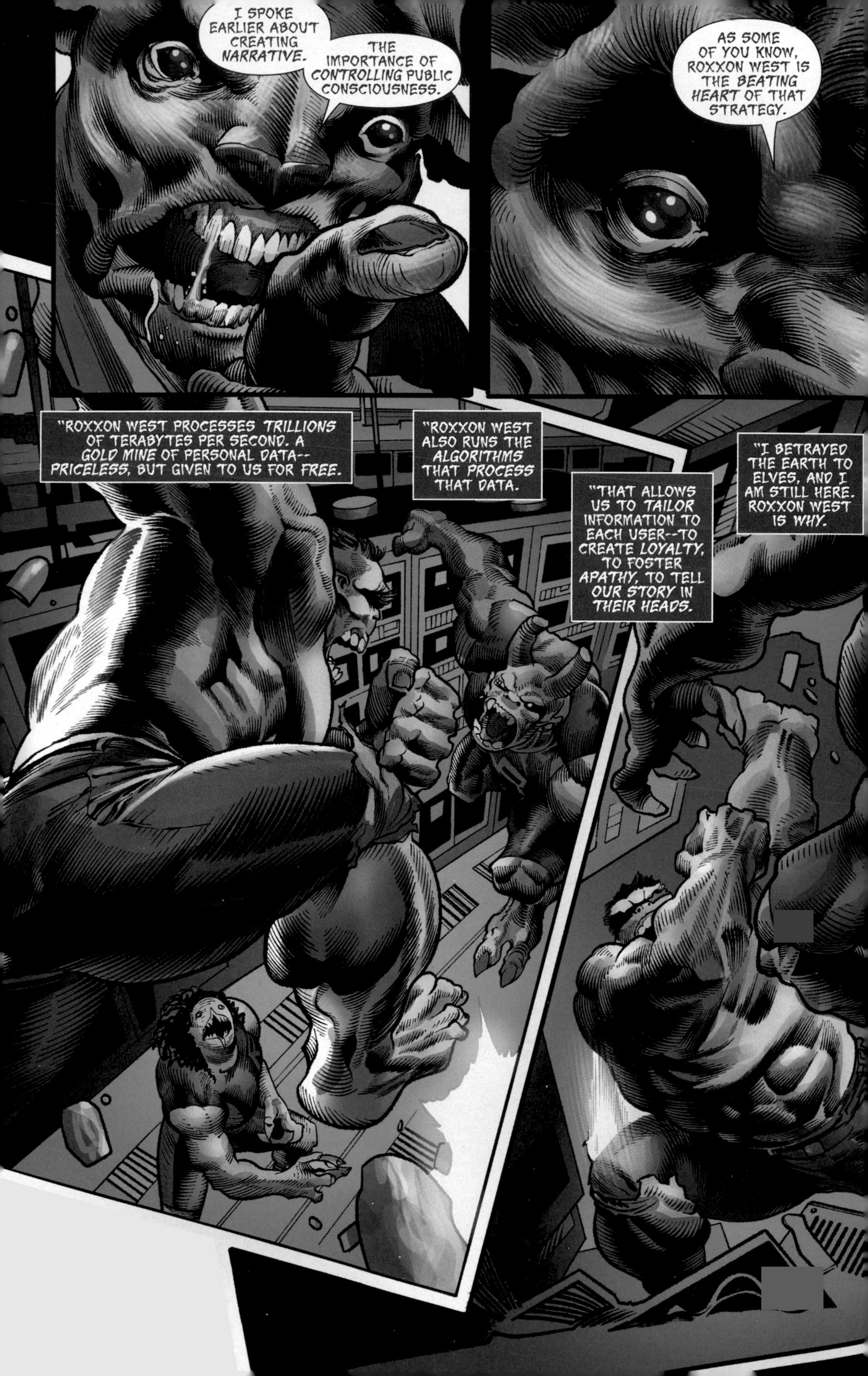
I SPOKE EARLIER ABOUT CREATING NARRATIVE.
THE IMPORTANCE OF CONTROLLING PUBLIC CONSCIOUSNESS.
AS SOME OF YOU KNOW, ROXXON WEST IS THE BEATING HEART OF THAT STRATEGY.
"ROXXON WEST PROCESSES TRILLIONS OF TERABYTES PER SECOND. A GOLD MINE OF PERSONAL DATA--PRICELESS, BUT GIVEN TO US FOR FREE.
"ROXXON WEST ALSO RUNS THE ALGORITHMS THAT PROCESS THAT DATA.
"THAT ALLOWS US TO TAILOR INFORMATION TO EACH USER--TO CREATE LOYALTY, TO FOSTER APATHY, TO TELL OUR STORY IN THEIR HEADS.
"I BETRAYED THE EARTH TO ELVES, AND I AM STILL HERE. ROXXON WEST IS WHY.

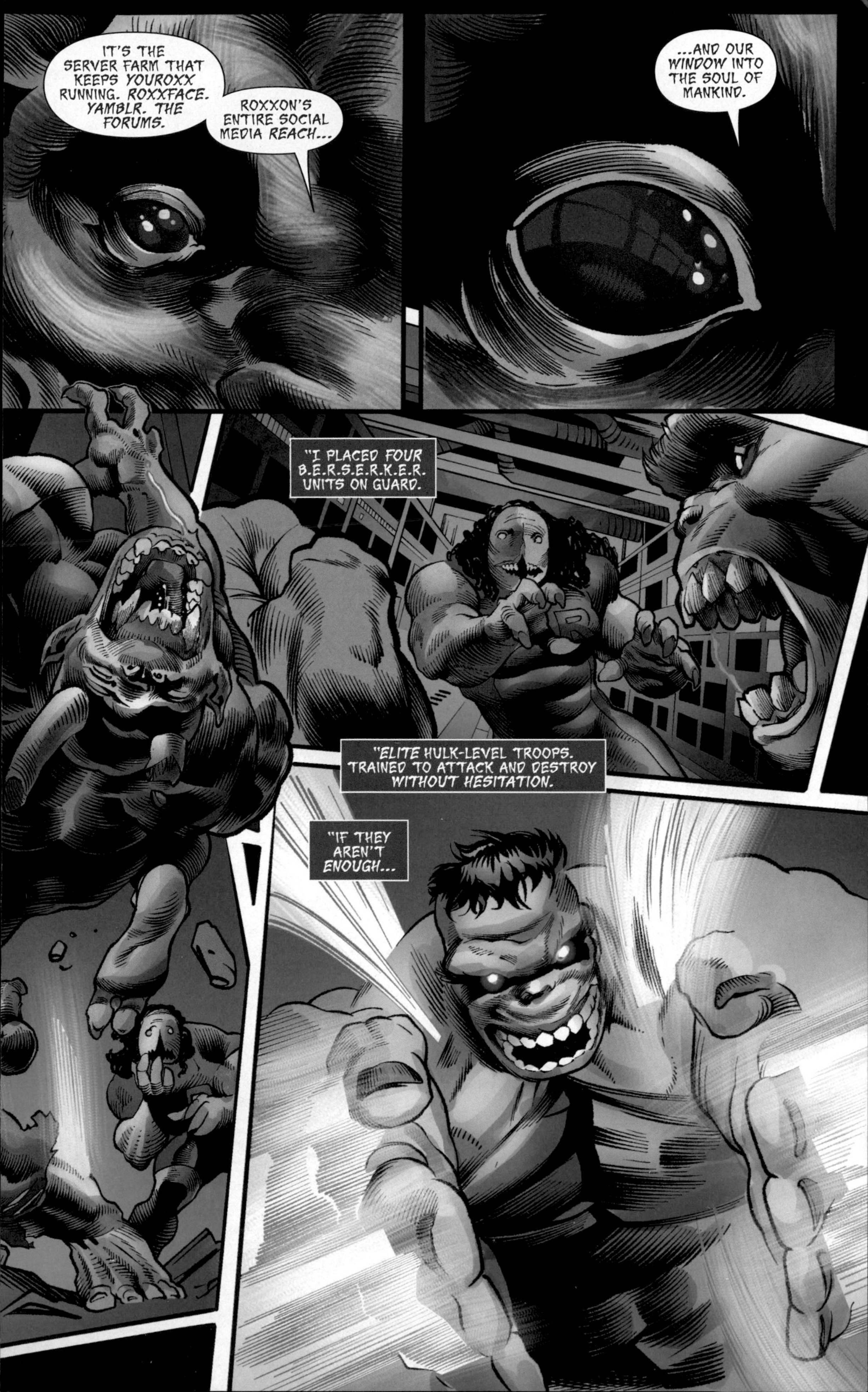
IT'S THE SERVER FARM THAT KEEPS YOUROXX RUNNING. ROXXFACE. YAMBLR. THE FORUMS.
ROXXON'S ENTIRE SOCIAL MEDIA REACH...
...AND OUR WINDOW INTO THE SOUL OF MANKIND.
"I PLACED FOUR B.E.R.S.E.R.K.E.R. UNITS ON GUARD.
"ELITE HULK-LEVEL TROOPS. TRAINED TO ATTACK AND DESTROY WITHOUT HESITATION.
"IF THEY AREN'T ENOUGH...

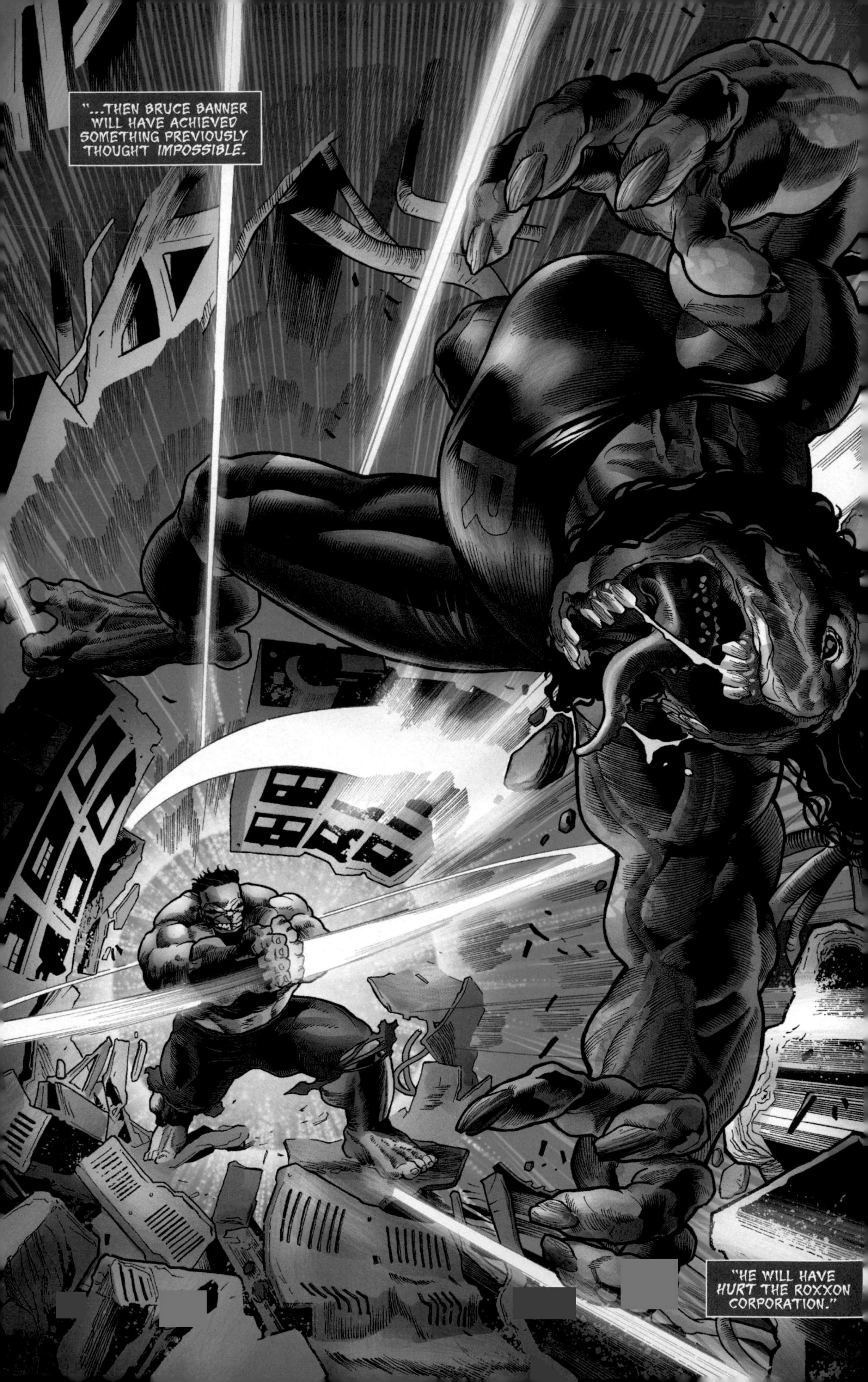
"...THEN BRUCE BANNER WILL HAVE ACHIEVED SOMETHING PREVIOUSLY THOUGHT *IMPOSSIBLE*.
"HE WILL HAVE HURT THE ROXXON CORPORATION."

THE...THE SERVERS ARE *DOWN*, SIR. ALL OF THEM. THE BACKUPS SAVED WHAT THEY *COULD*, BUT...

...WELL, THE SYSTEM ISN'T *DESIGNED* FOR...

NO. AND NEITHER ARE WE.

NOT *YET*.

MEETING ADJOURNED.

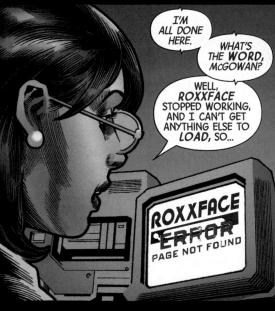

I'M ALL DONE HERE.

WHAT'S THE *WORD*, McGOWAN?

WELL, *ROXXFACE* STOPPED WORKING, AND I CAN'T GET ANYTHING ELSE TO *LOAD*, SO...

ROXXFACE
ERROR
PAGE NOT FOUND

...I GUESS DR. BANNER WAS *RIGHT*. THAT'S HOW YOU HURT THEM.

WE SHOULD TRANSLOCATE YOU *BACK*--IT'S ALMOST *SUNRISE*--

YEAH. FIGURED I'D *WATCH* IT.

WHAT?

I--I THOUGHT--THE *SUNLIGHT*--

YEAH. THE DAY AIN'T *MY* TIME. BUT BANNER SHOWED ME I...HRRHH...I COULD *FIGHT* THAT.

WE CAN FIGHT THAT. WE WORK *TOGETHER*, McGOWAN.

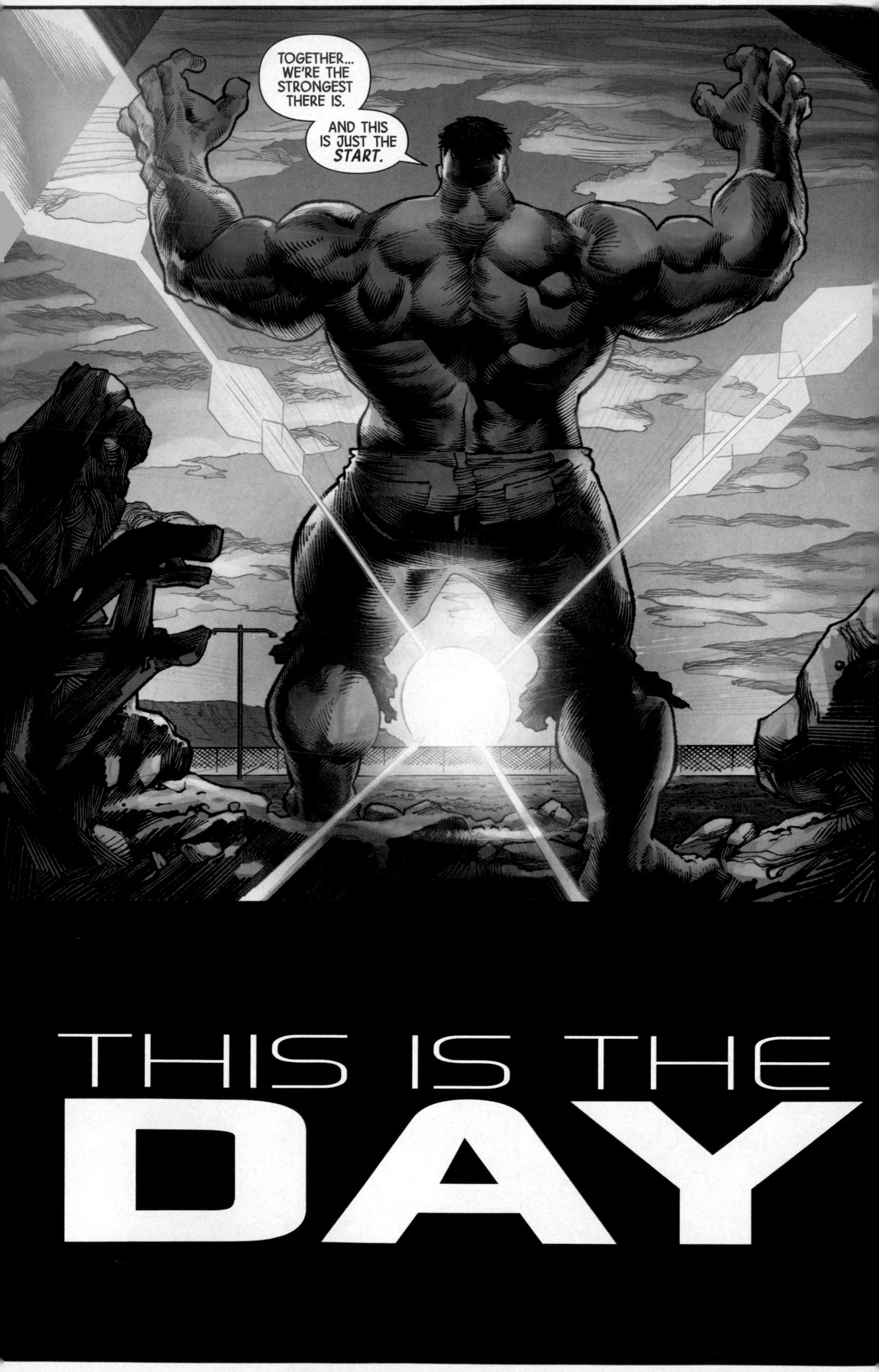
TOGETHER... WE'RE THE STRONGEST THERE IS.
AND THIS IS JUST THE *START.*

THIS IS THE
DAY

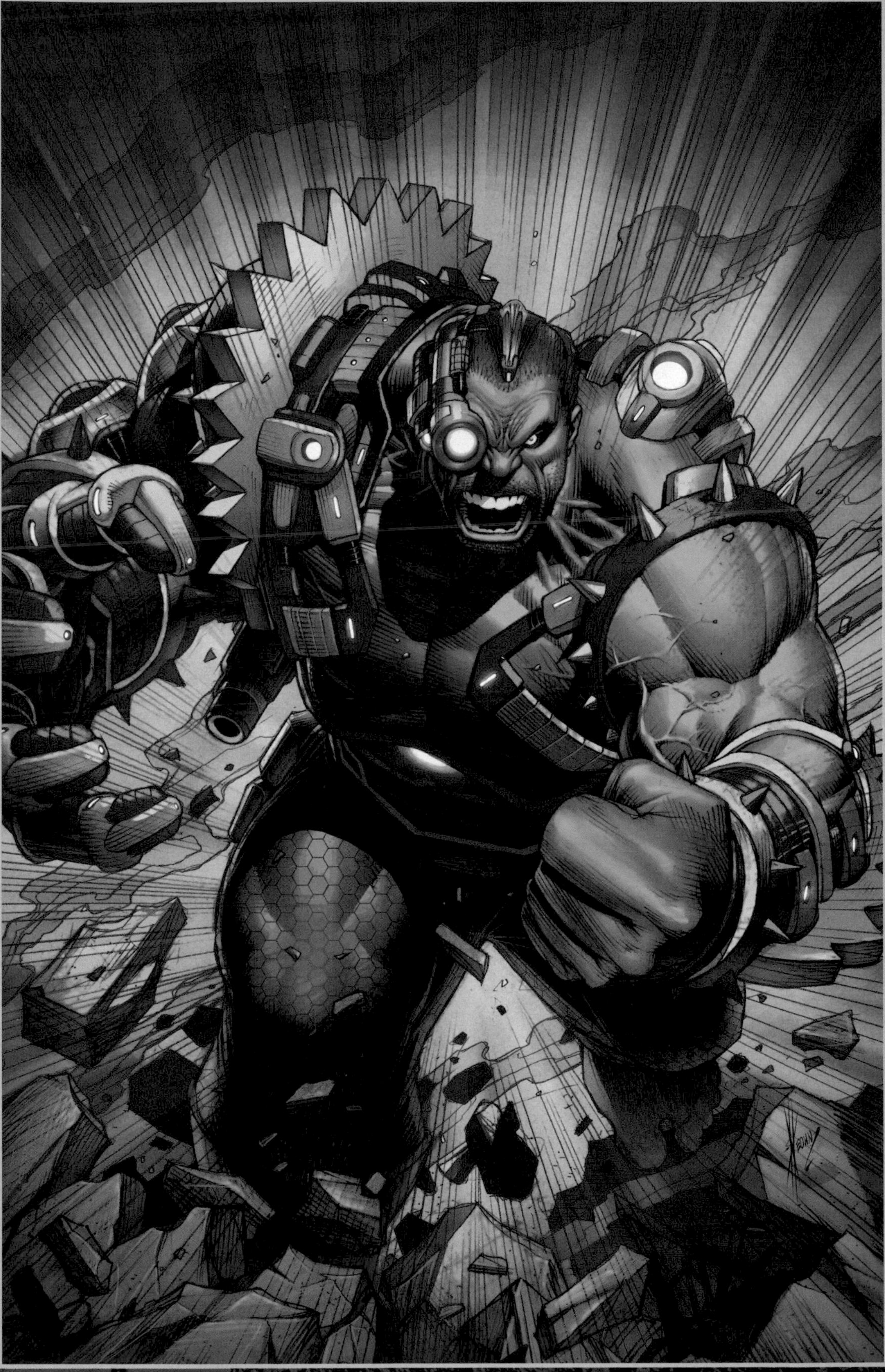

DALE KEOWN & JASON KEITH
#28 2020 VARIANT

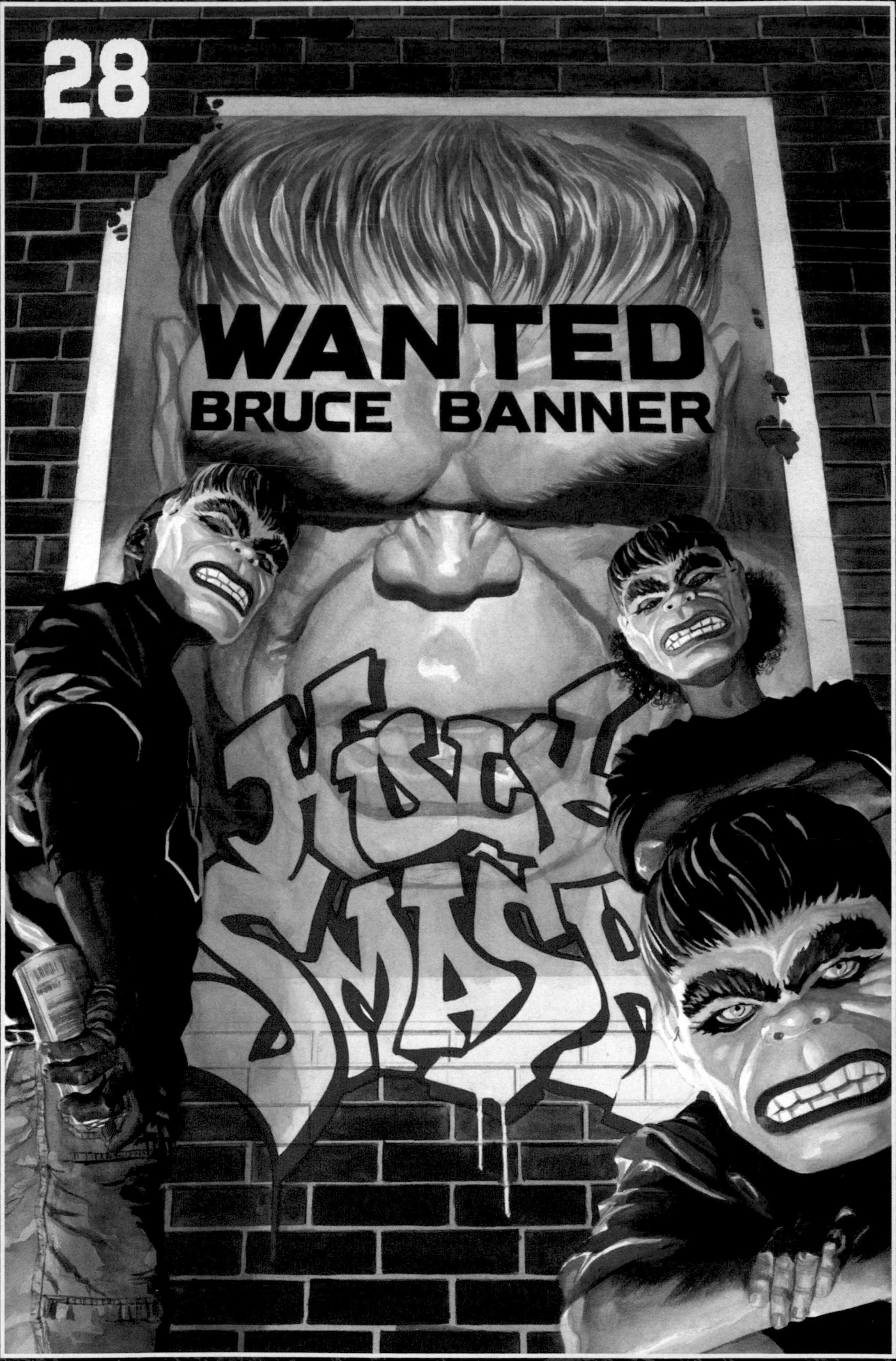

28
WANTED
BRUCE BANNER

"WE CONSIDERED OURSELVES TO BE A POWERFUL CULTURE."

— U.S. DEPARTMENT OF ENERGY

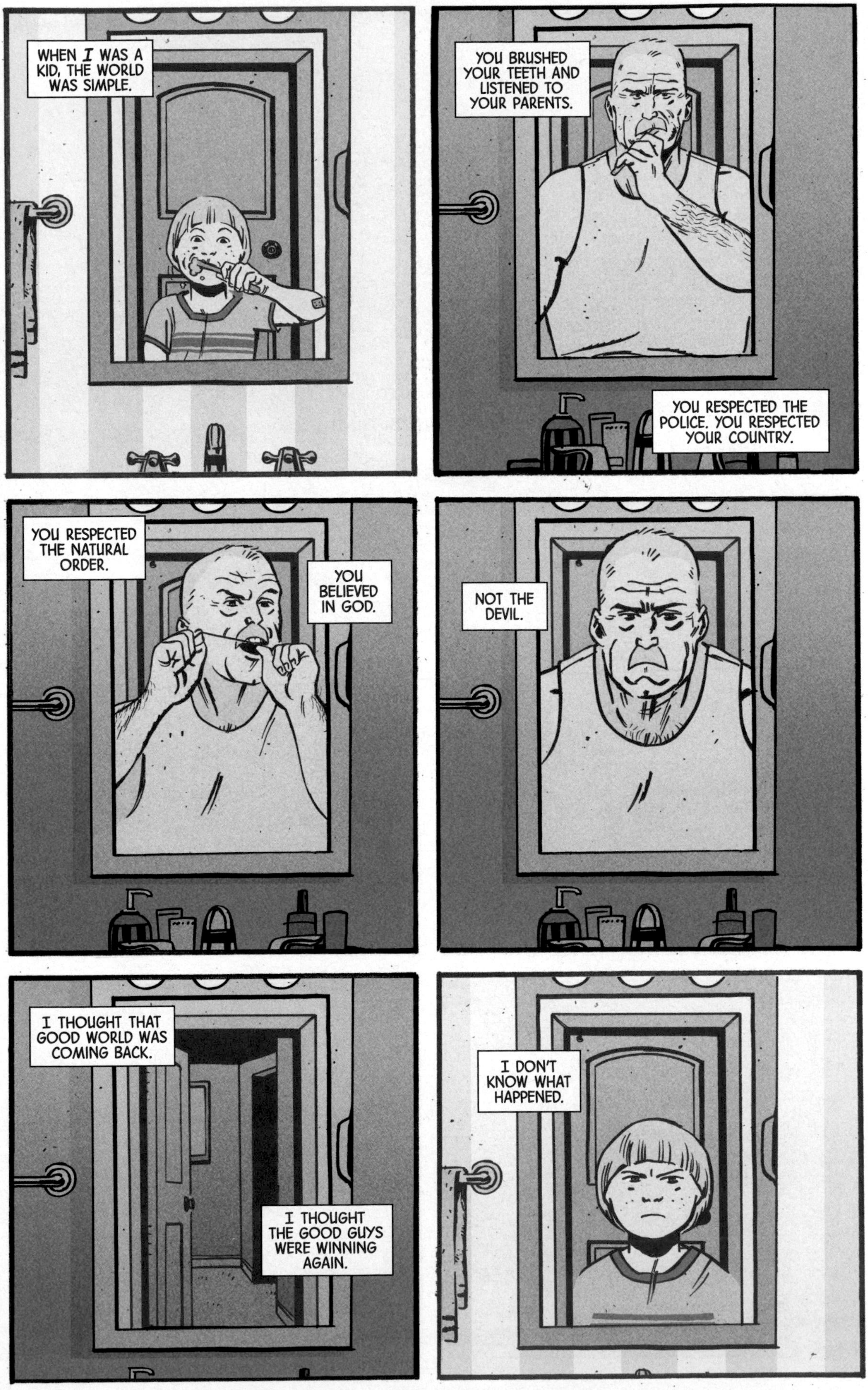
WHEN I WAS A KID, THE WORLD WAS SIMPLE.
YOU BRUSHED YOUR TEETH AND LISTENED TO YOUR PARENTS.
YOU RESPECTED THE POLICE. YOU RESPECTED YOUR COUNTRY.
YOU RESPECTED THE NATURAL ORDER.
YOU BELIEVED IN GOD.
NOT THE DEVIL.
I THOUGHT THAT GOOD WORLD WAS COMING BACK.
I THOUGHT THE GOOD GUYS WERE WINNING AGAIN.
I DON'T KNOW WHAT HAPPENED.

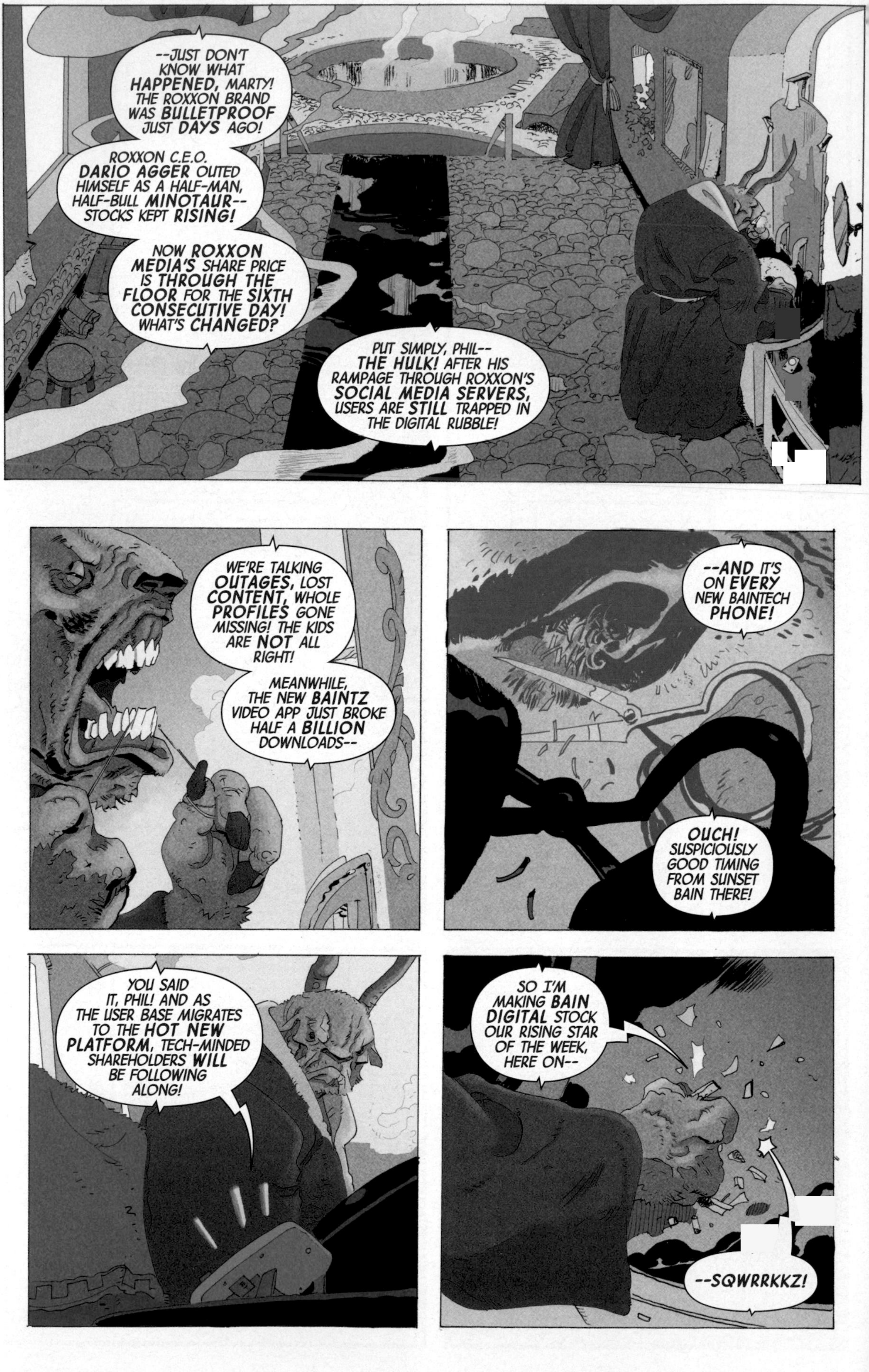
--JUST DON'T KNOW WHAT HAPPENED, MARTY! THE ROXXON BRAND WAS BULLETPROOF JUST DAYS AGO!
ROXXON C.E.O. DARIO AGGER OUTED HIMSELF AS A HALF-MAN, HALF-BULL MINOTAUR-- STOCKS KEPT RISING!
NOW ROXXON MEDIA'S SHARE PRICE IS THROUGH THE FLOOR FOR THE SIXTH CONSECUTIVE DAY! WHAT'S CHANGED?
PUT SIMPLY, PHIL-- THE HULK! AFTER HIS RAMPAGE THROUGH ROXXON'S SOCIAL MEDIA SERVERS, USERS ARE STILL TRAPPED IN THE DIGITAL RUBBLE!
WE'RE TALKING OUTAGES, LOST CONTENT, WHOLE PROFILES GONE MISSING! THE KIDS ARE NOT ALL RIGHT!
MEANWHILE, THE NEW BAINTZ VIDEO APP JUST BROKE HALF A BILLION DOWNLOADS--
--AND IT'S ON EVERY NEW BAINTECH PHONE!
OUCH! SUSPICIOUSLY GOOD TIMING FROM SUNSET BAIN THERE!
YOU SAID IT, PHIL! AND AS THE USER BASE MIGRATES TO THE HOT NEW PLATFORM, TECH-MINDED SHAREHOLDERS WILL BE FOLLOWING ALONG!
SO I'M MAKING BAIN DIGITAL STOCK OUR RISING STAR OF THE WEEK, HERE ON--
--SQWRRKKZ!

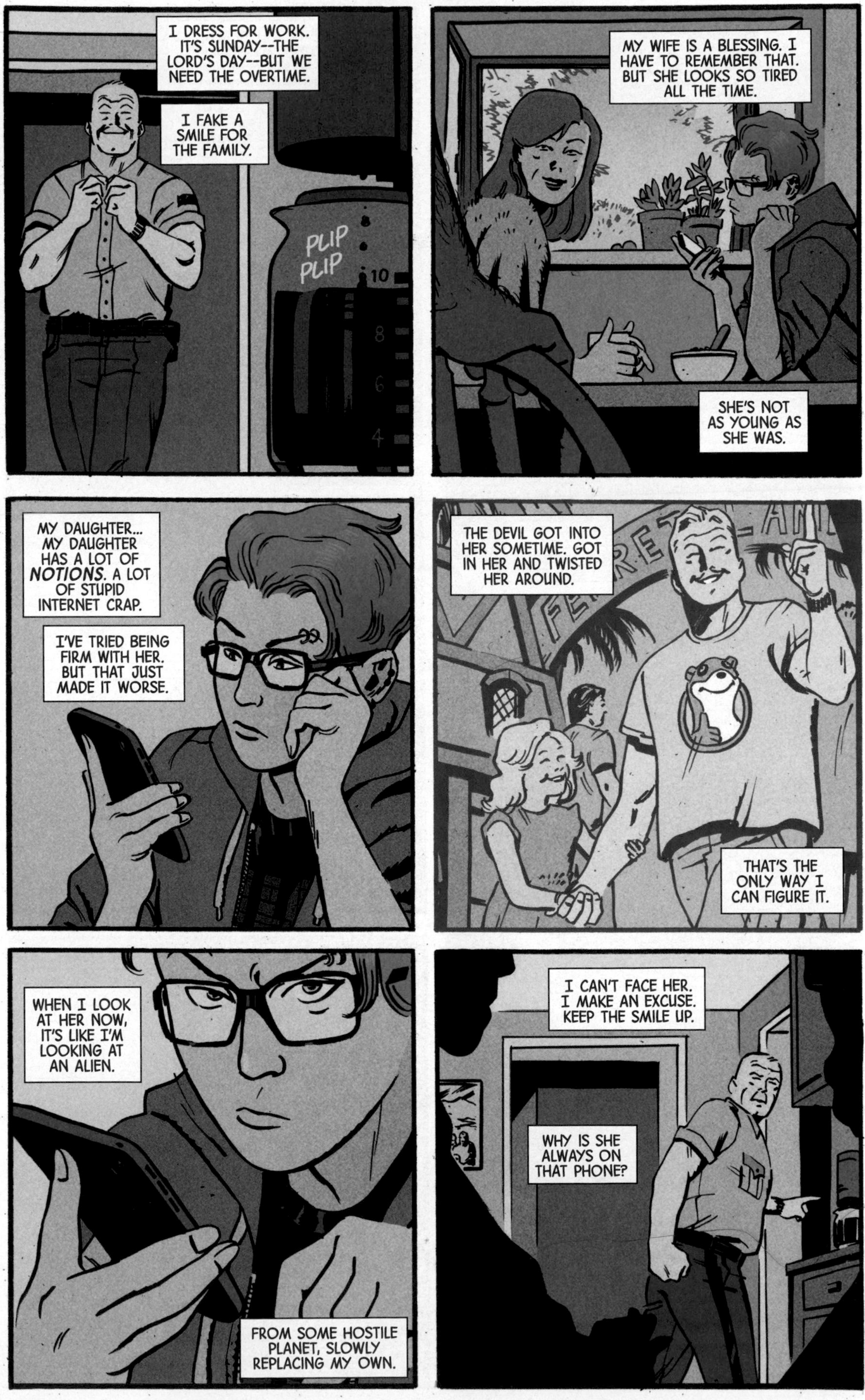
I DRESS FOR WORK. IT'S SUNDAY--THE LORD'S DAY--BUT WE NEED THE OVERTIME.
I FAKE A SMILE FOR THE FAMILY.
PLIP PLIP
MY WIFE IS A BLESSING. I HAVE TO REMEMBER THAT. BUT SHE LOOKS SO TIRED ALL THE TIME.
SHE'S NOT AS YOUNG AS SHE WAS.
MY DAUGHTER... MY DAUGHTER HAS A LOT OF *NOTIONS*. A LOT OF STUPID INTERNET CRAP.
I'VE TRIED BEING FIRM WITH HER. BUT THAT JUST MADE IT WORSE.
THE DEVIL GOT INTO HER SOMETIME. GOT IN HER AND TWISTED HER AROUND.
THAT'S THE ONLY WAY I CAN FIGURE IT.
WHEN I LOOK AT HER NOW, IT'S LIKE I'M LOOKING AT AN ALIEN.
FROM SOME HOSTILE PLANET, SLOWLY REPLACING MY OWN.
I CAN'T FACE HER. I MAKE AN EXCUSE. KEEP THE SMILE UP.
WHY IS SHE ALWAYS ON THAT PHONE?

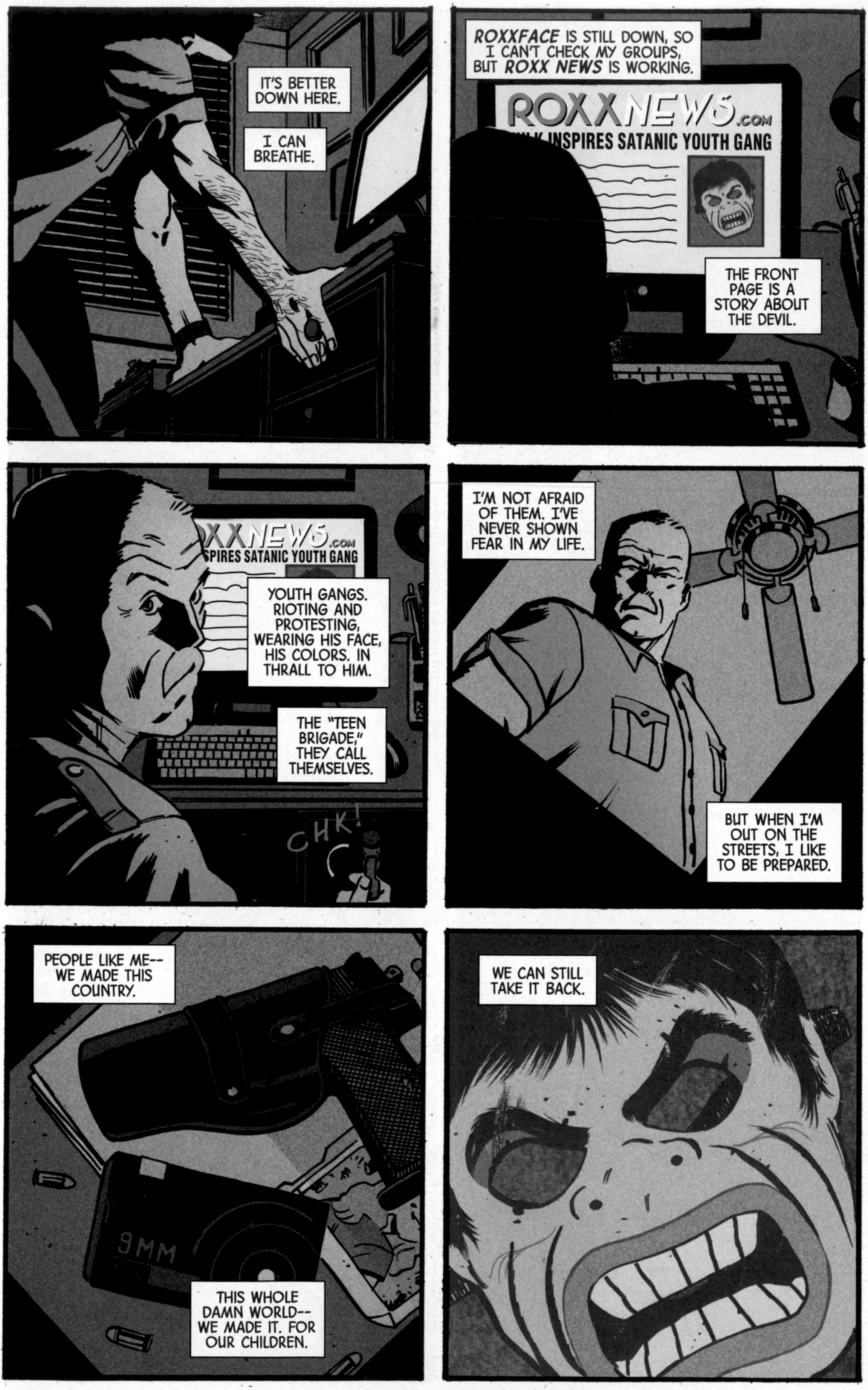
IT'S BETTER DOWN HERE.
I CAN BREATHE.
ROXXFACE IS STILL DOWN, SO I CAN'T CHECK MY GROUPS, BUT ROXX NEWS IS WORKING.
ROXXNEWS.com
INSPIRES SATANIC YOUTH GANG
THE FRONT PAGE IS A STORY ABOUT THE DEVIL.
XXNEWS.com
SPIRES SATANIC YOUTH GANG
YOUTH GANGS. RIOTING AND PROTESTING, WEARING HIS FACE, HIS COLORS. IN THRALL TO HIM.
THE "TEEN BRIGADE," THEY CALL THEMSELVES.
CHK!
I'M NOT AFRAID OF THEM. I'VE NEVER SHOWN FEAR IN MY LIFE.
BUT WHEN I'M OUT ON THE STREETS, I LIKE TO BE PREPARED.
PEOPLE LIKE ME-- WE MADE THIS COUNTRY.
9MM
THIS WHOLE DAMN WORLD-- WE MADE IT. FOR OUR CHILDREN.
WE CAN STILL TAKE IT BACK.

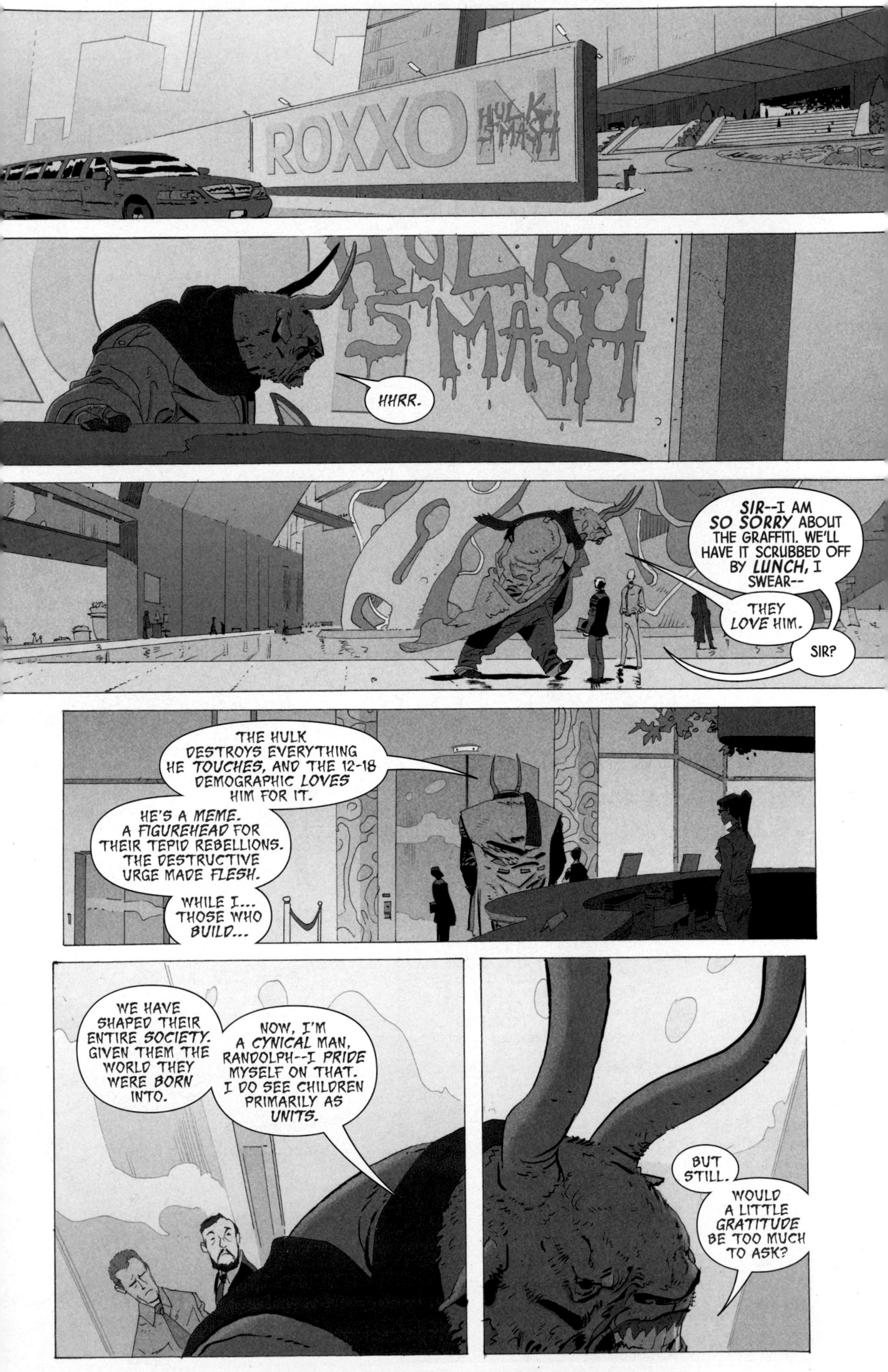
ROXXO
HULK SMASH
HHRR.
SIR--I AM SO SORRY ABOUT THE GRAFFITI. WE'LL HAVE IT SCRUBBED OFF BY LUNCH, I SWEAR--
THEY LOVE HIM.
SIR?
THE HULK DESTROYS EVERYTHING HE TOUCHES, AND THE 12-18 DEMOGRAPHIC LOVES HIM FOR IT.
HE'S A MEME. A FIGUREHEAD FOR THEIR TEPID REBELLIONS. THE DESTRUCTIVE URGE MADE FLESH.
WHILE I... THOSE WHO BUILD...
WE HAVE SHAPED THEIR ENTIRE SOCIETY. GIVEN THEM THE WORLD THEY WERE BORN INTO.
NOW, I'M A CYNICAL MAN, RANDOLPH--I PRIDE MYSELF ON THAT. I DO SEE CHILDREN PRIMARILY AS UNITS.
BUT STILL.
WOULD A LITTLE GRATITUDE BE TOO MUCH TO ASK?

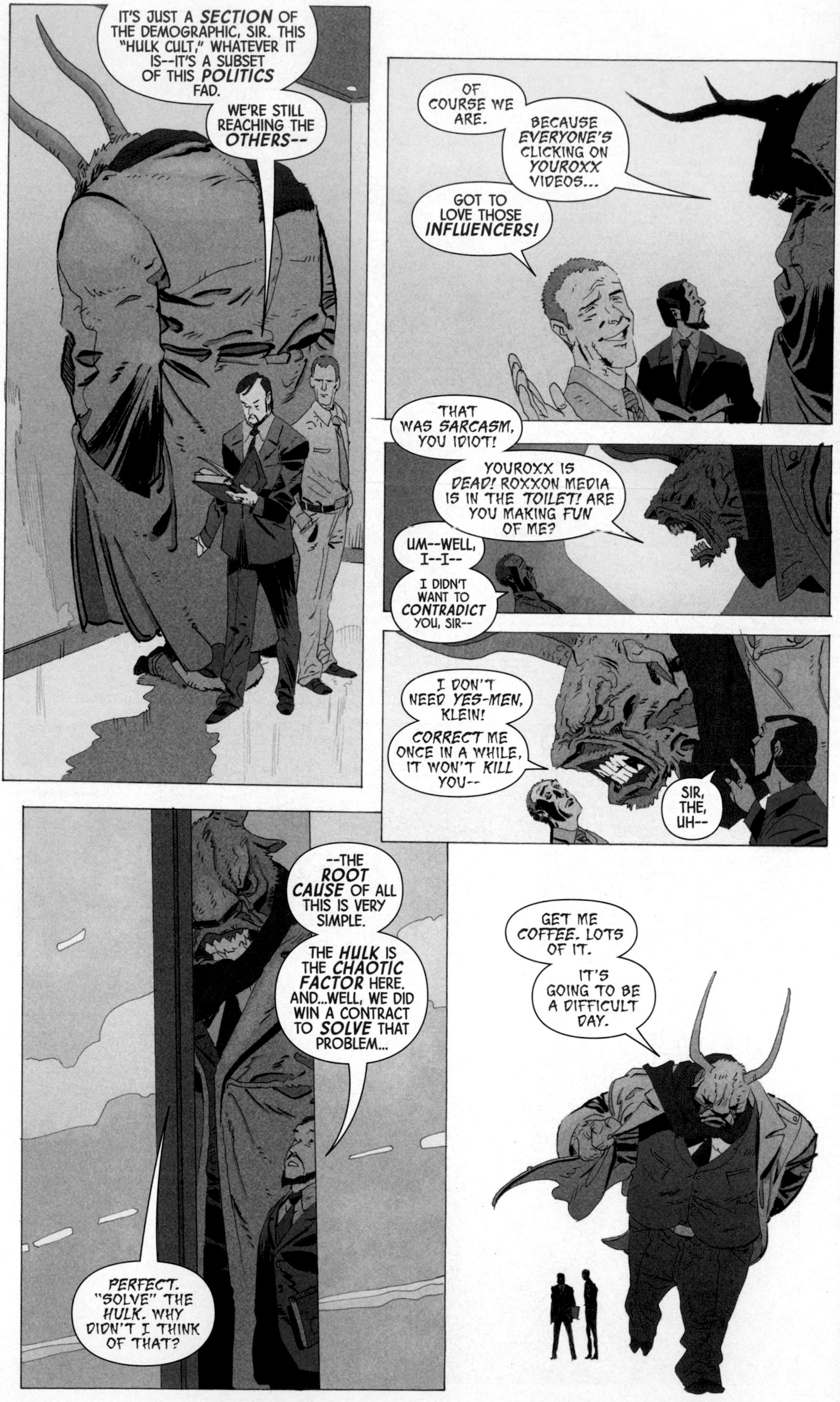
IT'S JUST A SECTION OF THE DEMOGRAPHIC, SIR. THIS "HULK CULT," WHATEVER IT IS--IT'S A SUBSET OF THIS POLITICS FAD.
WE'RE STILL REACHING THE OTHERS--
OF COURSE WE ARE.
BECAUSE EVERYONE'S CLICKING ON YOUROXX VIDEOS...
GOT TO LOVE THOSE INFLUENCERS!
THAT WAS SARCASM, YOU IDIOT!
YOUROXX IS DEAD! ROXXON MEDIA IS IN THE TOILET! ARE YOU MAKING FUN OF ME?
UM--WELL, I--I--
I DIDN'T WANT TO CONTRADICT YOU, SIR--
I DON'T NEED YES-MEN, KLEIN!
CORRECT ME ONCE IN A WHILE, IT WON'T KILL YOU--
SIR, THE, UH--
--THE ROOT CAUSE OF ALL THIS IS VERY SIMPLE.
THE HULK IS THE CHAOTIC FACTOR HERE. AND...WELL, WE DID WIN A CONTRACT TO SOLVE THAT PROBLEM...
PERFECT. "SOLVE" THE HULK. WHY DIDN'T I THINK OF THAT?
GET ME COFFEE. LOTS OF IT.
IT'S GOING TO BE A DIFFICULT DAY.

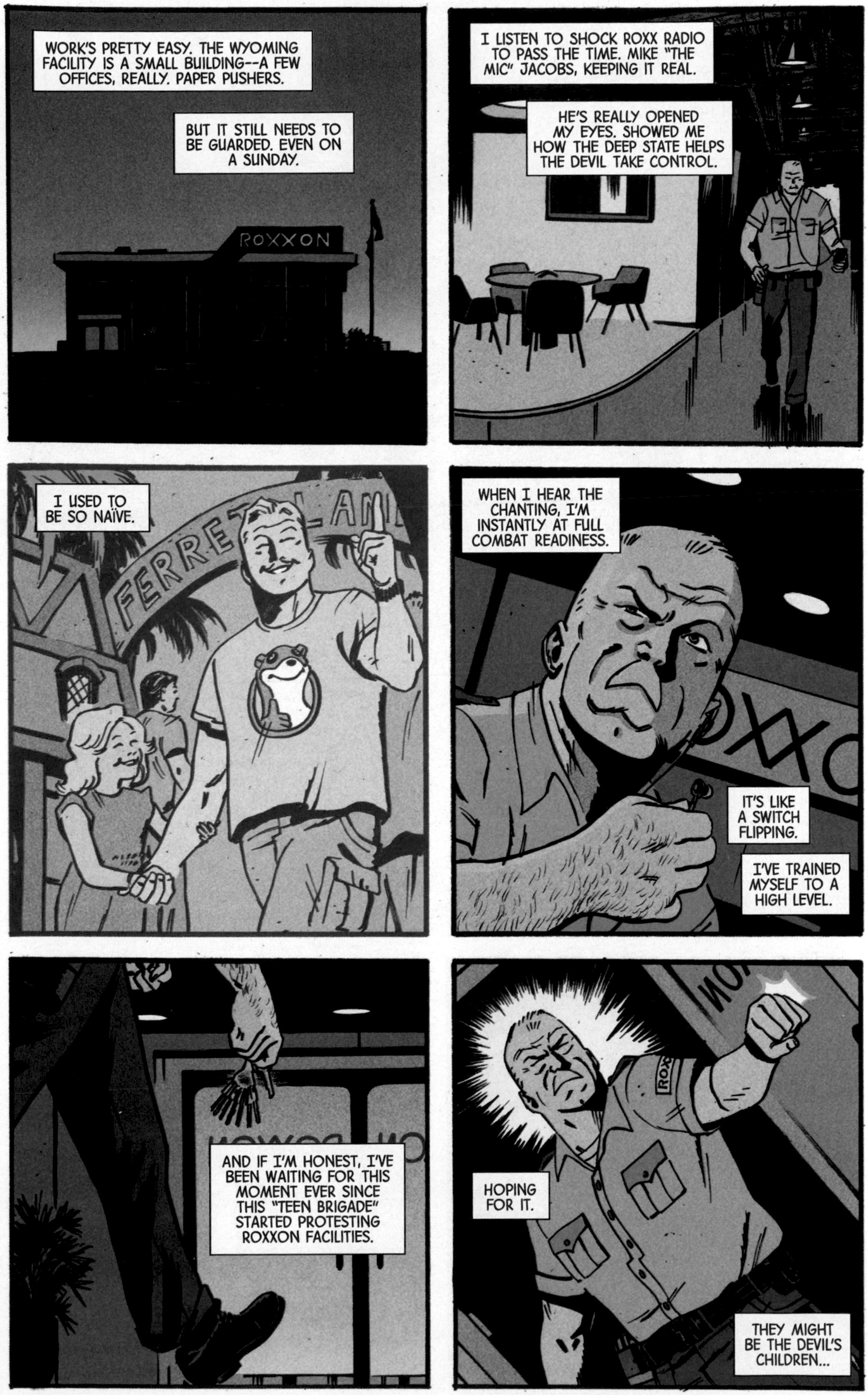
WORK'S PRETTY EASY. THE WYOMING FACILITY IS A SMALL BUILDING--A FEW OFFICES, REALLY. PAPER PUSHERS.
BUT IT STILL NEEDS TO BE GUARDED. EVEN ON A SUNDAY.
ROXXON
I LISTEN TO SHOCK ROXX RADIO TO PASS THE TIME. MIKE "THE MIC" JACOBS, KEEPING IT REAL.
HE'S REALLY OPENED MY EYES. SHOWED ME HOW THE DEEP STATE HELPS THE DEVIL TAKE CONTROL.
I USED TO BE SO NAÏVE.
FERRET LAN
WHEN I HEAR THE CHANTING, I'M INSTANTLY AT FULL COMBAT READINESS.
IT'S LIKE A SWITCH FLIPPING.
I'VE TRAINED MYSELF TO A HIGH LEVEL.
AND IF I'M HONEST, I'VE BEEN WAITING FOR THIS MOMENT EVER SINCE THIS "TEEN BRIGADE" STARTED PROTESTING ROXXON FACILITIES.
HOPING FOR IT.
THEY MIGHT BE THE DEVIL'S CHILDREN...

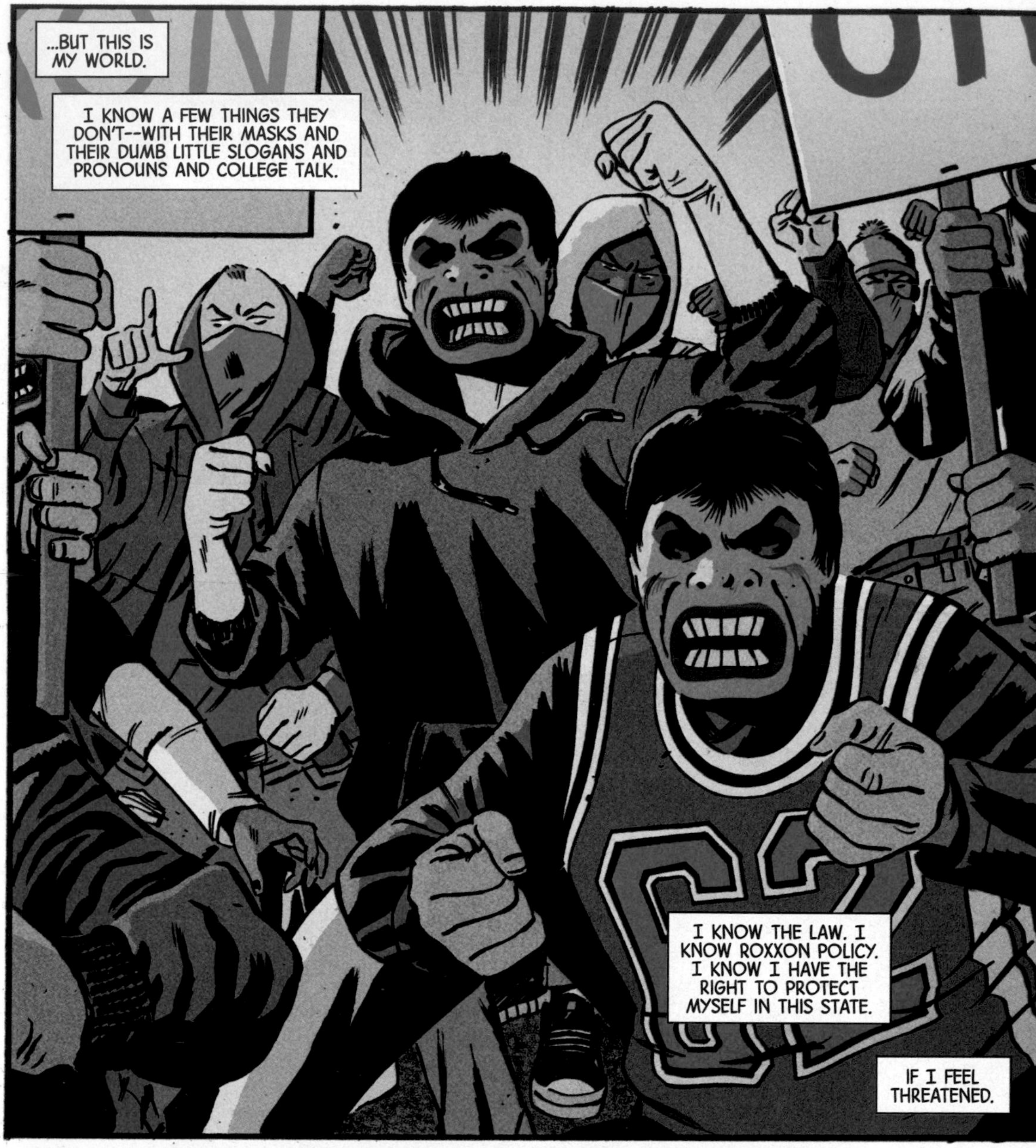
...BUT THIS IS MY WORLD.
I KNOW A FEW THINGS THEY DON'T--WITH THEIR MASKS AND THEIR DUMB LITTLE SLOGANS AND PRONOUNS AND COLLEGE TALK.
I KNOW THE LAW. I KNOW ROXXON POLICY. I KNOW I HAVE THE RIGHT TO PROTECT MYSELF IN THIS STATE.
IF I FEEL THREATENED.

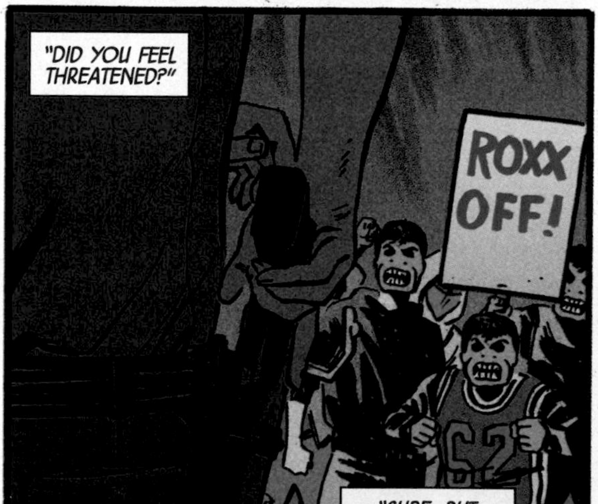
"DID YOU FEEL THREATENED?"
ROXX OFF!
"SURE. BUT NEVER AFRAID, YOUR HONOR.

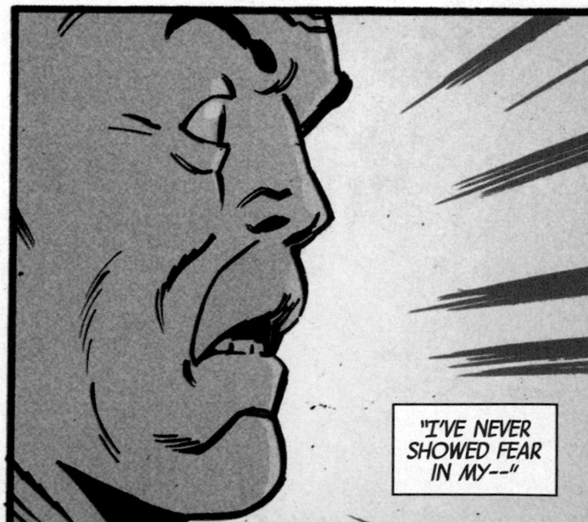
"I'VE NEVER SHOWED FEAR IN MY--"

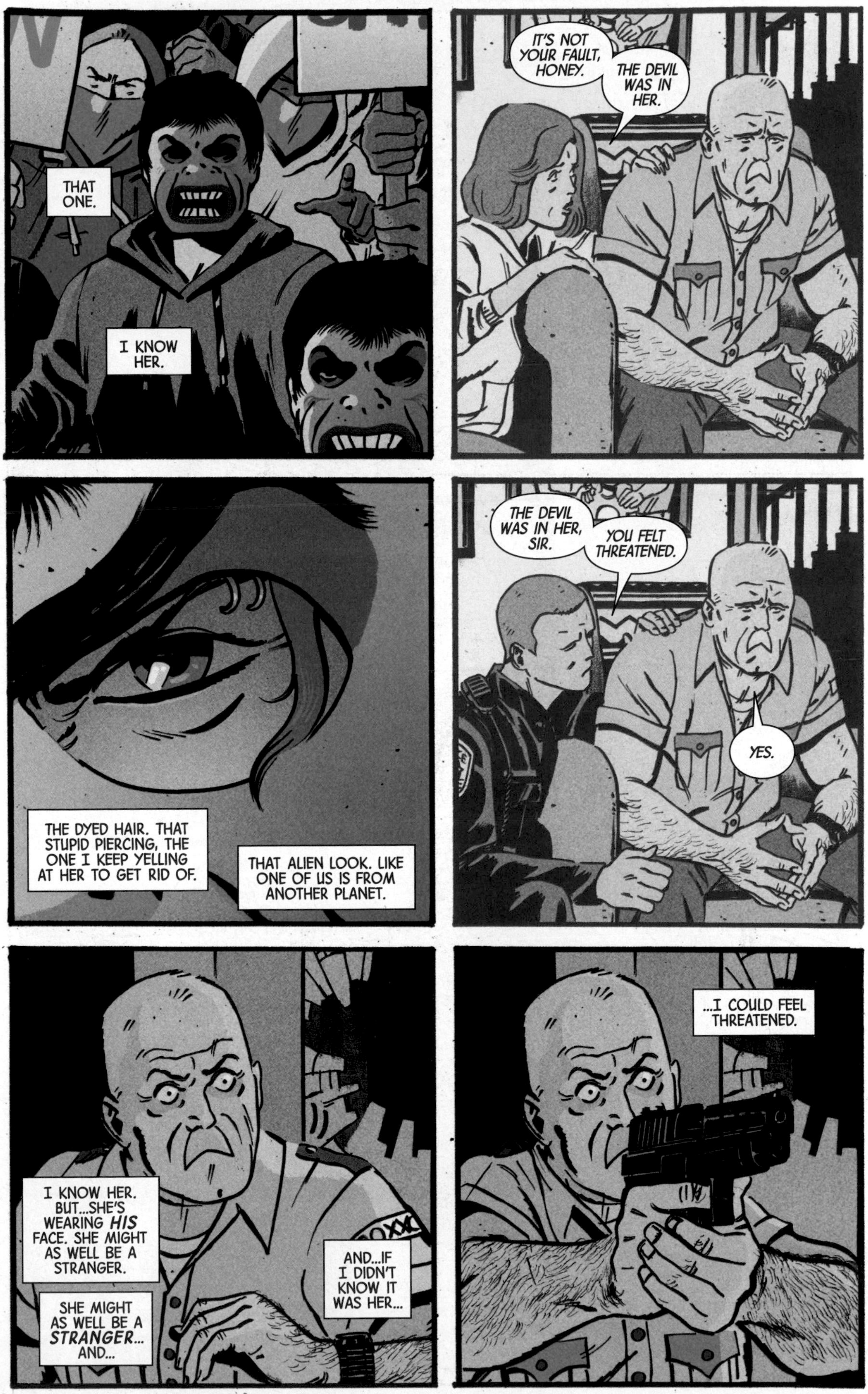
THAT ONE.
I KNOW HER.
IT'S NOT YOUR FAULT, HONEY.
THE DEVIL WAS IN HER.
THE DYED HAIR. THAT STUPID PIERCING, THE ONE I KEEP YELLING AT HER TO GET RID OF.
THAT ALIEN LOOK. LIKE ONE OF US IS FROM ANOTHER PLANET.
THE DEVIL WAS IN HER, SIR.
YOU FELT THREATENED.
YES.
I KNOW HER. BUT...SHE'S WEARING *HIS* FACE. SHE MIGHT AS WELL BE A STRANGER.
SHE MIGHT AS WELL BE A *STRANGER*... AND...
AND...IF I DIDN'T KNOW IT WAS HER...
...I COULD FEEL THREATENED.

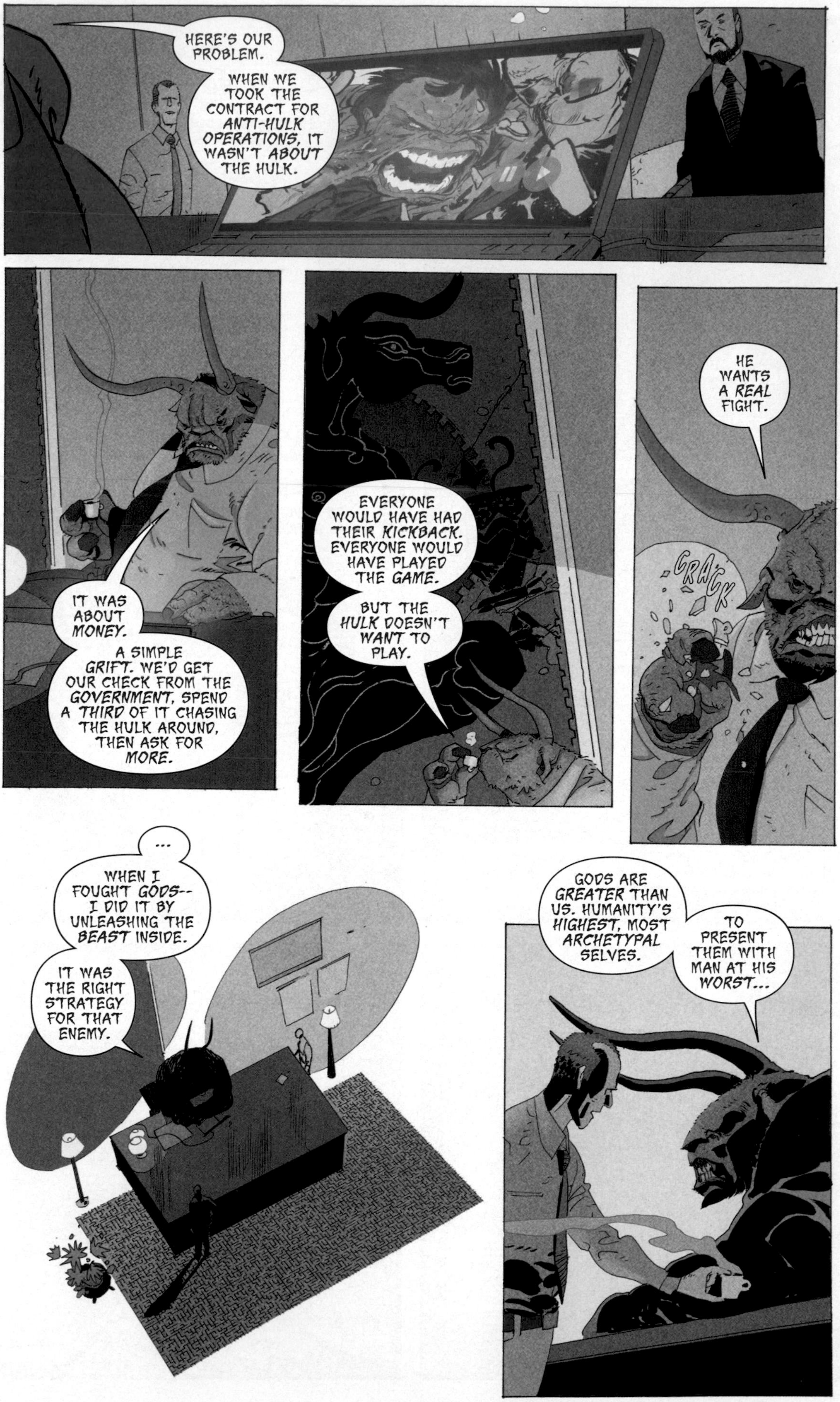
HERE'S OUR PROBLEM.
WHEN WE TOOK THE CONTRACT FOR ANTI-HULK OPERATIONS, IT WASN'T ABOUT THE HULK.
IT WAS ABOUT MONEY.
A SIMPLE GRIFT. WE'D GET OUR CHECK FROM THE GOVERNMENT, SPEND A THIRD OF IT CHASING THE HULK AROUND, THEN ASK FOR MORE.
EVERYONE WOULD HAVE HAD THEIR KICKBACK. EVERYONE WOULD HAVE PLAYED THE GAME.
BUT THE HULK DOESN'T WANT TO PLAY.
HE WANTS A REAL FIGHT.
CRACK
...
WHEN I FOUGHT GODS-- I DID IT BY UNLEASHING THE BEAST INSIDE.
IT WAS THE RIGHT STRATEGY FOR THAT ENEMY.
GODS ARE GREATER THAN US. HUMANITY'S HIGHEST, MOST ARCHETYPAL SELVES.
TO PRESENT THEM WITH MAN AT HIS WORST...

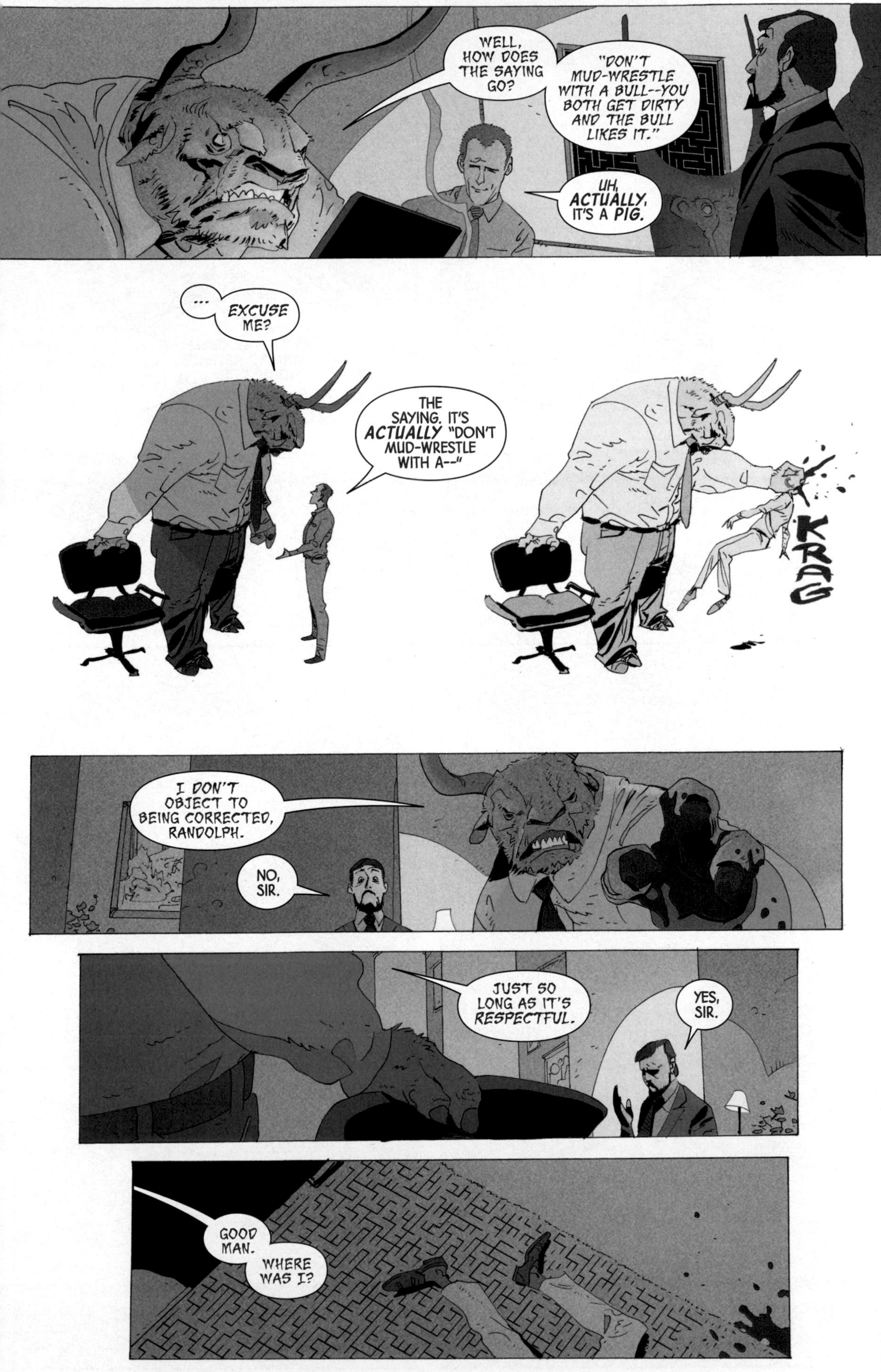
WELL, HOW DOES THE SAYING GO?
"DON'T MUD-WRESTLE WITH A BULL--YOU BOTH GET DIRTY AND THE BULL LIKES IT."
UH, ACTUALLY, IT'S A PIG.
...
EXCUSE ME?
THE SAYING. IT'S ACTUALLY "DON'T MUD-WRESTLE WITH A--"
KRAG
I DON'T OBJECT TO BEING CORRECTED, RANDOLPH.
NO, SIR.
JUST SO LONG AS IT'S RESPECTFUL.
YES, SIR.
GOOD MAN.
WHERE WAS I?

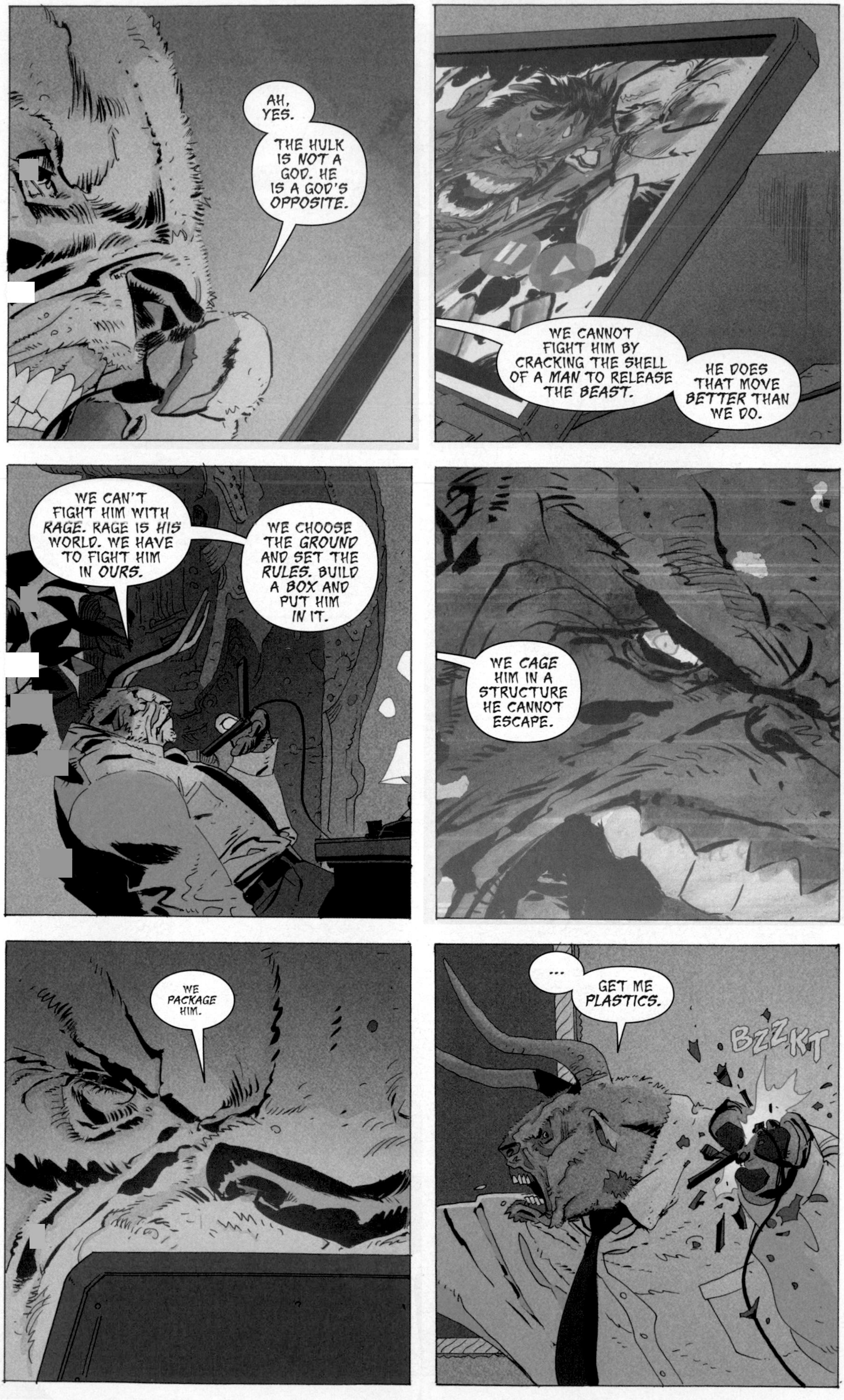
AH, YES.
THE HULK IS NOT A GOD. HE IS A GOD'S OPPOSITE.
WE CANNOT FIGHT HIM BY CRACKING THE SHELL OF A MAN TO RELEASE THE BEAST.
HE DOES THAT MOVE BETTER THAN WE DO.
WE CAN'T FIGHT HIM WITH RAGE. RAGE IS HIS WORLD. WE HAVE TO FIGHT HIM IN OURS.
WE CHOOSE THE GROUND AND SET THE RULES. BUILD A BOX AND PUT HIM IN IT.
WE CAGE HIM IN A STRUCTURE HE CANNOT ESCAPE.
WE PACKAGE HIM.
...
GET ME PLASTICS.
BZZKT

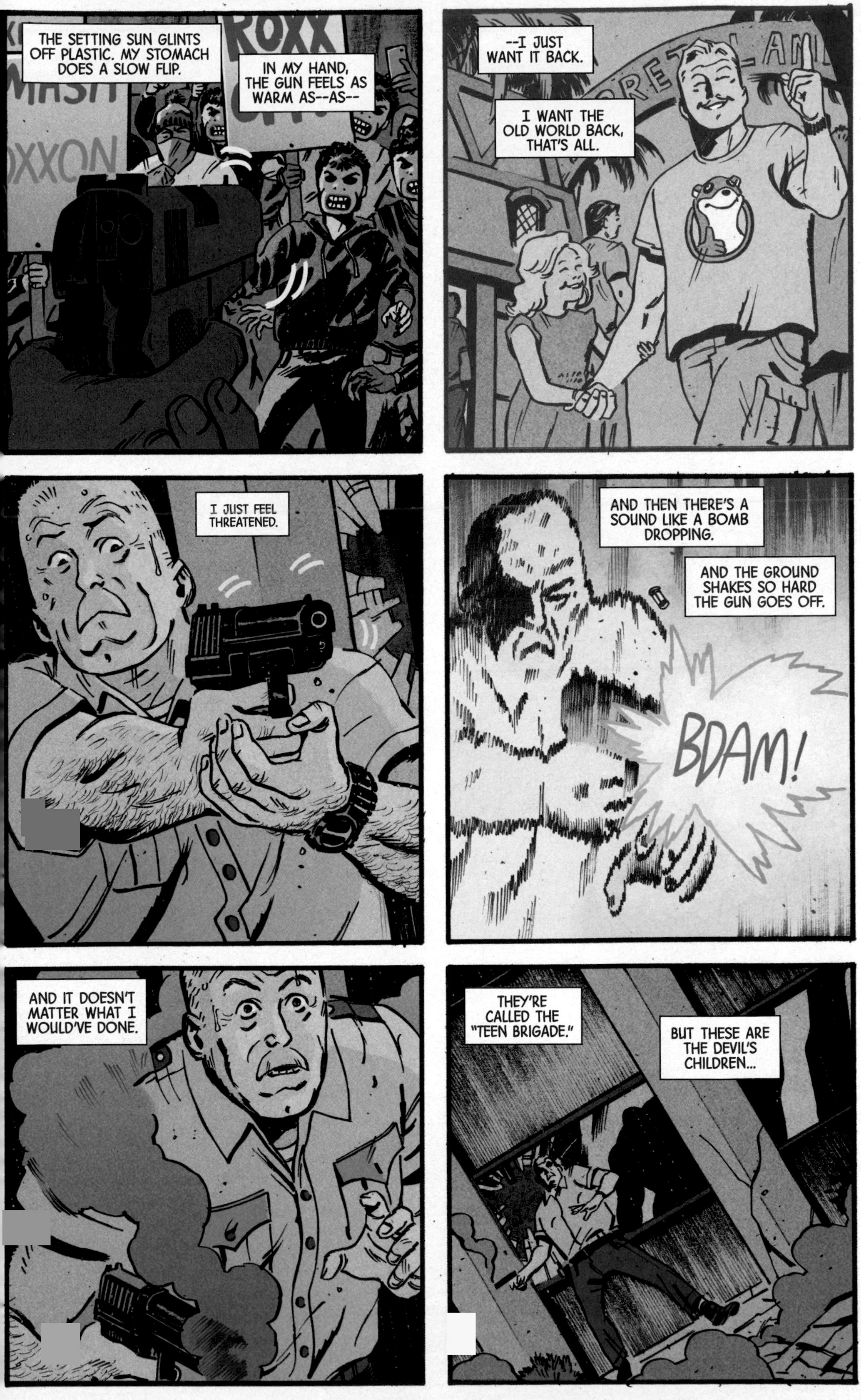
THE SETTING SUN GLINTS OFF PLASTIC. MY STOMACH DOES A SLOW FLIP.
IN MY HAND, THE GUN FEELS AS WARM AS--AS--
--I JUST WANT IT BACK.
I WANT THE OLD WORLD BACK, THAT'S ALL.
I JUST FEEL THREATENED.
AND THEN THERE'S A SOUND LIKE A BOMB DROPPING.
AND THE GROUND SHAKES SO HARD THE GUN GOES OFF.
BDAM!
AND IT DOESN'T MATTER WHAT I WOULD'VE DONE.
THEY'RE CALLED THE "TEEN BRIGADE."
BUT THESE ARE THE DEVIL'S CHILDREN...

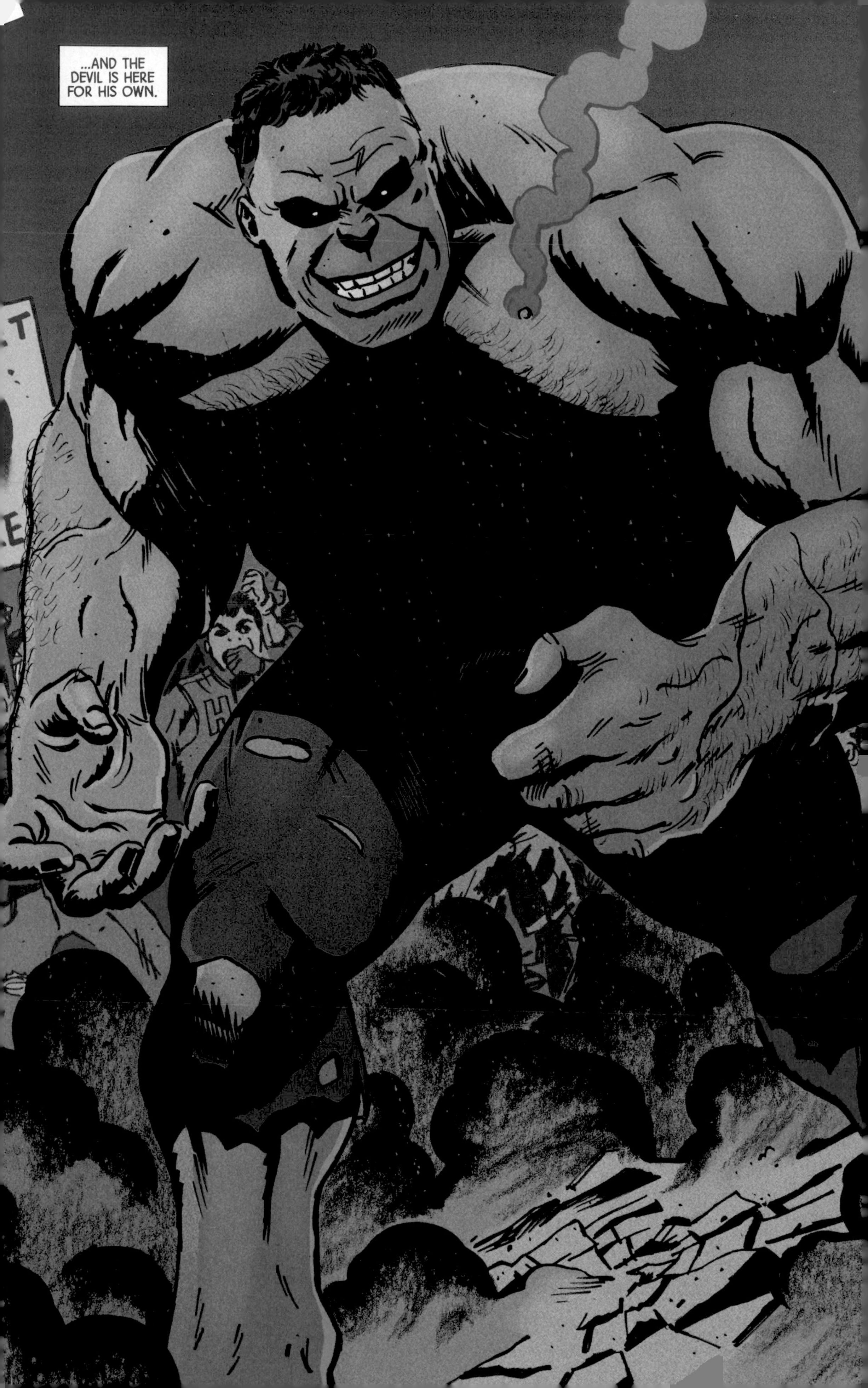
...AND THE DEVIL IS HERE FOR HIS OWN.

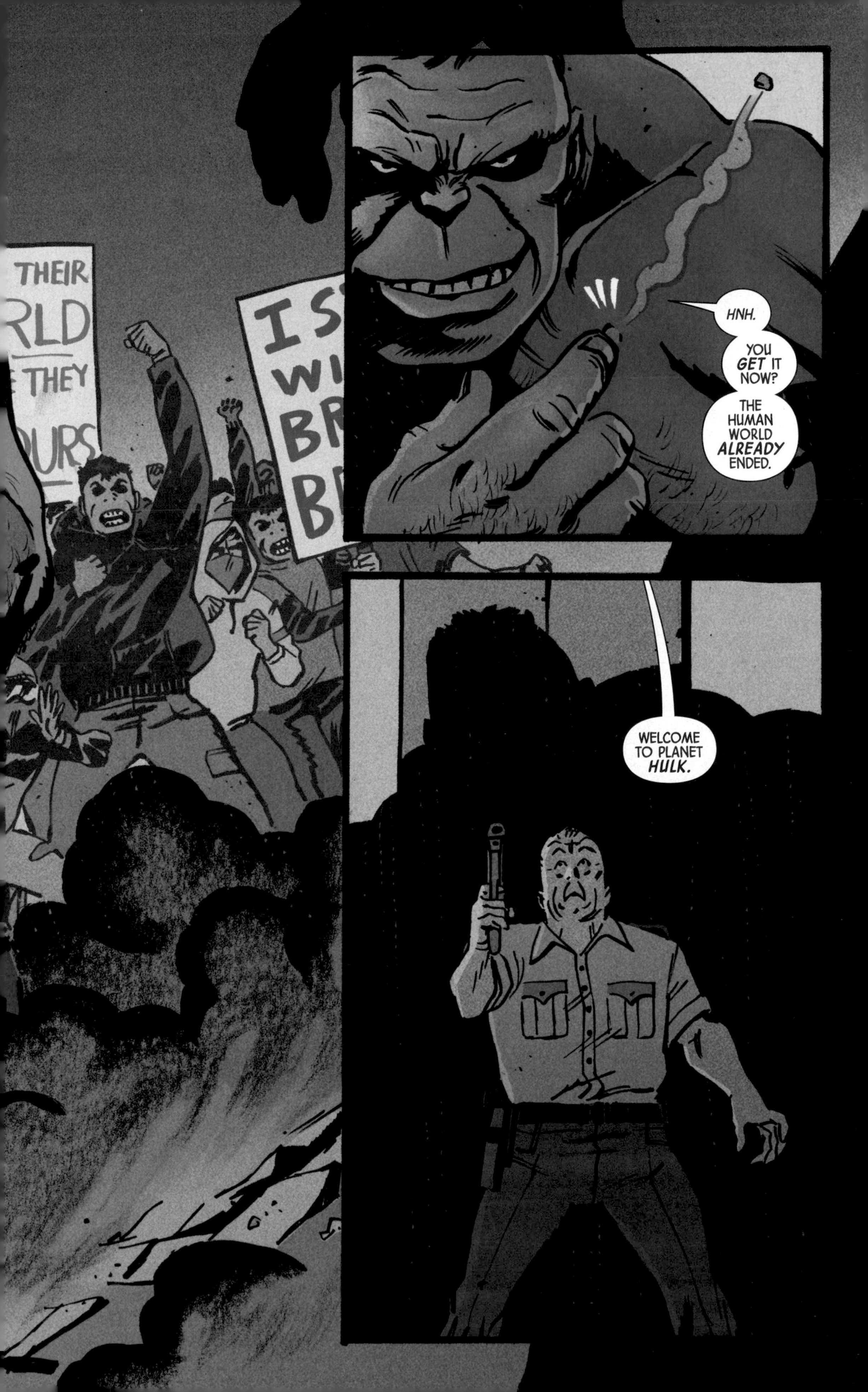
THEIR
HNH.
YOU GET IT NOW?
THE HUMAN WORLD ALREADY ENDED.
WELCOME TO PLANET HULK.

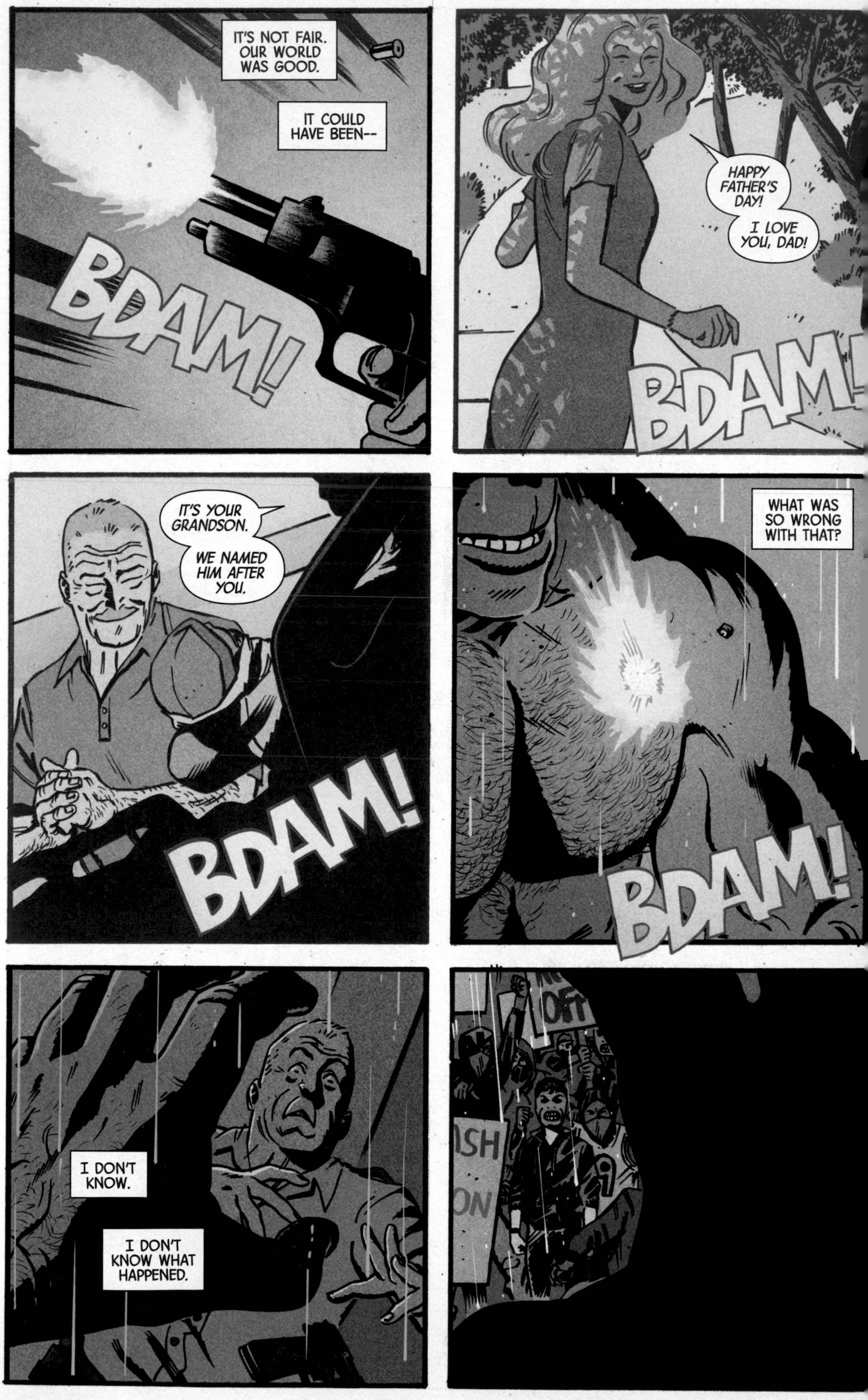
IT'S NOT FAIR. OUR WORLD WAS GOOD.
IT COULD HAVE BEEN--
BDAM!
HAPPY FATHER'S DAY!
I LOVE YOU, DAD!
BDAM!
IT'S YOUR GRANDSON.
WE NAMED HIM AFTER YOU.
BDAM!
WHAT WAS SO WRONG WITH THAT?
BDAM!
I DON'T KNOW.
I DON'T KNOW WHAT HAPPENED.

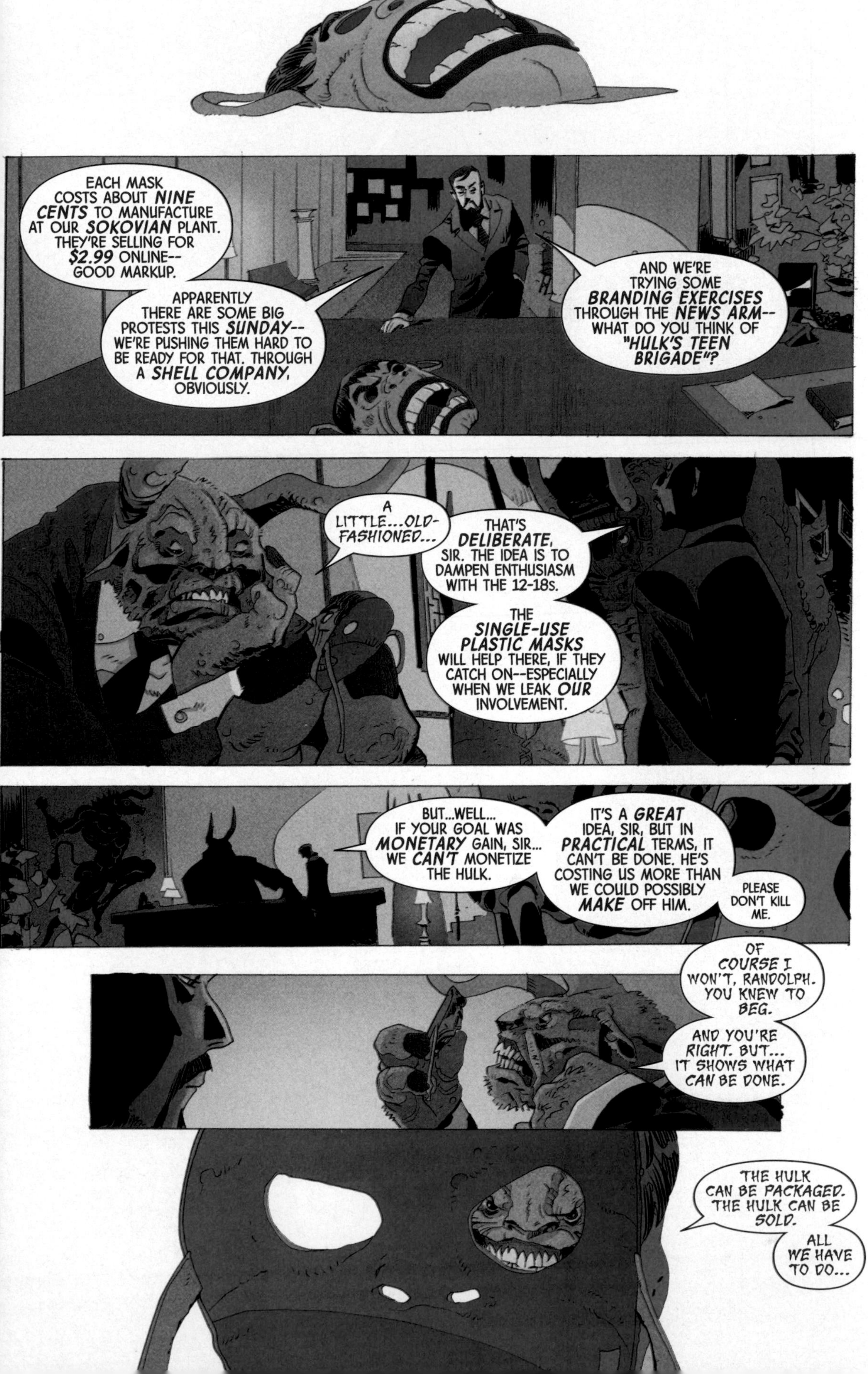
EACH MASK COSTS ABOUT NINE CENTS TO MANUFACTURE AT OUR SOKOVIAN PLANT. THEY'RE SELLING FOR $2.99 ONLINE--GOOD MARKUP.
APPARENTLY THERE ARE SOME BIG PROTESTS THIS SUNDAY--WE'RE PUSHING THEM HARD TO BE READY FOR THAT. THROUGH A SHELL COMPANY, OBVIOUSLY.
AND WE'RE TRYING SOME BRANDING EXERCISES THROUGH THE NEWS ARM--WHAT DO YOU THINK OF "HULK'S TEEN BRIGADE"?
A LITTLE...OLD-FASHIONED...
THAT'S DELIBERATE, SIR. THE IDEA IS TO DAMPEN ENTHUSIASM WITH THE 12-18s.
THE SINGLE-USE PLASTIC MASKS WILL HELP THERE, IF THEY CATCH ON--ESPECIALLY WHEN WE LEAK OUR INVOLVEMENT.
BUT...WELL... IF YOUR GOAL WAS MONETARY GAIN, SIR... WE CAN'T MONETIZE THE HULK.
IT'S A GREAT IDEA, SIR, BUT IN PRACTICAL TERMS, IT CAN'T BE DONE. HE'S COSTING US MORE THAN WE COULD POSSIBLY MAKE OFF HIM.
PLEASE DON'T KILL ME.
OF COURSE I WON'T, RANDOLPH. YOU KNEW TO BEG.
AND YOU'RE RIGHT. BUT... IT SHOWS WHAT CAN BE DONE.
THE HULK CAN BE PACKAGED. THE HULK CAN BE SOLD.
ALL WE HAVE TO DO...

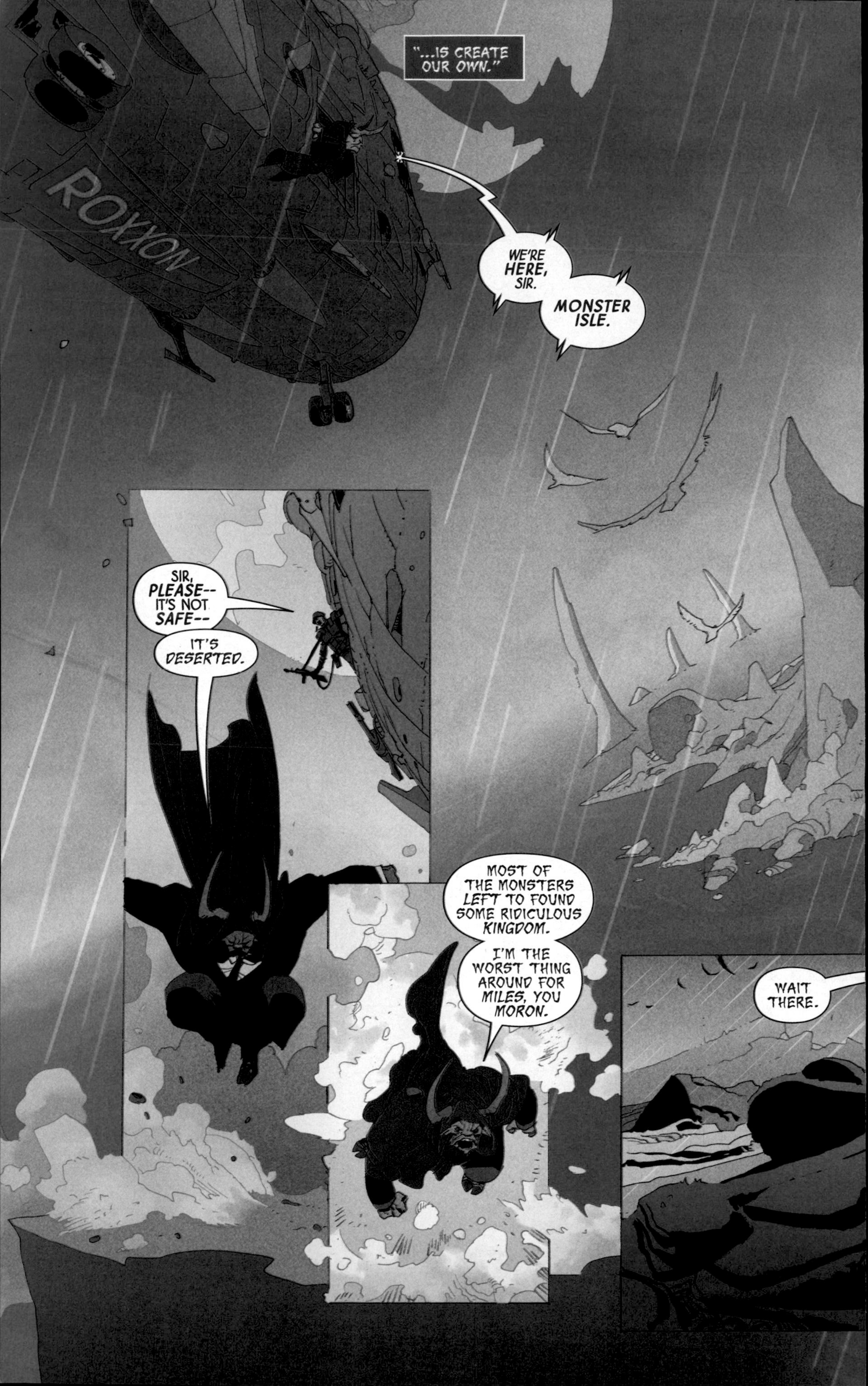
"...IS CREATE OUR OWN."
ROXXON
WE'RE HERE, SIR.
MONSTER ISLE.
SIR, PLEASE-- IT'S NOT SAFE--
IT'S DESERTED.
MOST OF THE MONSTERS LEFT TO FOUND SOME RIDICULOUS KINGDOM.
I'M THE WORST THING AROUND FOR MILES, YOU MORON.
WAIT THERE.

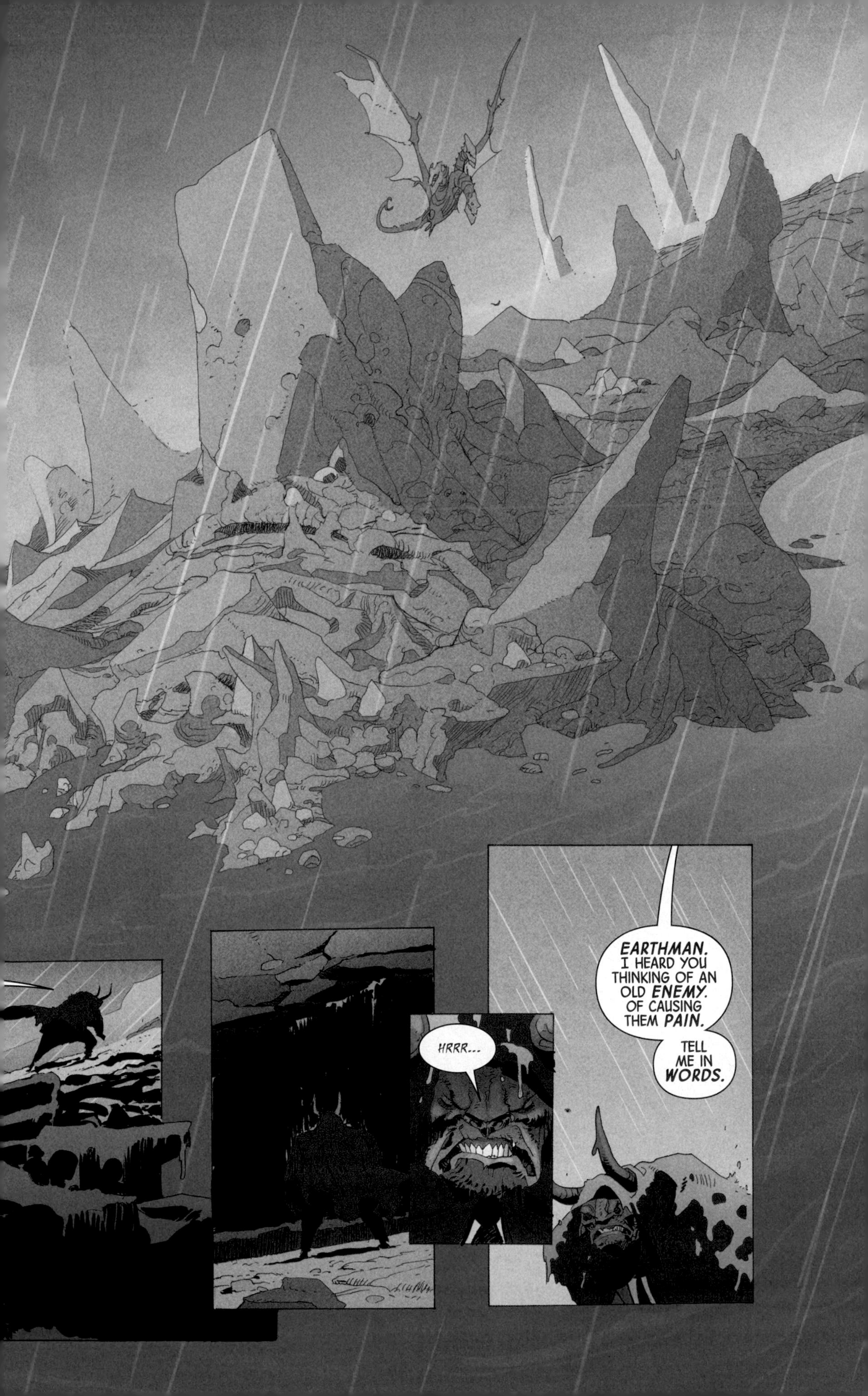
HRRR...
EARTHMAN. I HEARD YOU THINKING OF AN OLD ENEMY. OF CAUSING THEM PAIN.
TELL ME IN WORDS.

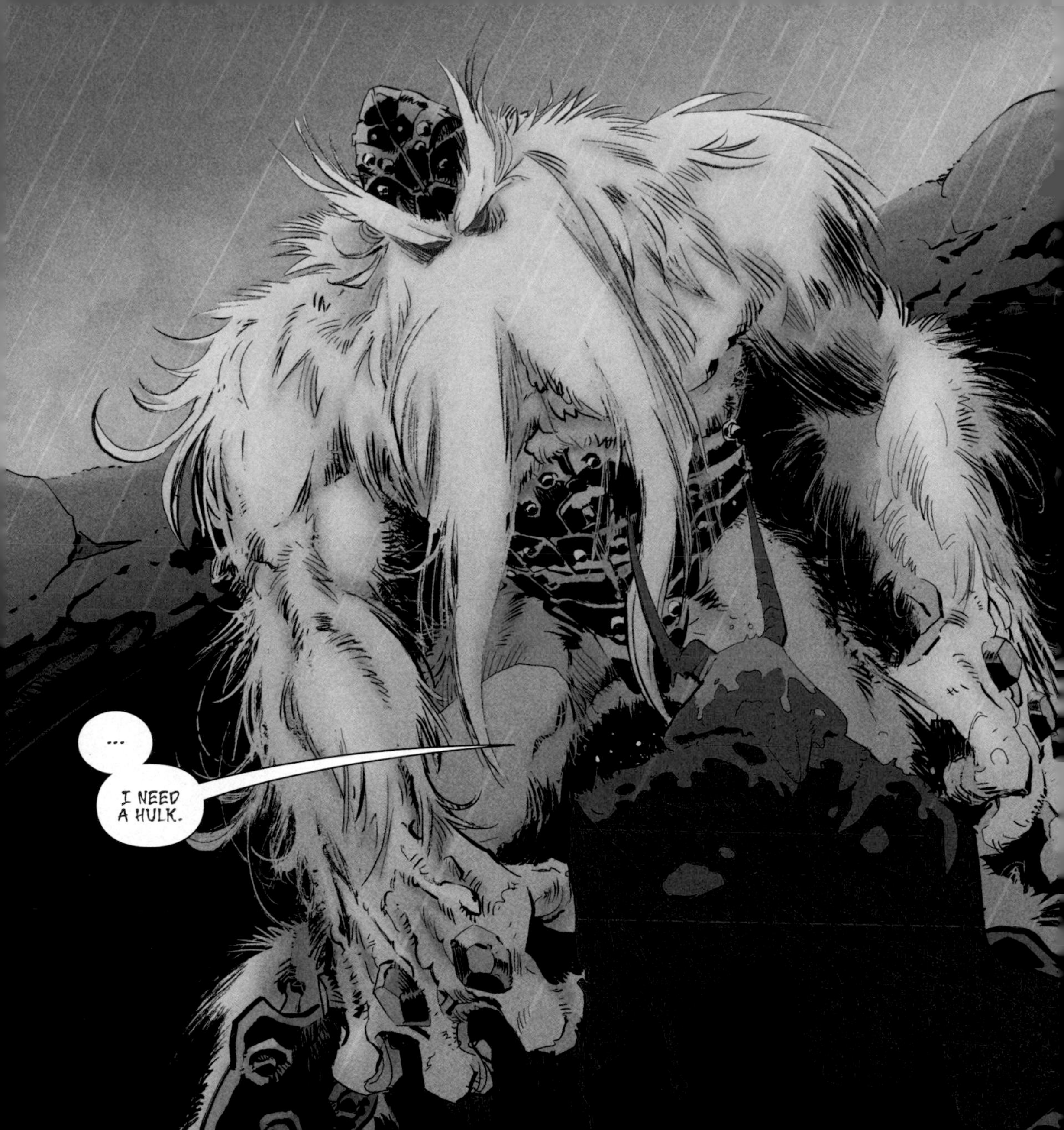
...
I NEED A HULK.

THE NEW WORLD

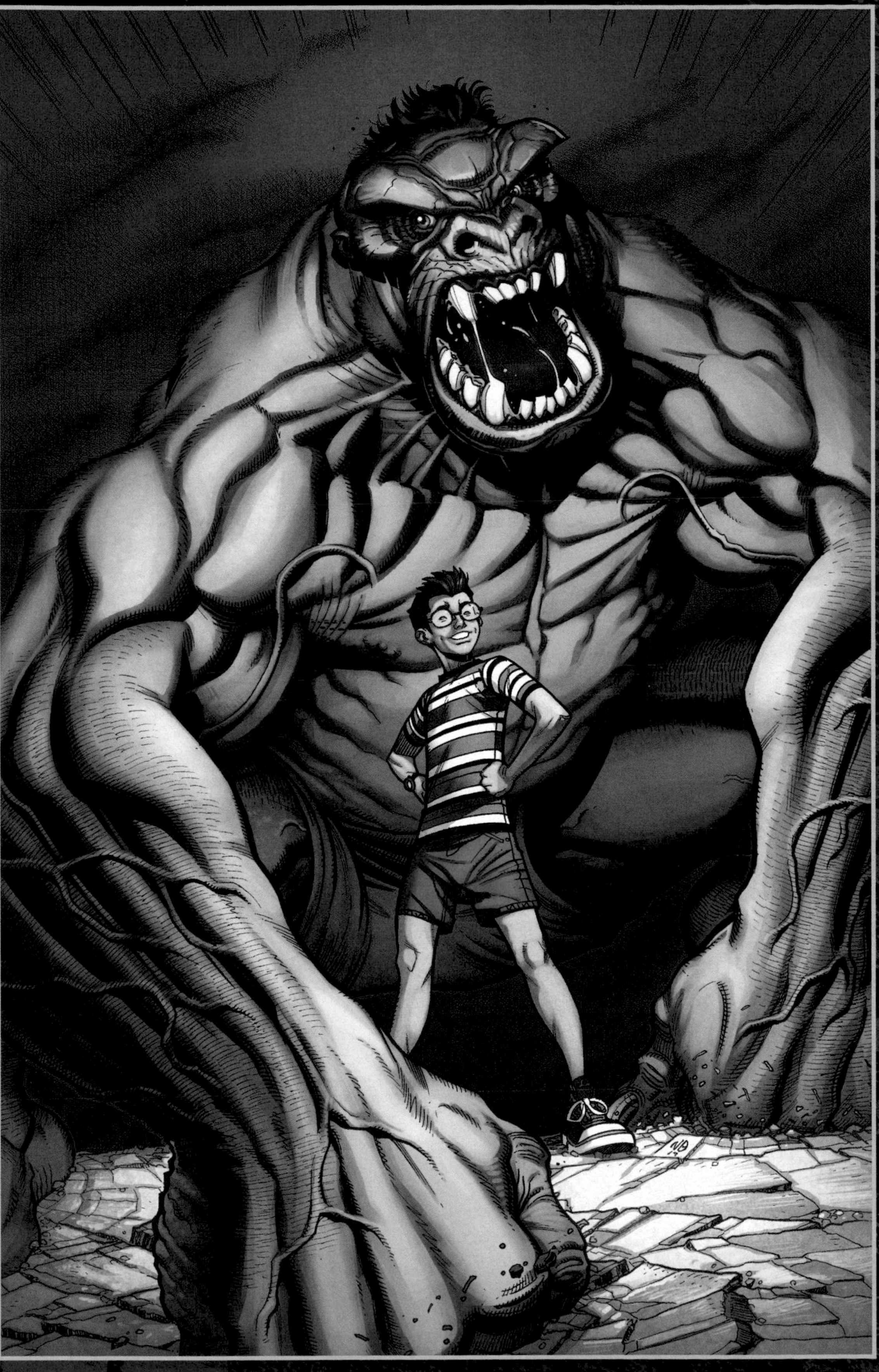

NICK BRADSHAW & JASON KEITH
#29 *MARVELS X* VARIANT

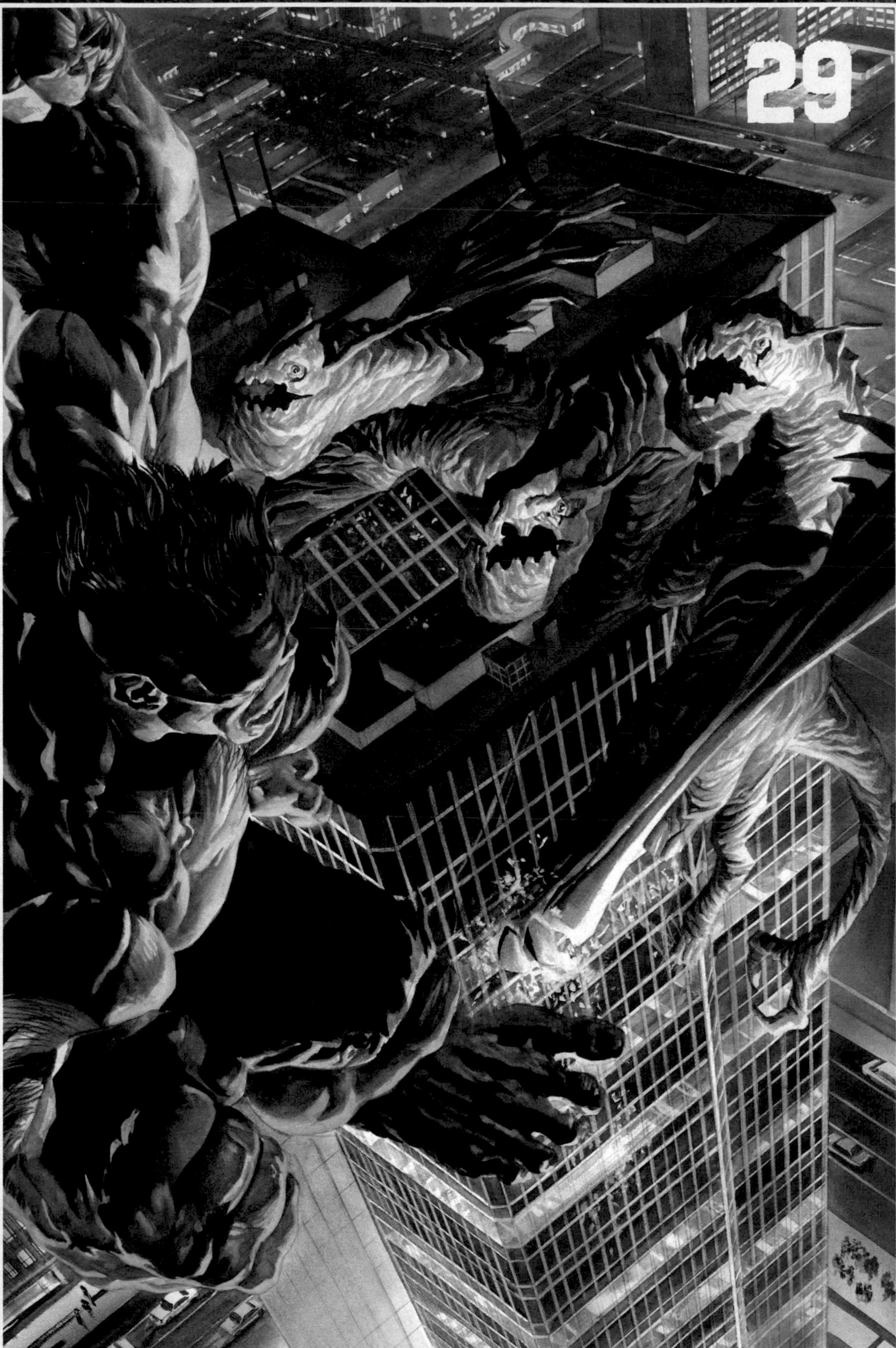
29

"SUCH IS THE CONDITION OF ORGANIC NATURE! WHOSE FIRST LAW MIGHT BE EXPRESSED IN THE WORDS, 'EAT OR BE EATEN!' AND WHICH WOULD SEEM TO BE ONE GREAT SLAUGHTER-HOUSE, ONE UNIVERSAL SCENE OF RAPACITY AND INJUSTICE!"

— ERASMUS DARWIN, *PHYTOLOGIA*

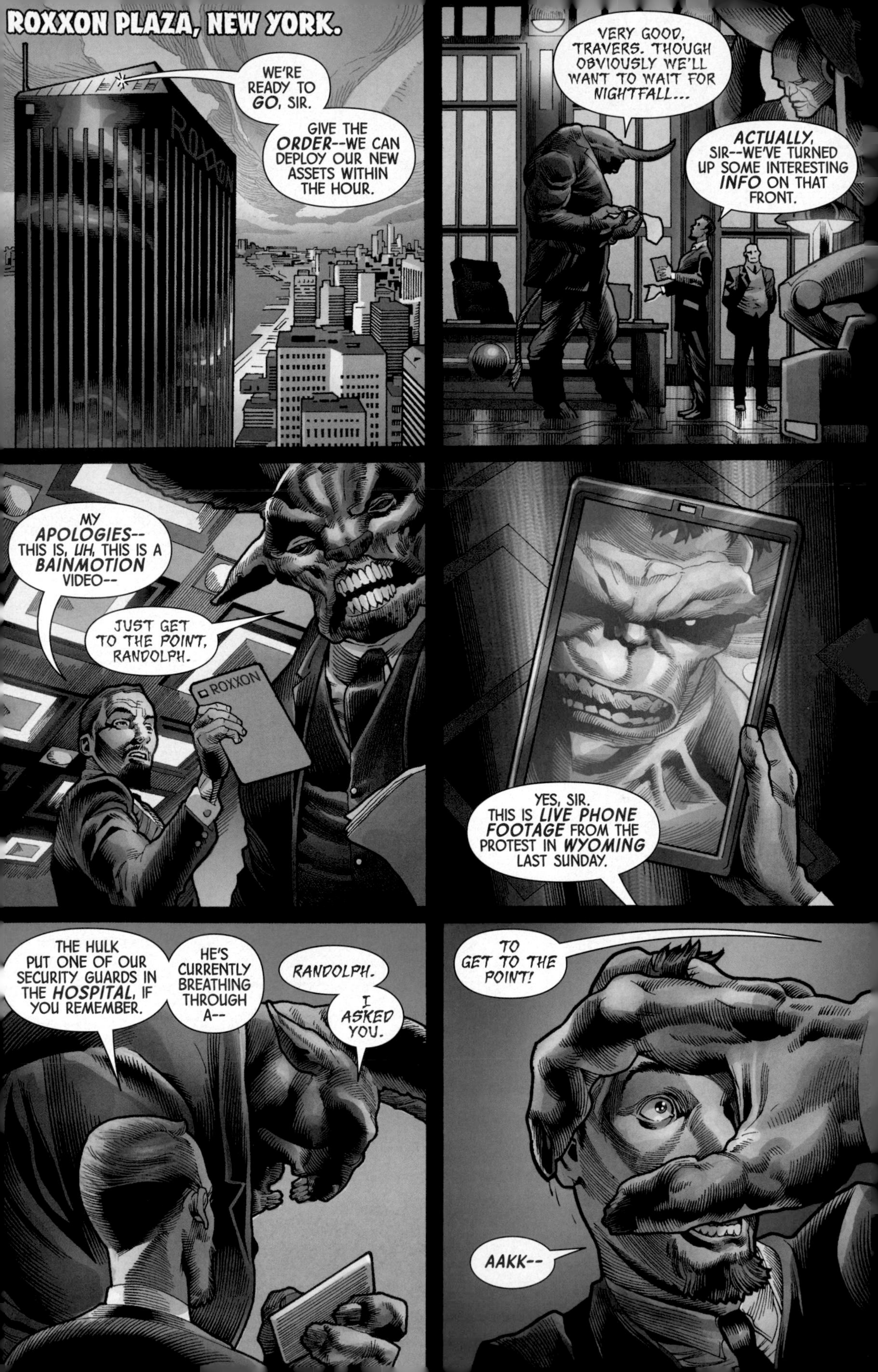
ROXXON PLAZA, NEW YORK.
WE'RE READY TO GO, SIR.
GIVE THE ORDER--WE CAN DEPLOY OUR NEW ASSETS WITHIN THE HOUR.
ROXXON
VERY GOOD, TRAVERS. THOUGH OBVIOUSLY WE'LL WANT TO WAIT FOR NIGHTFALL...
ACTUALLY, SIR--WE'VE TURNED UP SOME INTERESTING INFO ON THAT FRONT.
MY APOLOGIES-- THIS IS, UH, THIS IS A BAINMOTION VIDEO--
JUST GET TO THE POINT, RANDOLPH.
ROXXON
YES, SIR. THIS IS LIVE PHONE FOOTAGE FROM THE PROTEST IN WYOMING LAST SUNDAY.
THE HULK PUT ONE OF OUR SECURITY GUARDS IN THE HOSPITAL, IF YOU REMEMBER.
HE'S CURRENTLY BREATHING THROUGH A--
RANDOLPH.
I ASKED YOU.
TO GET TO THE POINT!
AAKK--

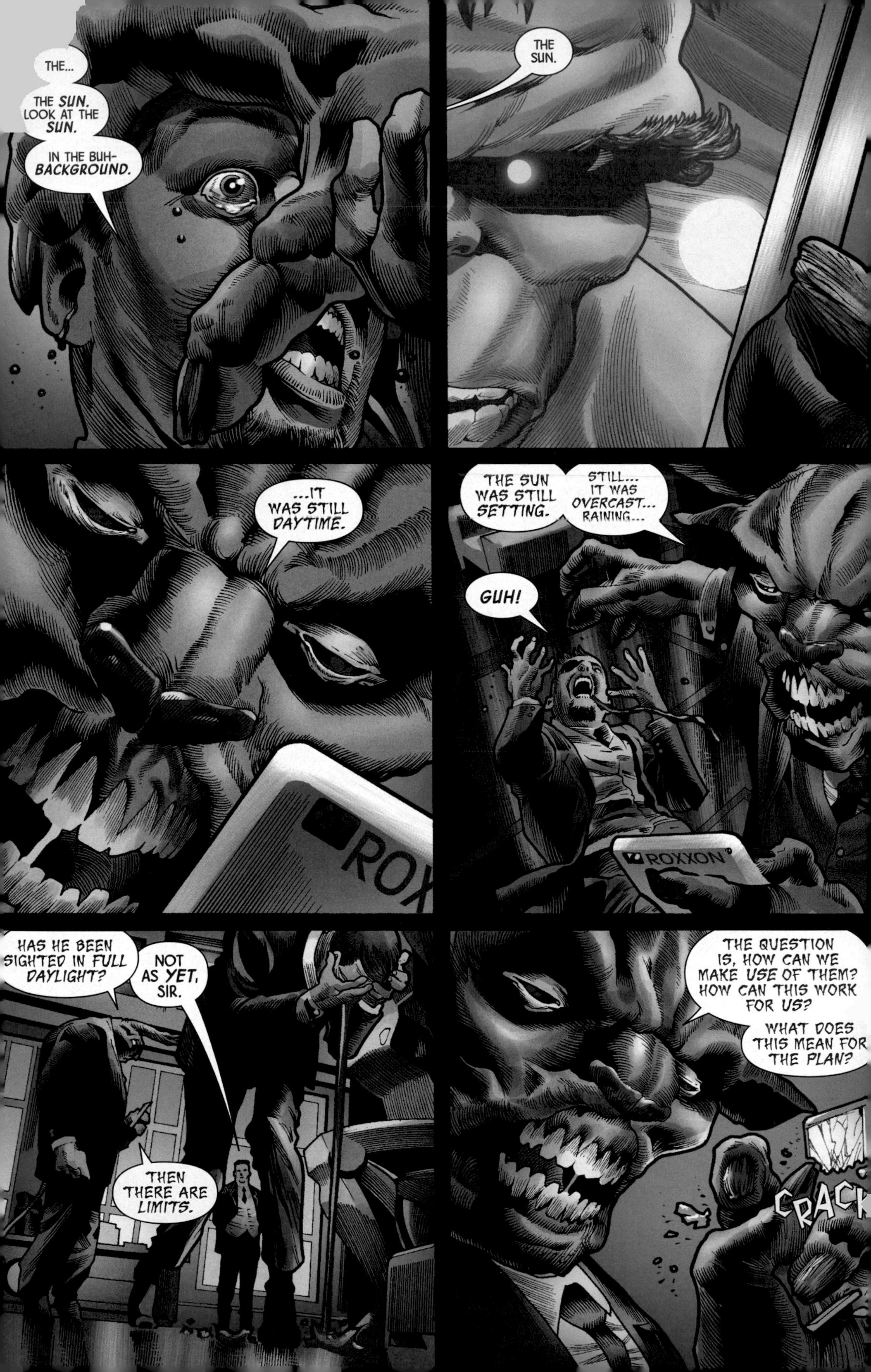
THE...
THE SUN. LOOK AT THE SUN.
IN THE BUH-BACKGROUND.
THE SUN.
...IT WAS STILL DAYTIME.
ROXX
THE SUN WAS STILL SETTING.
STILL... IT WAS OVERCAST... RAINING...
GUH!
ROXXON
HAS HE BEEN SIGHTED IN FULL DAYLIGHT?
NOT AS YET, SIR.
THEN THERE ARE LIMITS.
THE QUESTION IS, HOW CAN WE MAKE USE OF THEM? HOW CAN THIS WORK FOR US?
WHAT DOES THIS MEAN FOR THE PLAN?
CRACK

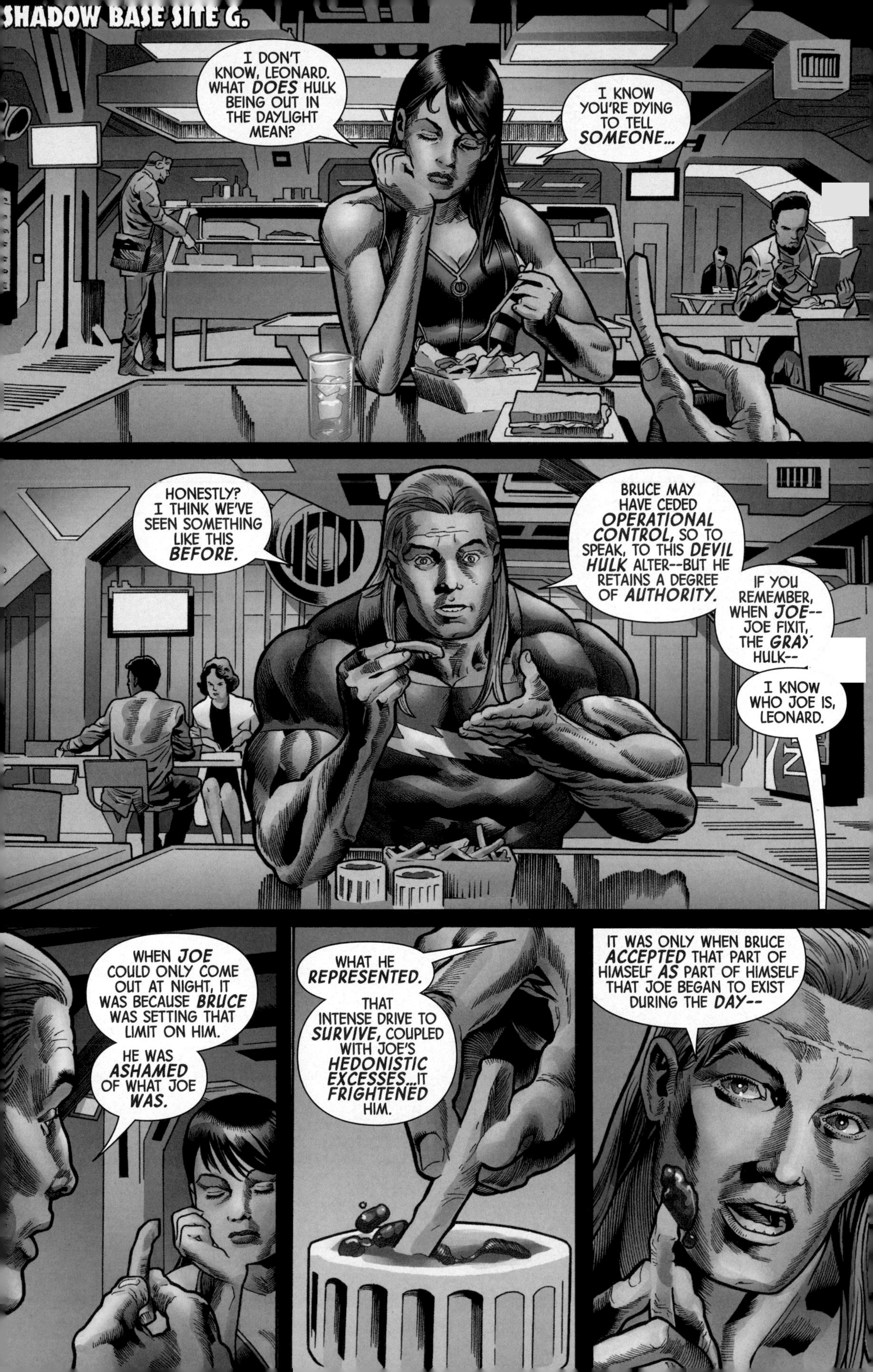
SHADOW BASE SITE G.
I DON'T KNOW, LEONARD. WHAT DOES HULK BEING OUT IN THE DAYLIGHT MEAN?
I KNOW YOU'RE DYING TO TELL SOMEONE...
HONESTLY? I THINK WE'VE SEEN SOMETHING LIKE THIS BEFORE.
BRUCE MAY HAVE CEDED OPERATIONAL CONTROL, SO TO SPEAK, TO THIS DEVIL HULK ALTER--BUT HE RETAINS A DEGREE OF AUTHORITY.
IF YOU REMEMBER, WHEN JOE--JOE FIXIT, THE GRAY HULK--
I KNOW WHO JOE IS, LEONARD.
WHEN JOE COULD ONLY COME OUT AT NIGHT, IT WAS BECAUSE BRUCE WAS SETTING THAT LIMIT ON HIM.
HE WAS ASHAMED OF WHAT JOE WAS.
WHAT HE REPRESENTED.
THAT INTENSE DRIVE TO SURVIVE, COUPLED WITH JOE'S HEDONISTIC EXCESSES...IT FRIGHTENED HIM.
IT WAS ONLY WHEN BRUCE ACCEPTED THAT PART OF HIMSELF AS PART OF HIMSELF THAT JOE BEGAN TO EXIST DURING THE DAY--

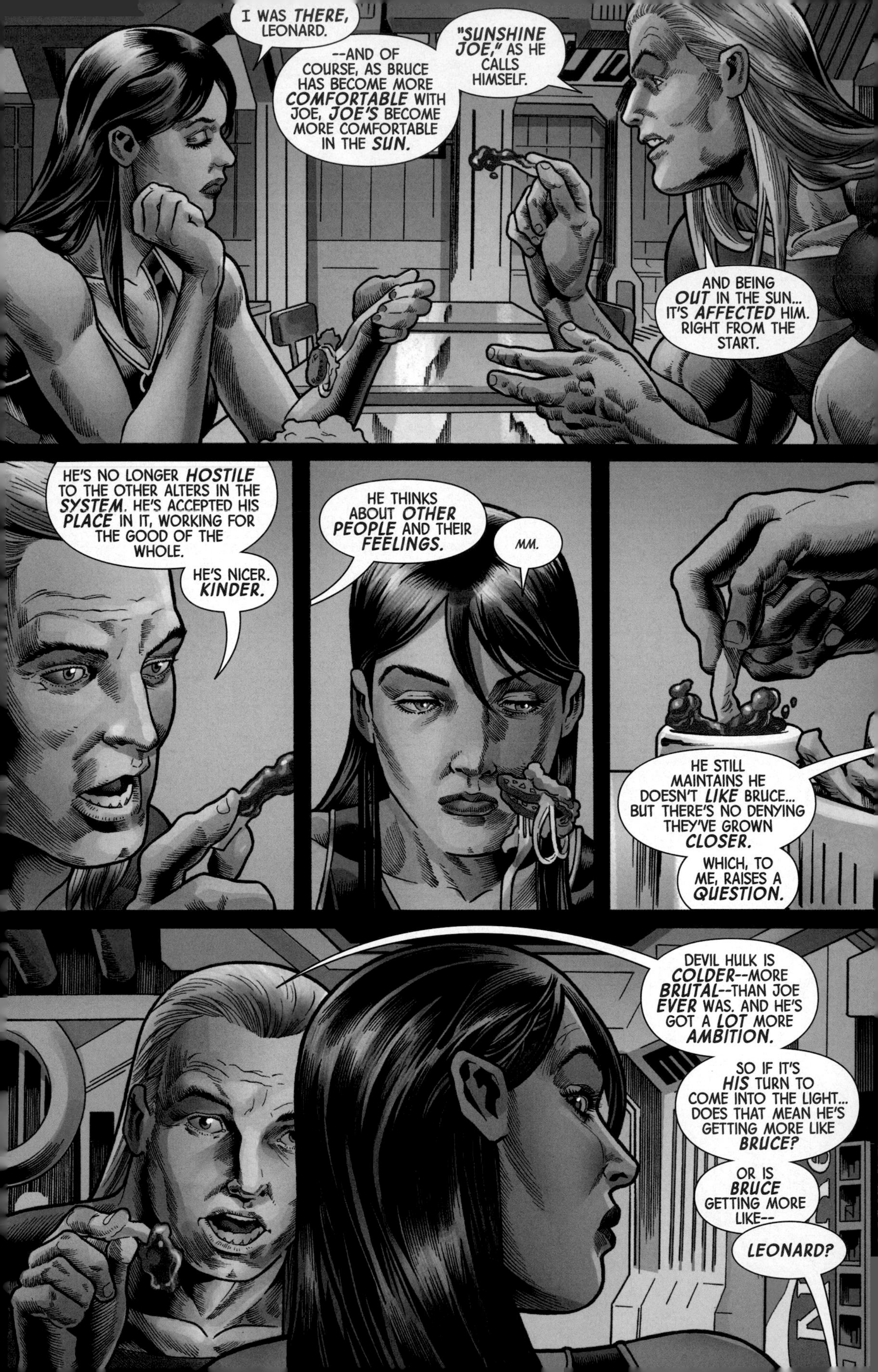
I WAS THERE, LEONARD.
--AND OF COURSE, AS BRUCE HAS BECOME MORE COMFORTABLE WITH JOE, JOE'S BECOME MORE COMFORTABLE IN THE SUN.
"SUNSHINE JOE," AS HE CALLS HIMSELF.
AND BEING OUT IN THE SUN... IT'S AFFECTED HIM. RIGHT FROM THE START.
HE'S NO LONGER HOSTILE TO THE OTHER ALTERS IN THE SYSTEM. HE'S ACCEPTED HIS PLACE IN IT, WORKING FOR THE GOOD OF THE WHOLE.
HE'S NICER. KINDER.
HE THINKS ABOUT OTHER PEOPLE AND THEIR FEELINGS.
MM.
HE STILL MAINTAINS HE DOESN'T LIKE BRUCE... BUT THERE'S NO DENYING THEY'VE GROWN CLOSER.
WHICH, TO ME, RAISES A QUESTION.
DEVIL HULK IS COLDER--MORE BRUTAL--THAN JOE EVER WAS. AND HE'S GOT A LOT MORE AMBITION.
SO IF IT'S HIS TURN TO COME INTO THE LIGHT... DOES THAT MEAN HE'S GETTING MORE LIKE BRUCE?
OR IS BRUCE GETTING MORE LIKE--
LEONARD?

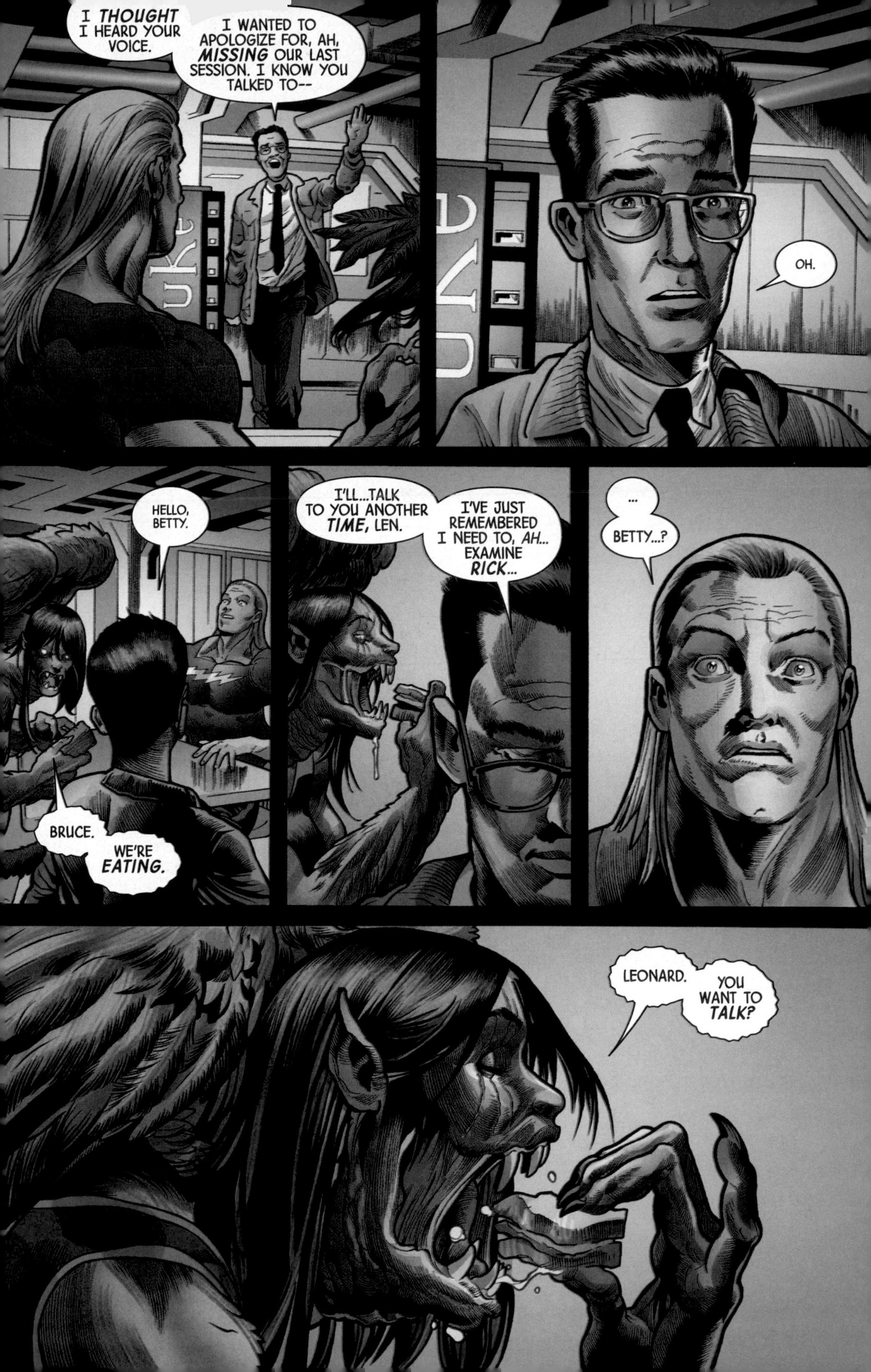
I THOUGHT I HEARD YOUR VOICE.
I WANTED TO APOLOGIZE FOR, AH, MISSING OUR LAST SESSION. I KNOW YOU TALKED TO--
OH.
HELLO, BETTY.
BRUCE.
WE'RE EATING.
I'LL...TALK TO YOU ANOTHER TIME, LEN.
I'VE JUST REMEMBERED I NEED TO, AH... EXAMINE RICK...
...
BETTY...?
LEONARD.
YOU WANT TO TALK?

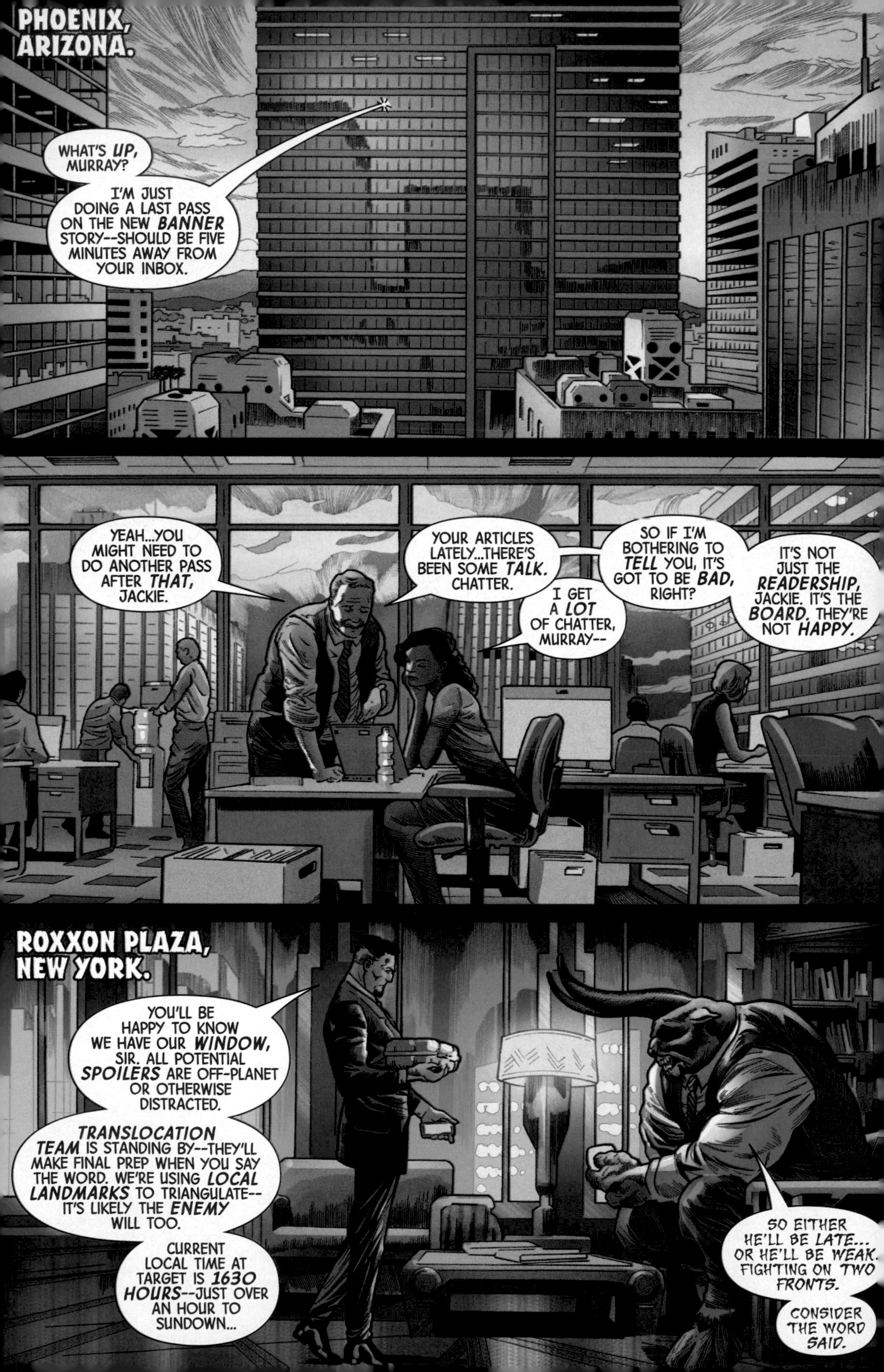

PHOENIX, ARIZONA.
WHAT'S UP, MURRAY?
I'M JUST DOING A LAST PASS ON THE NEW BANNER STORY--SHOULD BE FIVE MINUTES AWAY FROM YOUR INBOX.
YEAH...YOU MIGHT NEED TO DO ANOTHER PASS AFTER THAT, JACKIE.
YOUR ARTICLES LATELY...THERE'S BEEN SOME TALK. CHATTER.
I GET A LOT OF CHATTER, MURRAY--
SO IF I'M BOTHERING TO TELL YOU, IT'S GOT TO BE BAD, RIGHT?
IT'S NOT JUST THE READERSHIP, JACKIE. IT'S THE BOARD. THEY'RE NOT HAPPY.
ROXXON PLAZA, NEW YORK.
YOU'LL BE HAPPY TO KNOW WE HAVE OUR WINDOW, SIR. ALL POTENTIAL SPOILERS ARE OFF-PLANET OR OTHERWISE DISTRACTED.
TRANSLOCATION TEAM IS STANDING BY--THEY'LL MAKE FINAL PREP WHEN YOU SAY THE WORD. WE'RE USING LOCAL LANDMARKS TO TRIANGULATE--IT'S LIKELY THE ENEMY WILL TOO.
CURRENT LOCAL TIME AT TARGET IS 1630 HOURS--JUST OVER AN HOUR TO SUNDOWN...
SO EITHER HE'LL BE LATE... OR HE'LL BE WEAK. FIGHTING ON TWO FRONTS.
CONSIDER THE WORD SAID.

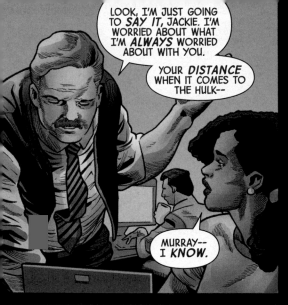

LOOK, I'M JUST GOING TO *SAY IT*, JACKIE. I'M WORRIED ABOUT WHAT I'M *ALWAYS* WORRIED ABOUT WITH YOU.

YOUR *DISTANCE* WHEN IT COMES TO THE HULK--

MURRAY-- I *KNOW*.

I KNOW YOU HAD TO PUSH ME BACK *INTO* THIS. I...I WAS *SCARED*, I ADMIT IT. OF THEM, OF THEIR *WORLD*.

BUT...I'M NOT *AFRAID* ANYMORE.

HOW ARE THE *ASSETS*? SUITABLY *FEARSOME*?

O'BRIEN'S LOOKING SKITTISH, BUT HE'LL BE FINE ONCE HIS BLOOD'S UP. *HARRYHAUSEN* IS RARING TO GO.

OH--AND THEY DIDN'T FEED *LOVECRAFT* TODAY...

SO HE'S *HUNGRY*.

I LIKE *THAT*.

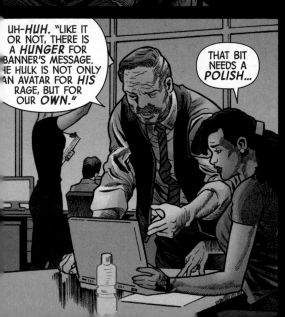

UH-*HUH*. "LIKE IT OR NOT, THERE IS A *HUNGER* FOR BANNER'S MESSAGE. THE HULK IS NOT ONLY AN AVATAR FOR *HIS* RAGE, BUT FOR *OUR OWN*."

THAT BIT NEEDS A *POLISH*...

"*OUR*" RAGE, THOUGH. YOU'RE EXPLICITLY *IDENTIFYING* WITH HIM IN THE PIECE.

THAT'S WHAT I MEAN ABOUT *DISTANCE*.

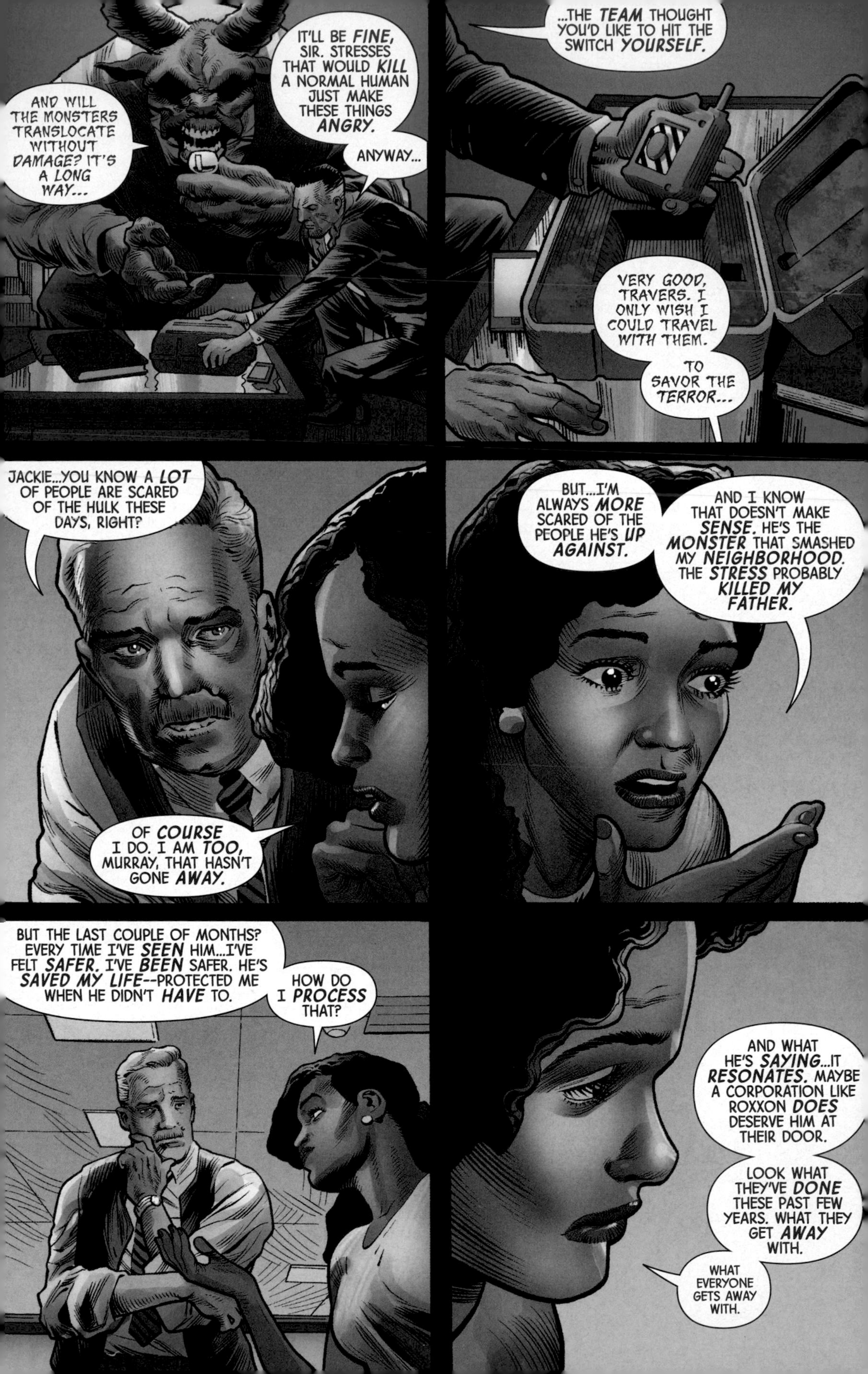
AND WILL THE MONSTERS TRANSLOCATE WITHOUT DAMAGE? IT'S A LONG WAY...
IT'LL BE FINE, SIR. STRESSES THAT WOULD KILL A NORMAL HUMAN JUST MAKE THESE THINGS ANGRY.
ANYWAY...
...THE TEAM THOUGHT YOU'D LIKE TO HIT THE SWITCH YOURSELF.
VERY GOOD, TRAVERS. I ONLY WISH I COULD TRAVEL WITH THEM.
TO SAVOR THE TERROR...
JACKIE...YOU KNOW A LOT OF PEOPLE ARE SCARED OF THE HULK THESE DAYS, RIGHT?
OF COURSE I DO. I AM TOO, MURRAY, THAT HASN'T GONE AWAY.
BUT...I'M ALWAYS MORE SCARED OF THE PEOPLE HE'S UP AGAINST.
AND I KNOW THAT DOESN'T MAKE SENSE. HE'S THE MONSTER THAT SMASHED MY NEIGHBORHOOD. THE STRESS PROBABLY KILLED MY FATHER.
BUT THE LAST COUPLE OF MONTHS? EVERY TIME I'VE SEEN HIM...I'VE FELT SAFER. I'VE BEEN SAFER. HE'S SAVED MY LIFE--PROTECTED ME WHEN HE DIDN'T HAVE TO.
HOW DO I PROCESS THAT?
AND WHAT HE'S SAYING...IT RESONATES. MAYBE A CORPORATION LIKE ROXXON DOES DESERVE HIM AT THEIR DOOR.
LOOK WHAT THEY'VE DONE THESE PAST FEW YEARS. WHAT THEY GET AWAY WITH.
WHAT EVERYONE GETS AWAY WITH.

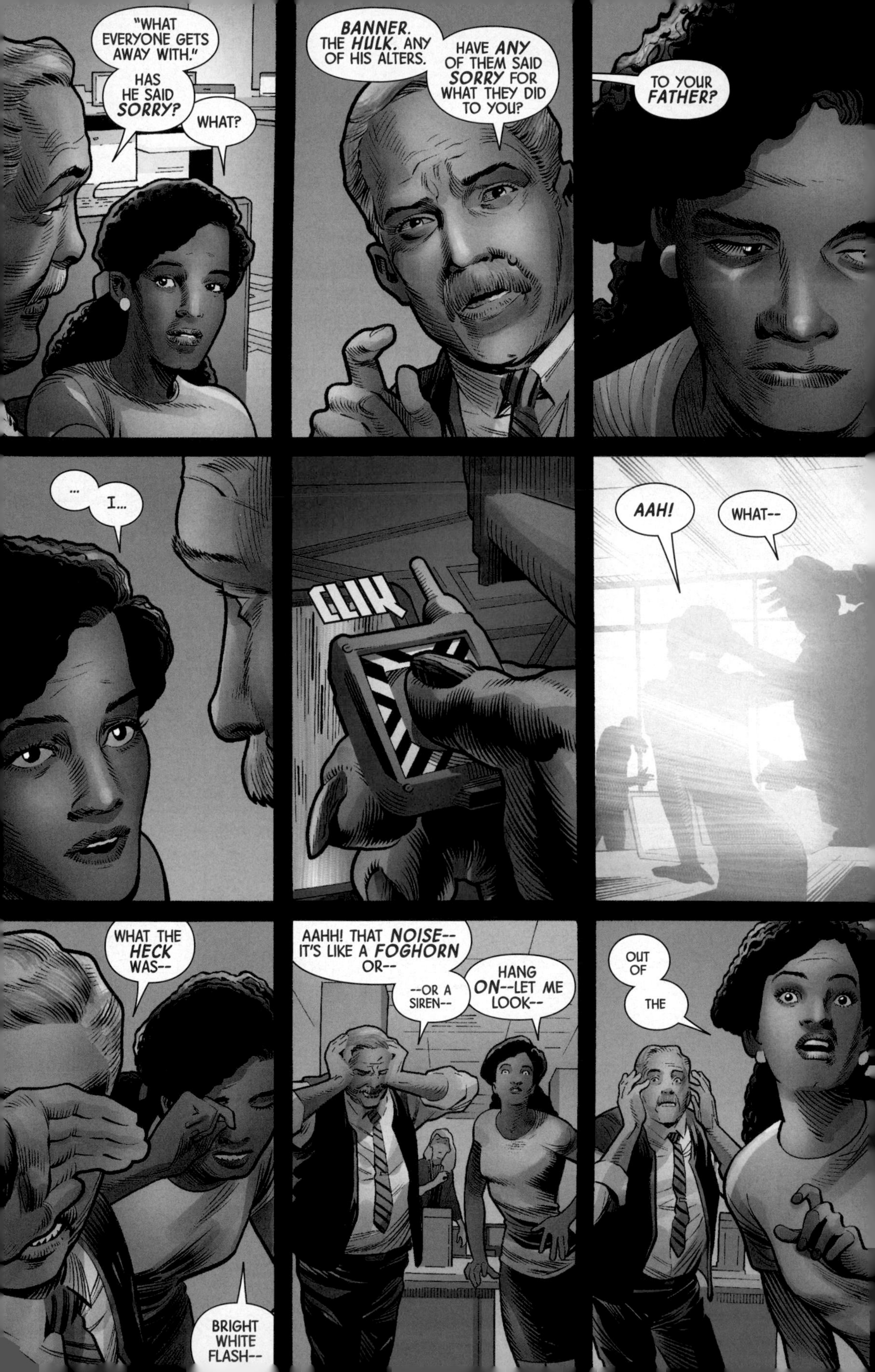
"WHAT EVERYONE GETS AWAY WITH."
HAS HE SAID SORRY?
WHAT?
BANNER. THE HULK. ANY OF HIS ALTERS.
HAVE ANY OF THEM SAID SORRY FOR WHAT THEY DID TO YOU?
TO YOUR FATHER?
...
I...
CLIK
AAH!
WHAT--
WHAT THE HECK WAS--
BRIGHT WHITE FLASH--
AAHH! THAT NOISE-- IT'S LIKE A FOGHORN OR--
--OR A SIREN--
HANG ON--LET ME LOOK--
OUT OF
THE

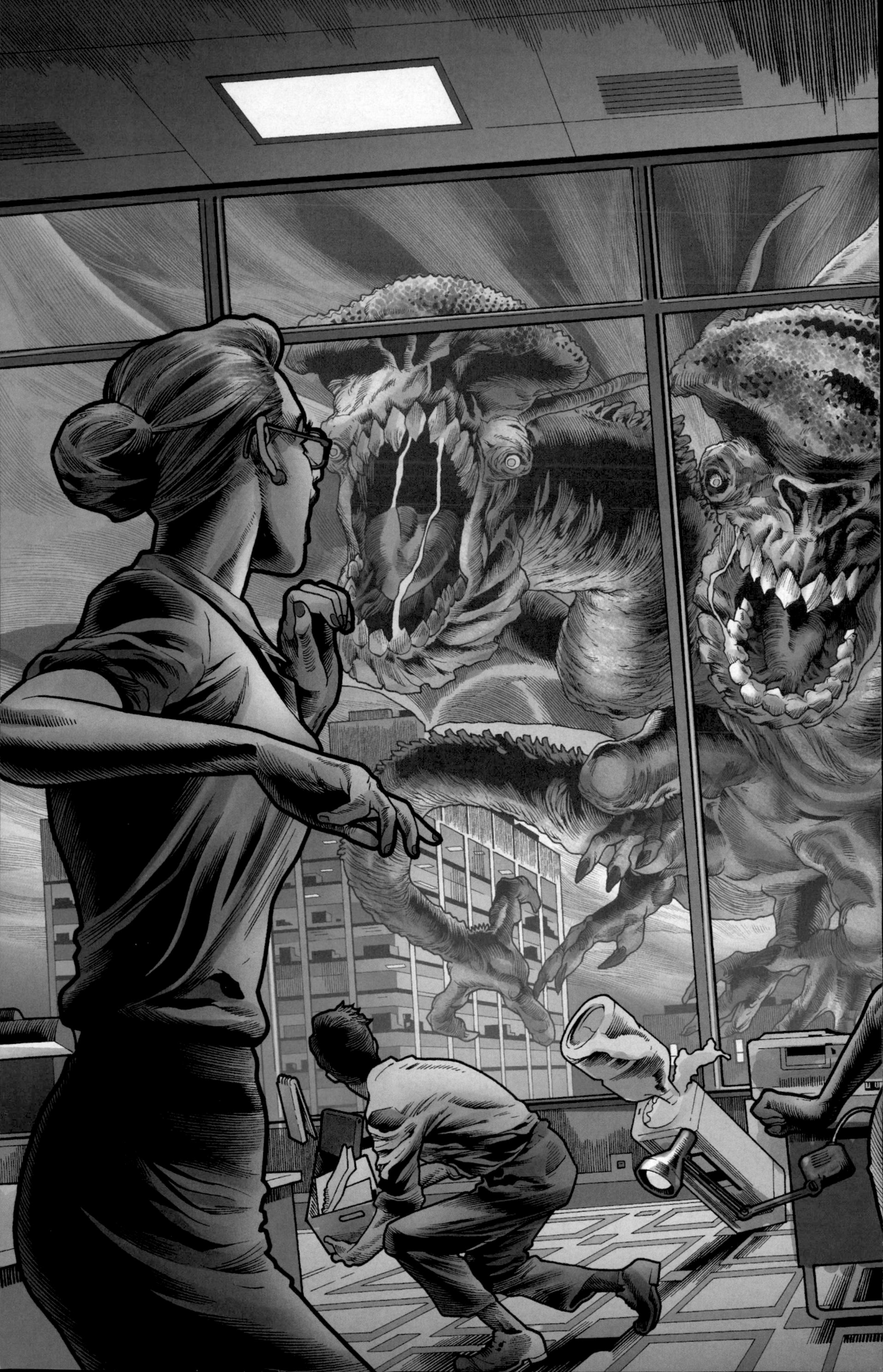

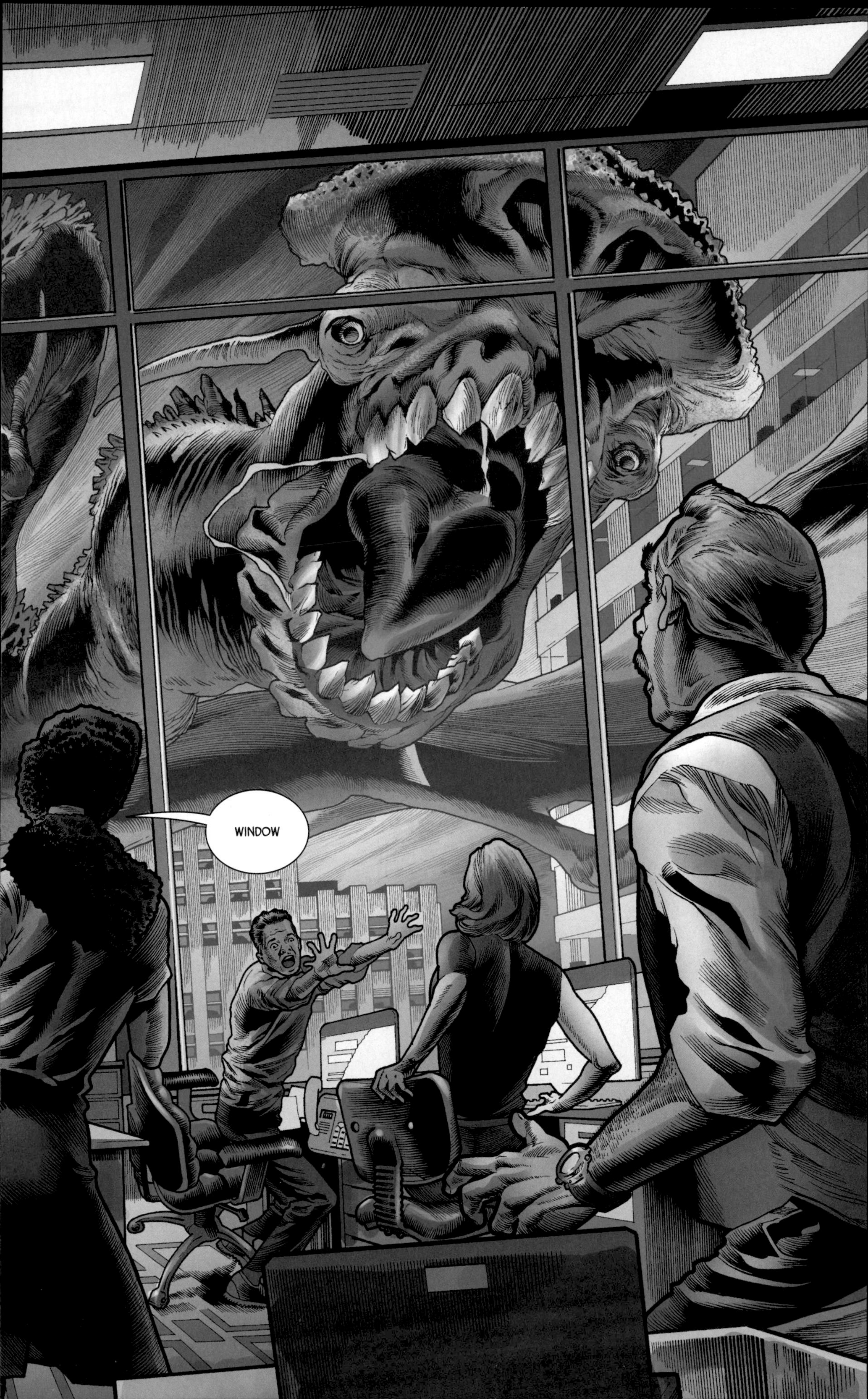
WINDOW

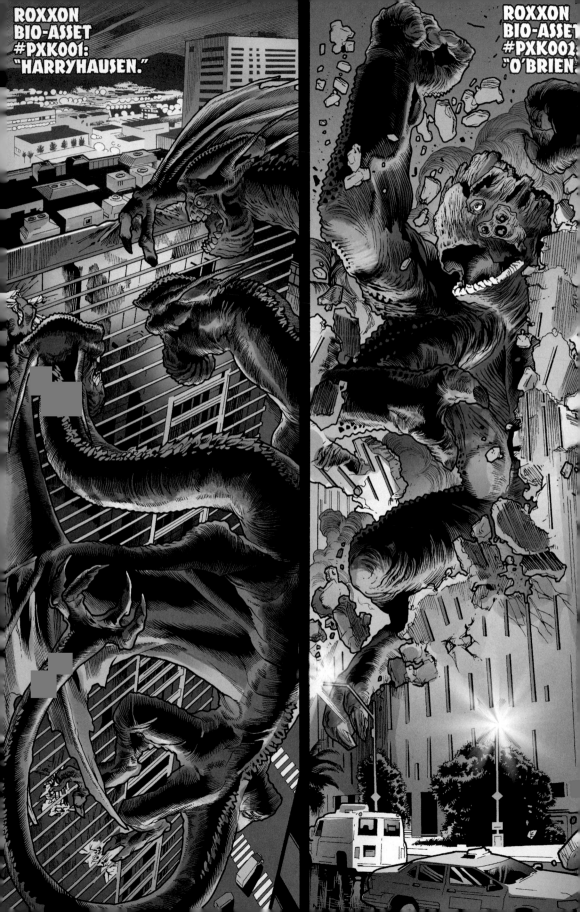

ROXXON
BIO-ASSET
#PXK001:
"HARRYHAUSEN."

ROXXON
BIO-ASSET
#PXK002:
"O'BRIEN."

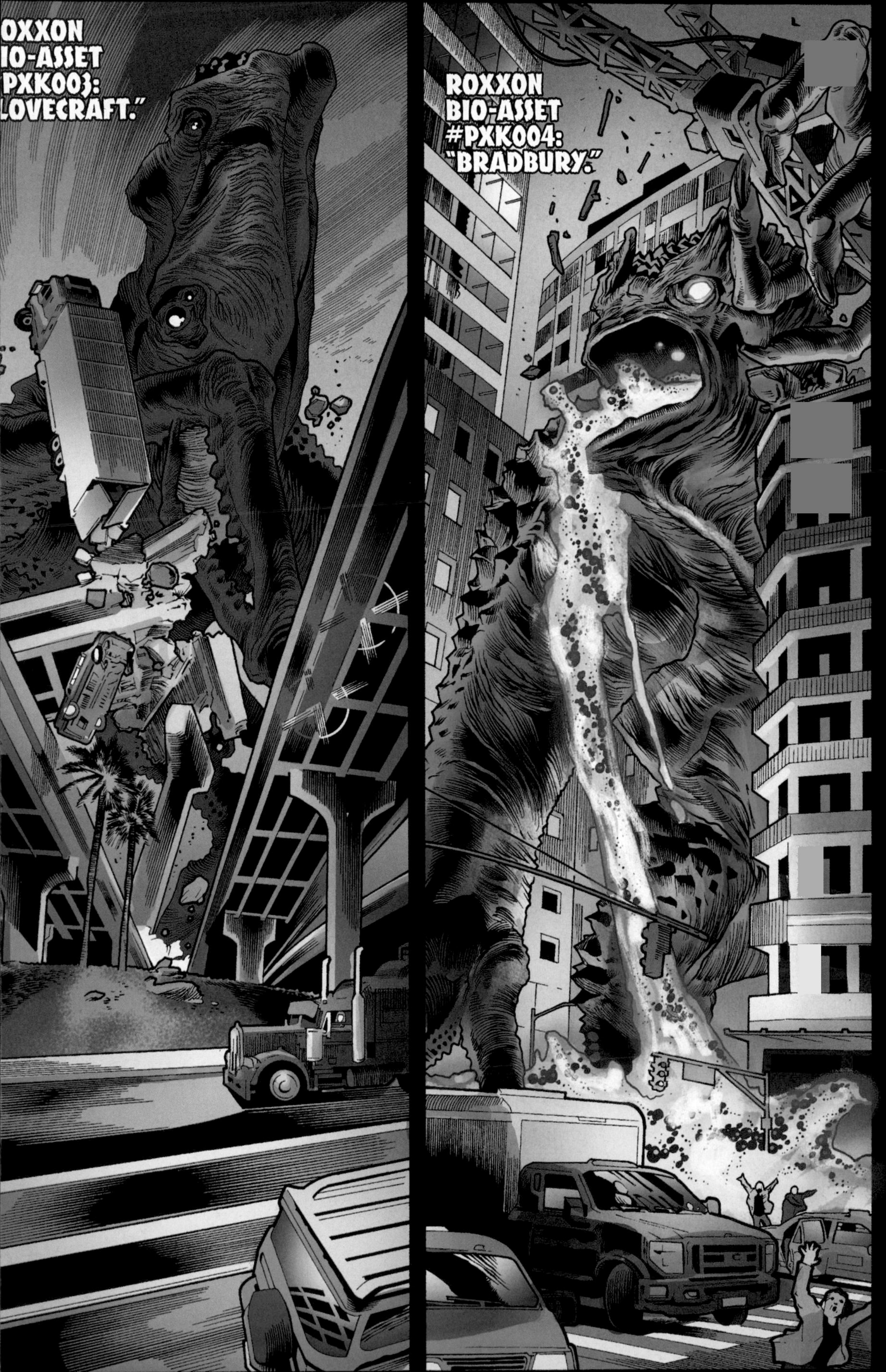
OXXON BIO-ASSET PXK003: LOVECRAFT."
ROXXON BIO-ASSET #PXK004: "BRADBURY."

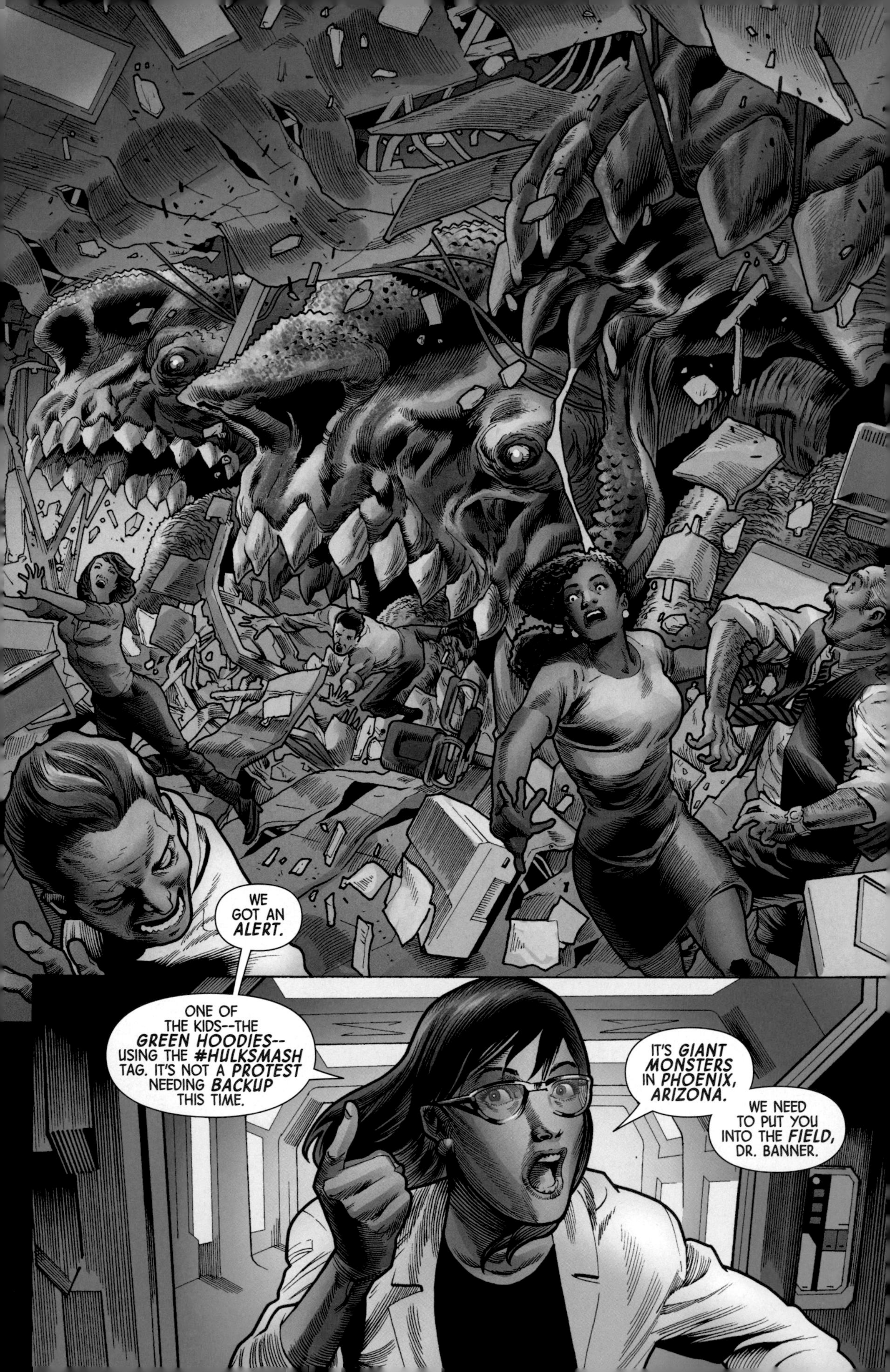
WE GOT AN ALERT.
ONE OF THE KIDS--THE GREEN HOODIES--USING THE #HULKSMASH TAG. IT'S NOT A PROTEST NEEDING BACKUP THIS TIME.
IT'S GIANT MONSTERS IN PHOENIX, ARIZONA.
WE NEED TO PUT YOU INTO THE FIELD, DR. BANNER.

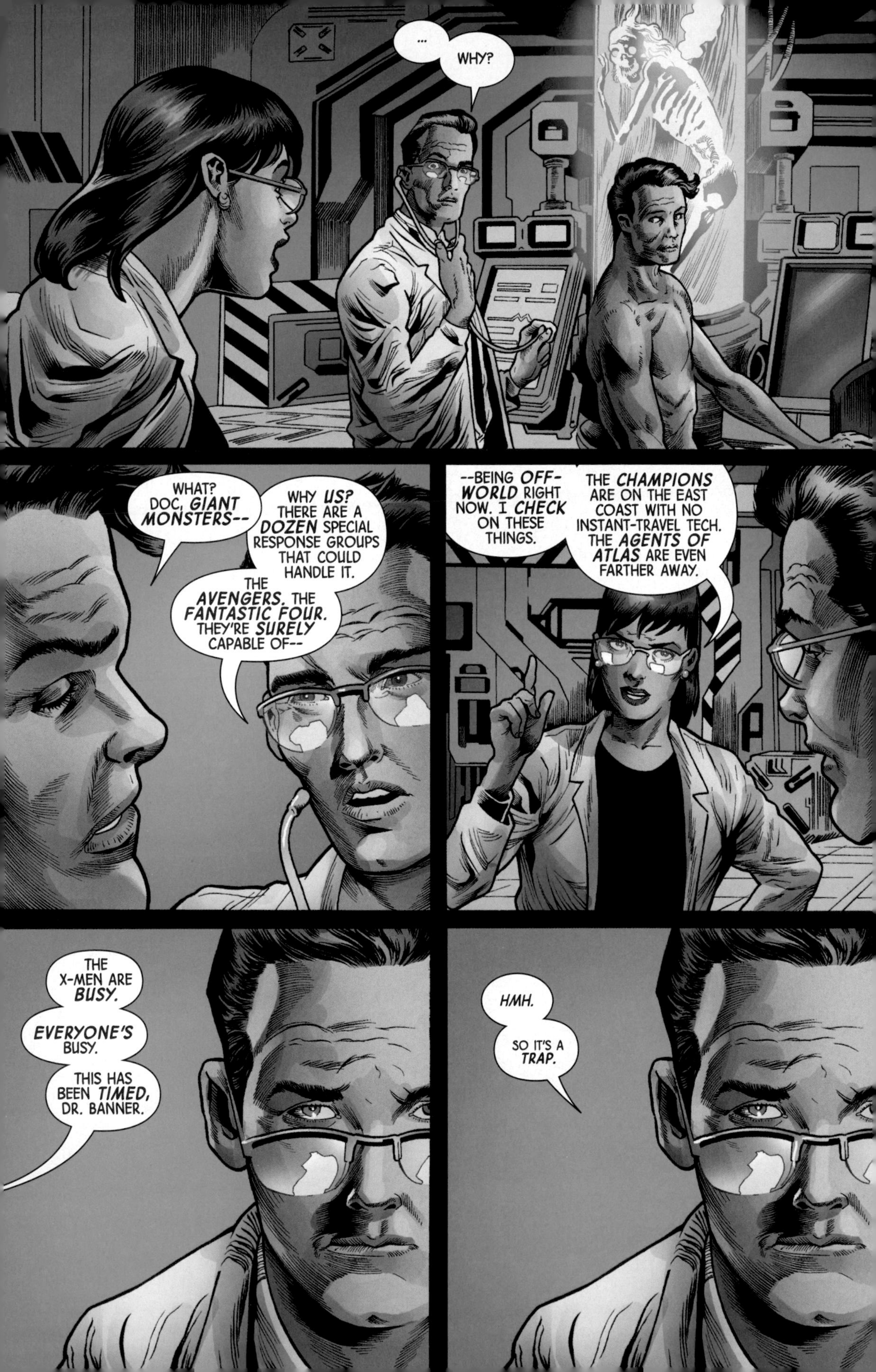
...
WHY?
WHAT? DOC, GIANT MONSTERS--
WHY US? THERE ARE A DOZEN SPECIAL RESPONSE GROUPS THAT COULD HANDLE IT.
THE AVENGERS. THE FANTASTIC FOUR. THEY'RE SURELY CAPABLE OF--
--BEING OFF-WORLD RIGHT NOW. I CHECK ON THESE THINGS.
THE CHAMPIONS ARE ON THE EAST COAST WITH NO INSTANT-TRAVEL TECH. THE AGENTS OF ATLAS ARE EVEN FARTHER AWAY.
THE X-MEN ARE BUSY.
EVERYONE'S BUSY.
THIS HAS BEEN TIMED, DR. BANNER.
HMH.
SO IT'S A TRAP.

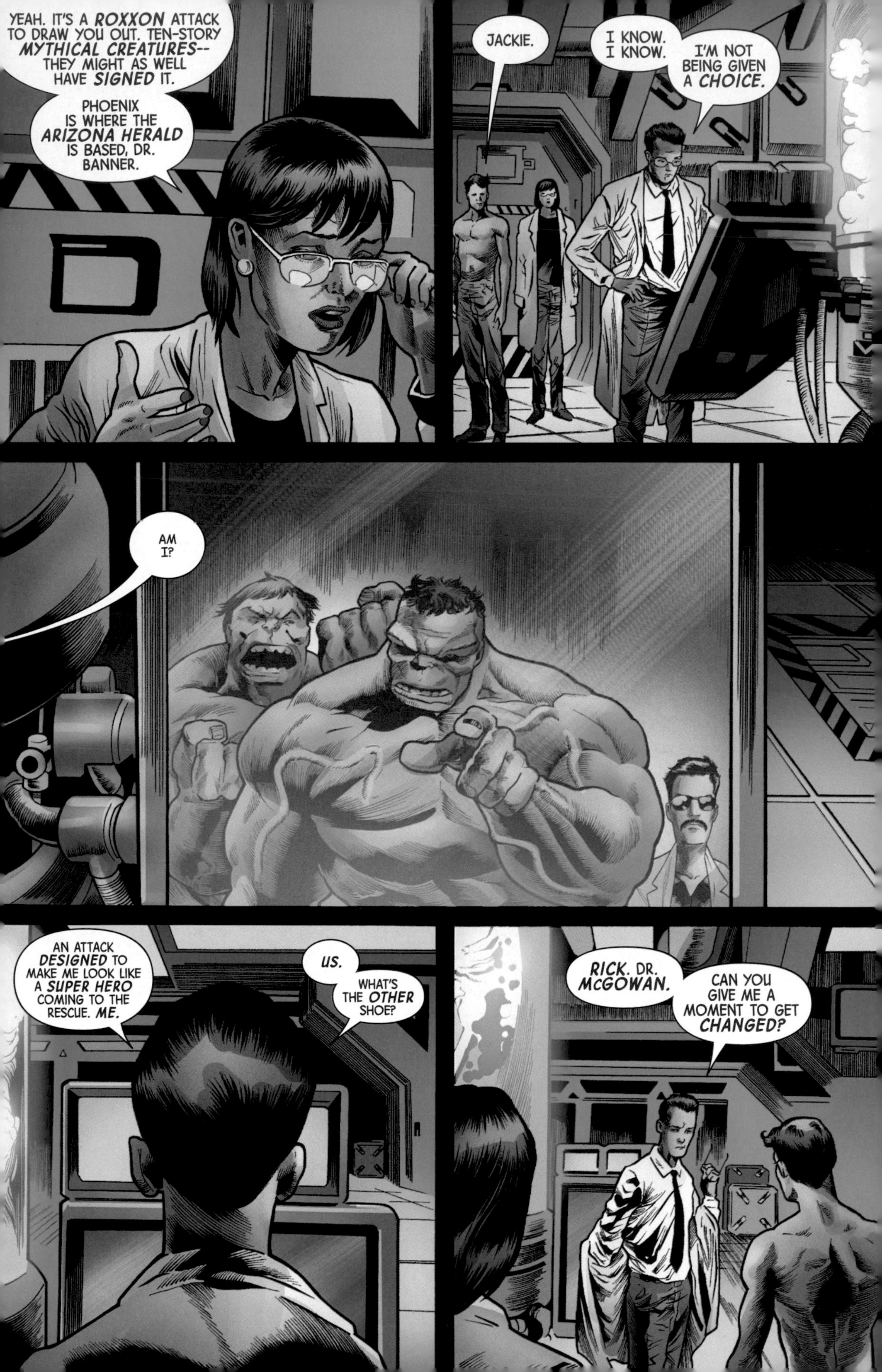
YEAH. IT'S A ROXXON ATTACK TO DRAW YOU OUT. TEN-STORY MYTHICAL CREATURES-- THEY MIGHT AS WELL HAVE SIGNED IT.
PHOENIX IS WHERE THE ARIZONA HERALD IS BASED, DR. BANNER.
JACKIE.
I KNOW. I KNOW.
I'M NOT BEING GIVEN A CHOICE.
AM I?
AN ATTACK DESIGNED TO MAKE ME LOOK LIKE A SUPER HERO COMING TO THE RESCUE. ME.
US.
WHAT'S THE OTHER SHOE?
RICK. DR. McGOWAN.
CAN YOU GIVE ME A MOMENT TO GET CHANGED?

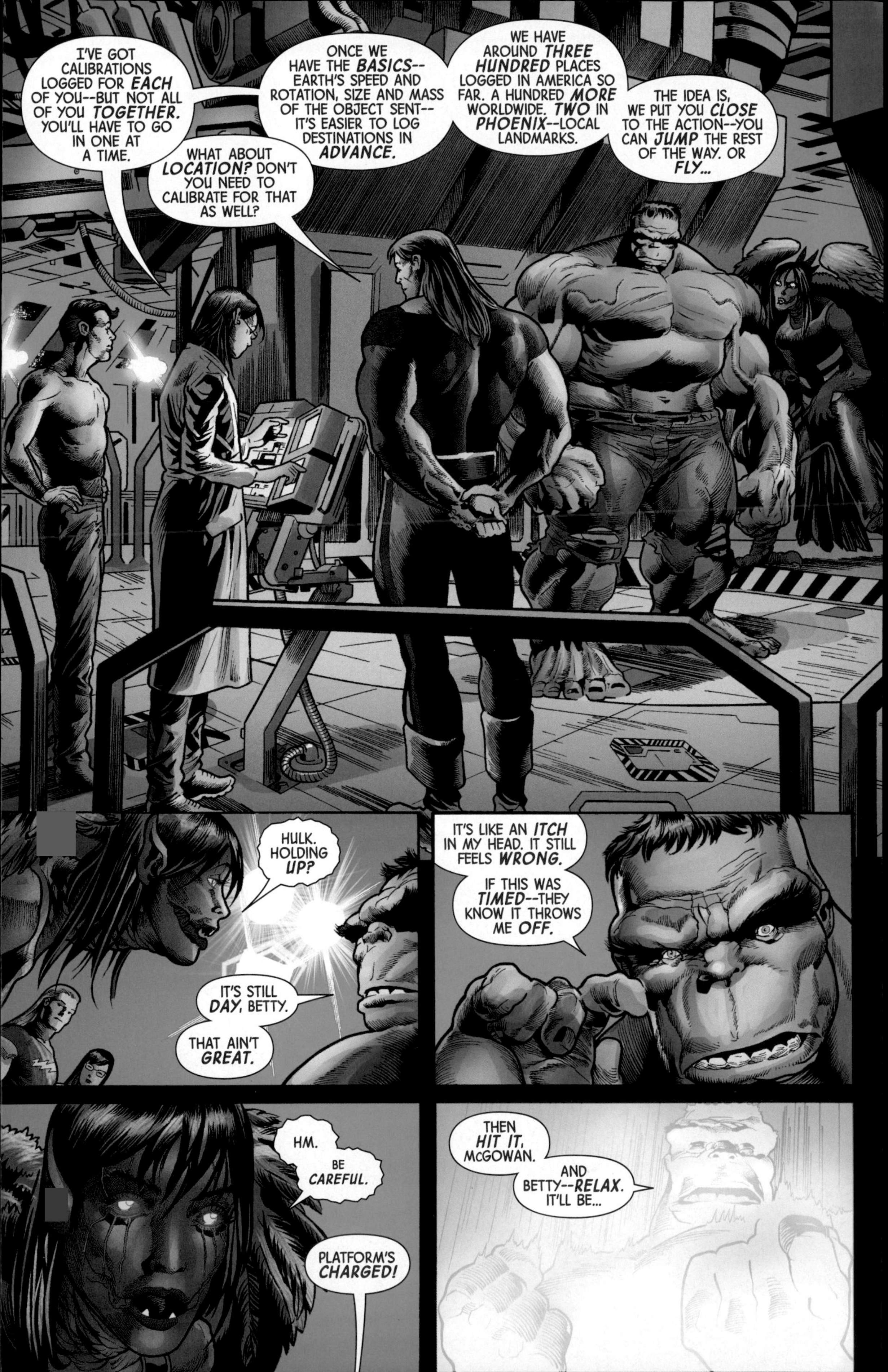
I'VE GOT CALIBRATIONS LOGGED FOR EACH OF YOU--BUT NOT ALL OF YOU TOGETHER. YOU'LL HAVE TO GO IN ONE AT A TIME.
WHAT ABOUT LOCATION? DON'T YOU NEED TO CALIBRATE FOR THAT AS WELL?
ONCE WE HAVE THE BASICS-- EARTH'S SPEED AND ROTATION, SIZE AND MASS OF THE OBJECT SENT-- IT'S EASIER TO LOG DESTINATIONS IN ADVANCE.
WE HAVE AROUND THREE HUNDRED PLACES LOGGED IN AMERICA SO FAR. A HUNDRED MORE WORLDWIDE. TWO IN PHOENIX--LOCAL LANDMARKS.
THE IDEA IS, WE PUT YOU CLOSE TO THE ACTION--YOU CAN JUMP THE REST OF THE WAY. OR FLY...
HULK. HOLDING UP?
IT'S STILL DAY, BETTY.
THAT AIN'T GREAT.
IT'S LIKE AN ITCH IN MY HEAD. IT STILL FEELS WRONG.
IF THIS WAS TIMED--THEY KNOW IT THROWS ME OFF.
HM.
BE CAREFUL.
PLATFORM'S CHARGED!
THEN HIT IT, McGOWAN.
AND BETTY--RELAX. IT'LL BE...

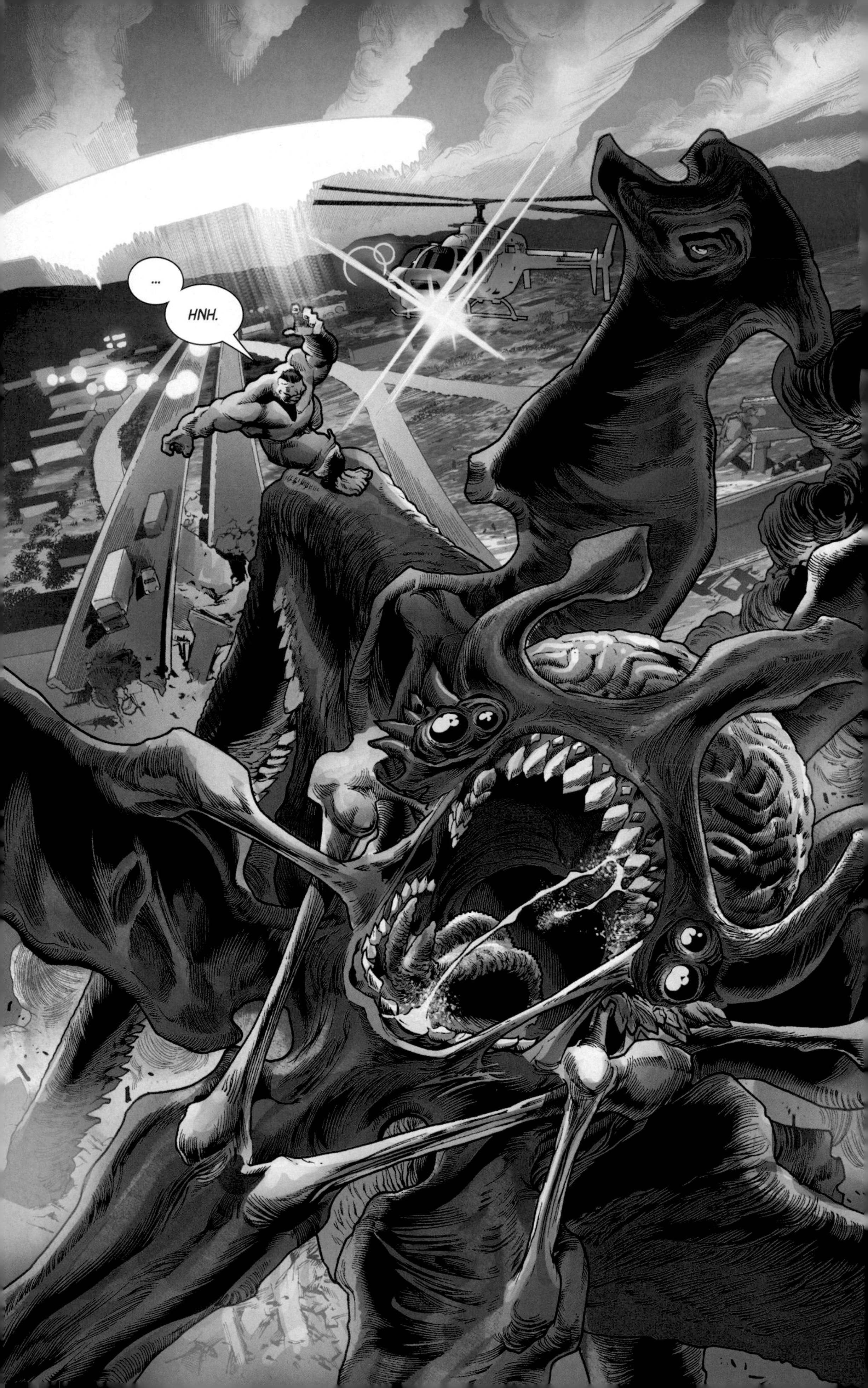
...
HNH.

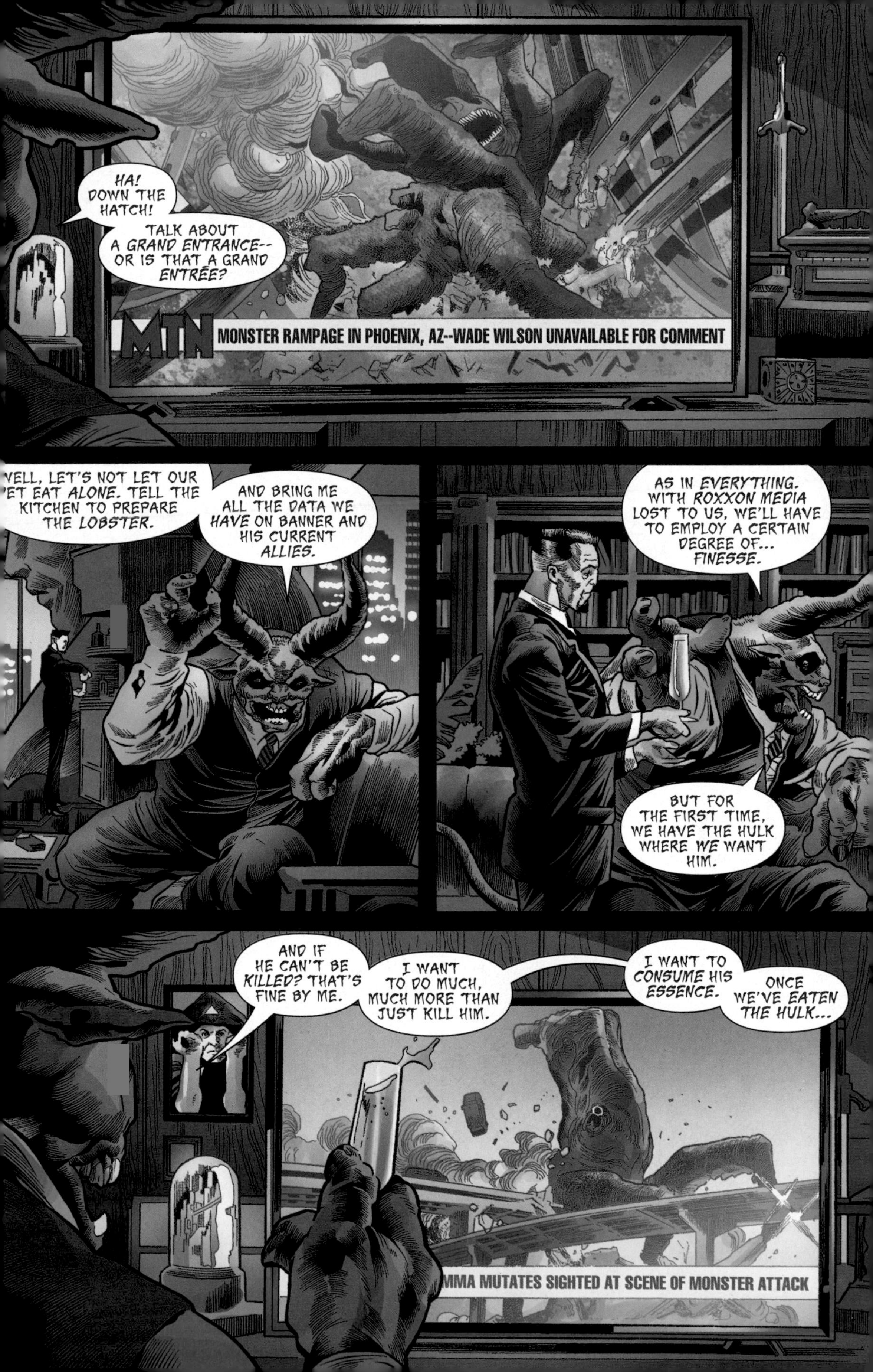
HA! DOWN THE HATCH!
TALK ABOUT A GRAND ENTRANCE-- OR IS THAT A GRAND ENTRÉE?
MTN
MONSTER RAMPAGE IN PHOENIX, AZ--WADE WILSON UNAVAILABLE FOR COMMENT
WELL, LET'S NOT LET OUR PET EAT ALONE. TELL THE KITCHEN TO PREPARE THE LOBSTER.
AND BRING ME ALL THE DATA WE HAVE ON BANNER AND HIS CURRENT ALLIES.
AS IN EVERYTHING. WITH ROXXON MEDIA LOST TO US, WE'LL HAVE TO EMPLOY A CERTAIN DEGREE OF... FINESSE.
BUT FOR THE FIRST TIME, WE HAVE THE HULK WHERE WE WANT HIM.
AND IF HE CAN'T BE KILLED? THAT'S FINE BY ME.
I WANT TO DO MUCH, MUCH MORE THAN JUST KILL HIM.
I WANT TO CONSUME HIS ESSENCE.
ONCE WE'VE EATEN THE HULK...
MMA MUTATES SIGHTED AT SCENE OF MONSTER ATTACK

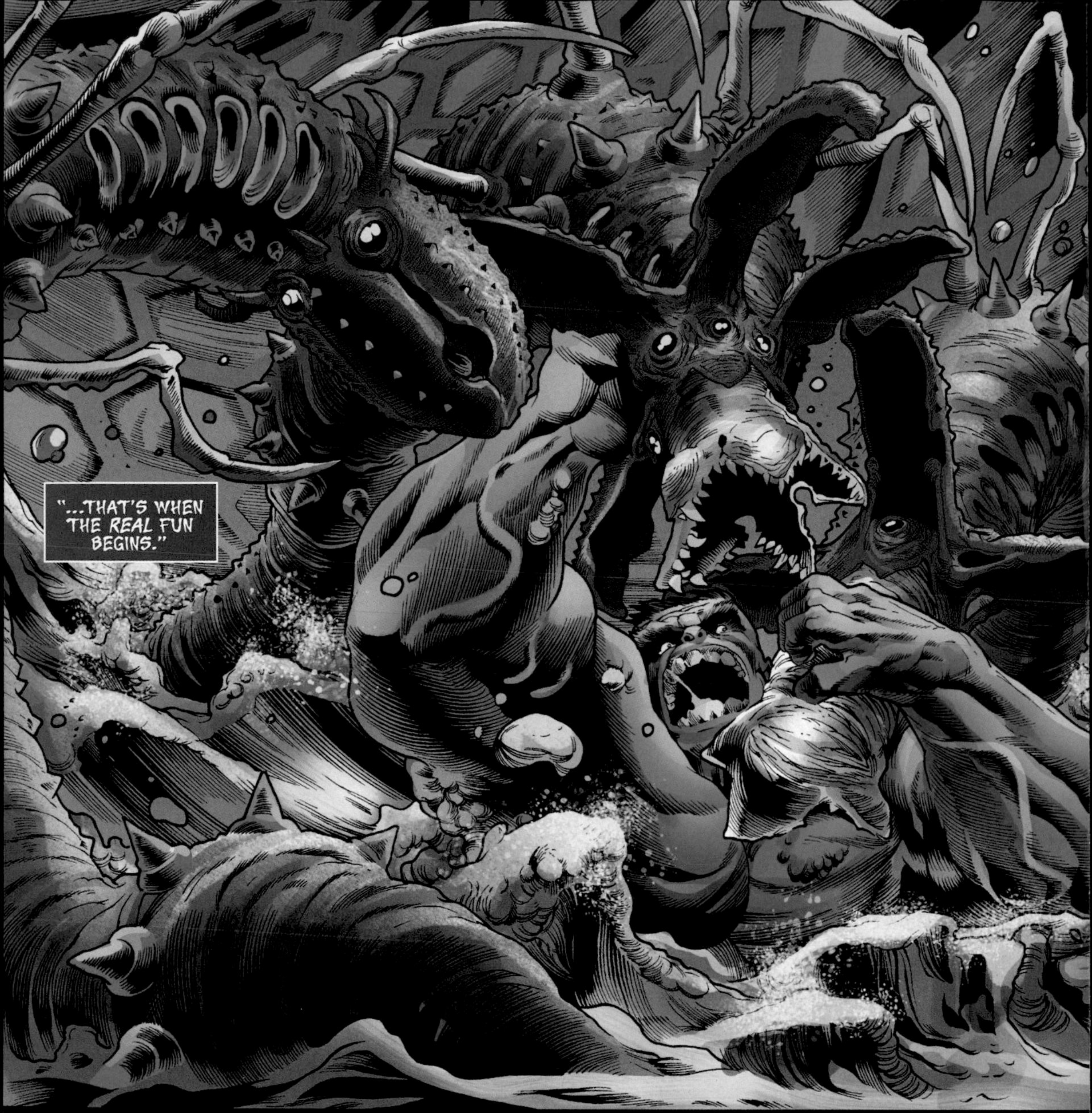
"...THAT'S WHEN THE REAL FUN BEGINS."

EAT OR BE EATEN

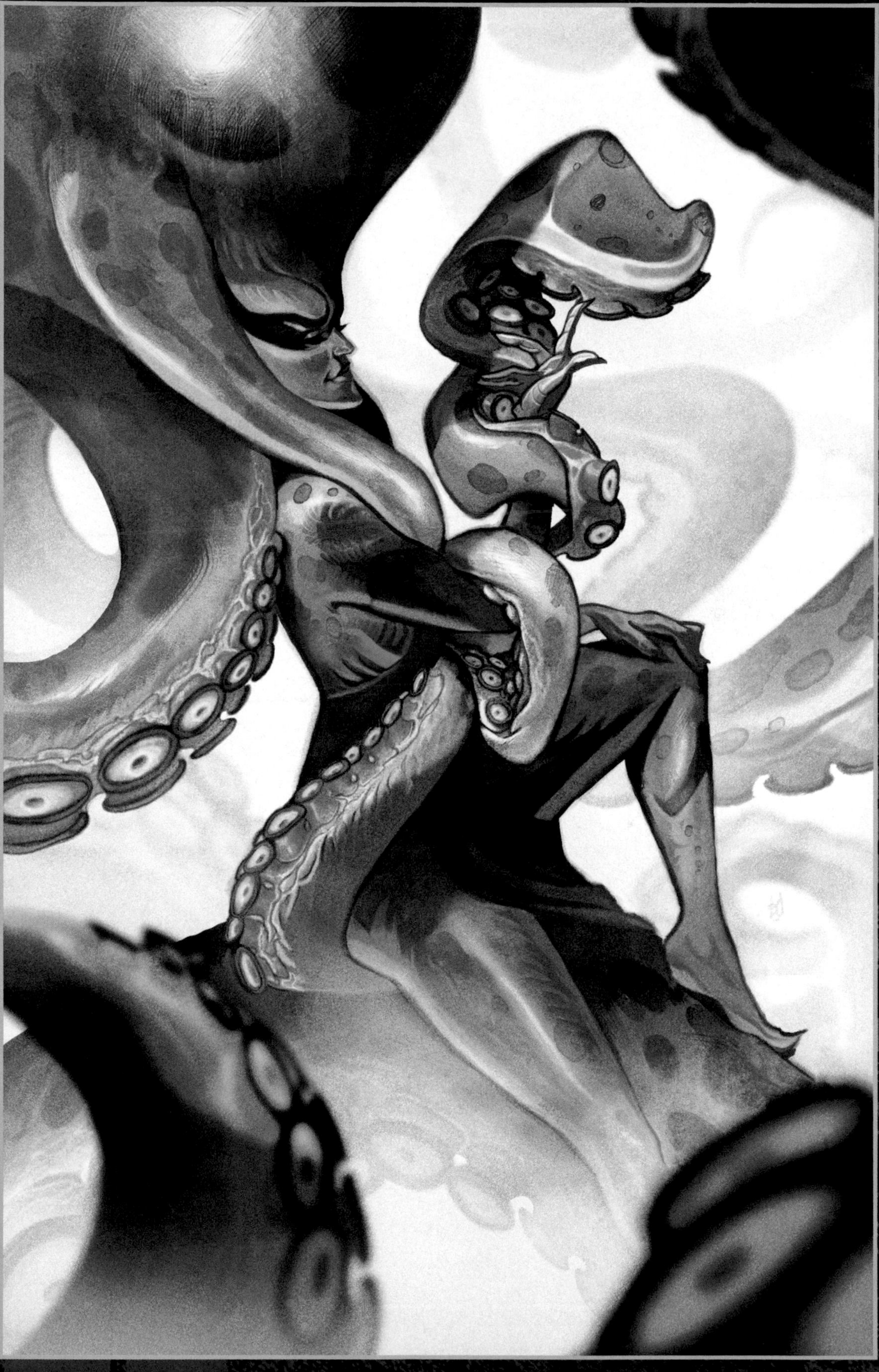

MIKE DEL MUNDO
#30 *MARVELS X* VARIANT

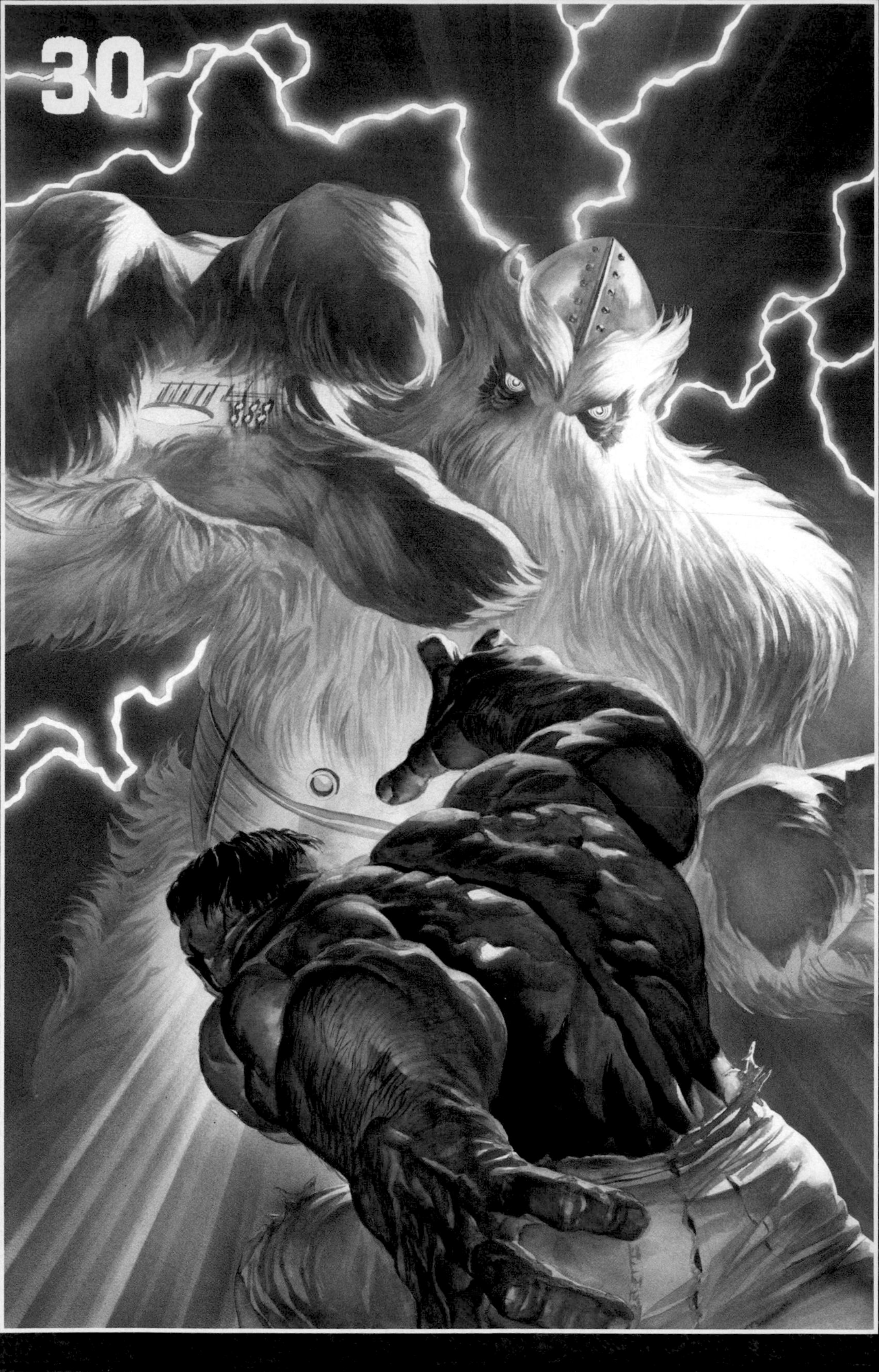
30

"WATCH THEREFORE: FOR YE KNOW NOT WHAT HOUR YOUR LORD DOTH COME."

– MATTHEW 24:42

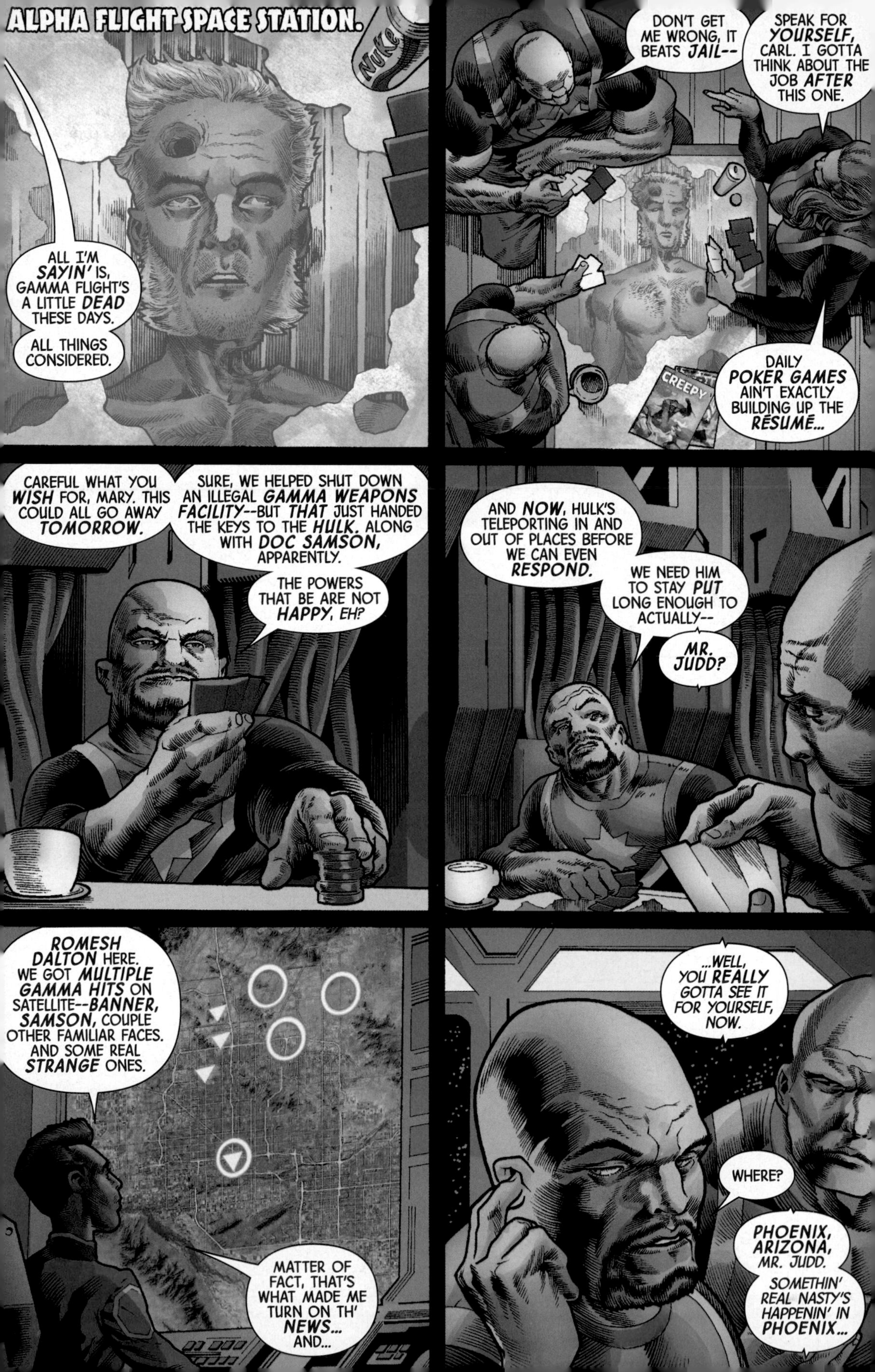
ALPHA FLIGHT SPACE STATION.
NUKE
ALL I'M SAYIN' IS, GAMMA FLIGHT'S A LITTLE DEAD THESE DAYS.
ALL THINGS CONSIDERED.
DON'T GET ME WRONG, IT BEATS JAIL--
SPEAK FOR YOURSELF, CARL. I GOTTA THINK ABOUT THE JOB AFTER THIS ONE.
DAILY POKER GAMES AIN'T EXACTLY BUILDING UP THE RÉSUMÉ...
CREEPY
CAREFUL WHAT YOU WISH FOR, MARY. THIS COULD ALL GO AWAY TOMORROW.
SURE, WE HELPED SHUT DOWN AN ILLEGAL GAMMA WEAPONS FACILITY--BUT THAT JUST HANDED THE KEYS TO THE HULK. ALONG WITH DOC SAMSON, APPARENTLY.
THE POWERS THAT BE ARE NOT HAPPY, EH?
AND NOW, HULK'S TELEPORTING IN AND OUT OF PLACES BEFORE WE CAN EVEN RESPOND.
WE NEED HIM TO STAY PUT LONG ENOUGH TO ACTUALLY--
MR. JUDD?
ROMESH DALTON HERE. WE GOT MULTIPLE GAMMA HITS ON SATELLITE--BANNER, SAMSON, COUPLE OTHER FAMILIAR FACES. AND SOME REAL STRANGE ONES.
MATTER OF FACT, THAT'S WHAT MADE ME TURN ON TH' NEWS... AND...
...WELL, YOU REALLY GOTTA SEE IT FOR YOURSELF, NOW.
WHERE?
PHOENIX, ARIZONA, MR. JUDD.
SOMETHIN' REAL NASTY'S HAPPENIN' IN PHOENIX...

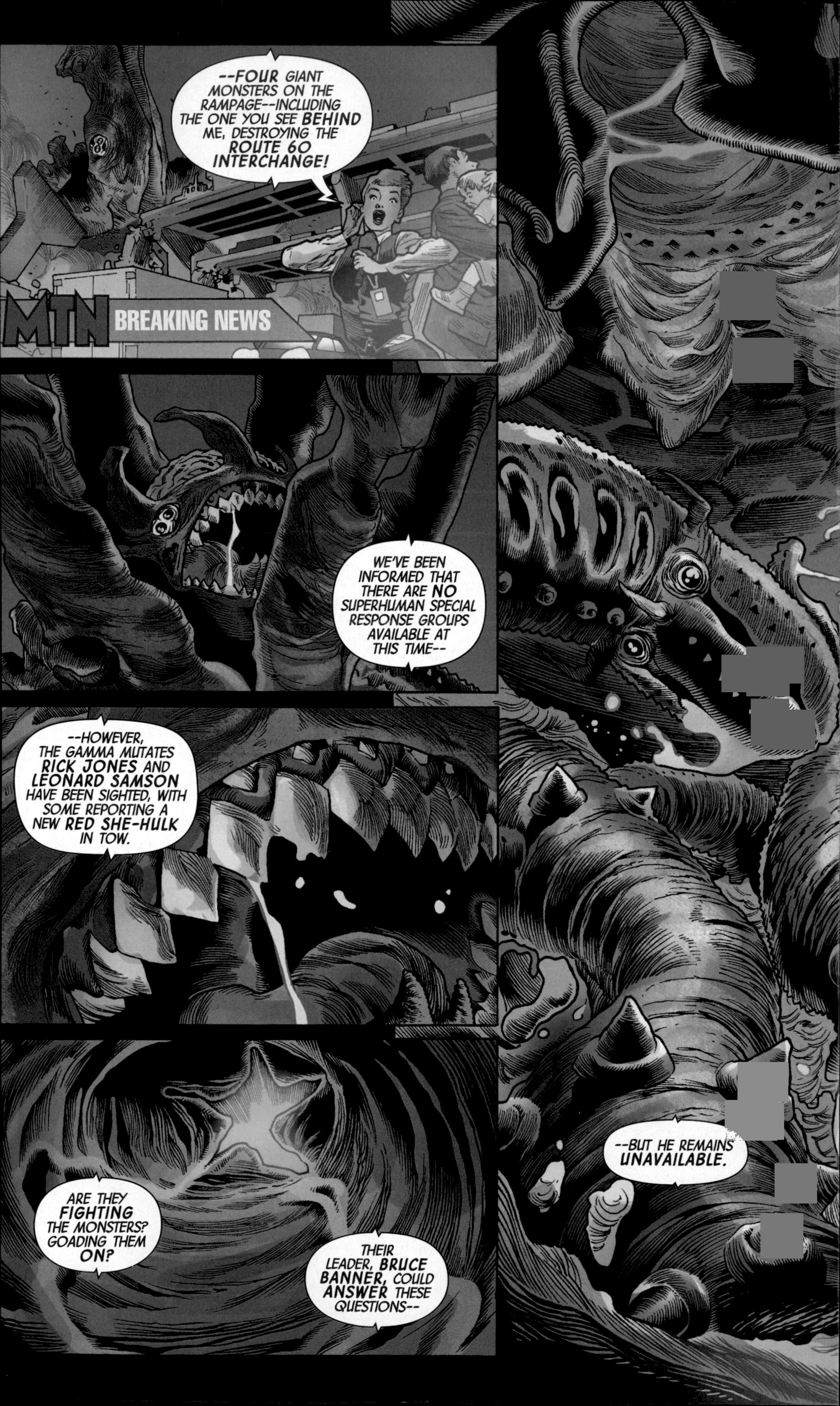
--FOUR GIANT MONSTERS ON THE RAMPAGE--INCLUDING THE ONE YOU SEE BEHIND ME, DESTROYING THE ROUTE 60 INTERCHANGE!
MTN BREAKING NEWS
WE'VE BEEN INFORMED THAT THERE ARE NO SUPERHUMAN SPECIAL RESPONSE GROUPS AVAILABLE AT THIS TIME--
--HOWEVER, THE GAMMA MUTATES RICK JONES AND LEONARD SAMSON HAVE BEEN SIGHTED, WITH SOME REPORTING A NEW RED SHE-HULK IN TOW.
ARE THEY FIGHTING THE MONSTERS? GOADING THEM ON?
THEIR LEADER, BRUCE BANNER, COULD ANSWER THESE QUESTIONS--
--BUT HE REMAINS UNAVAILABLE.

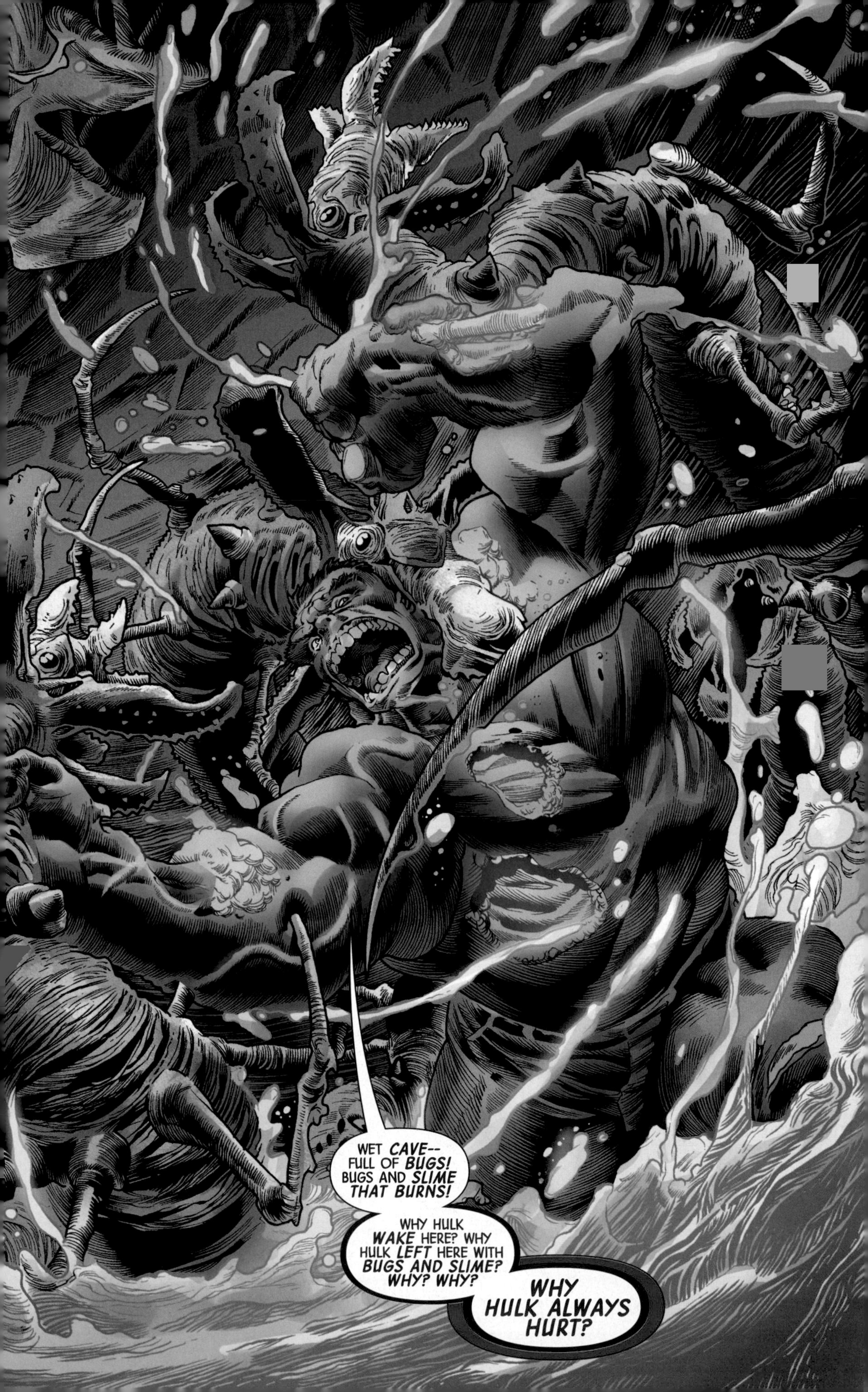
WET CAVE-- FULL OF BUGS! BUGS AND SLIME THAT BURNS!
WHY HULK WAKE HERE? WHY HULK LEFT HERE WITH BUGS AND SLIME? WHY? WHY?
WHY HULK ALWAYS HURT?

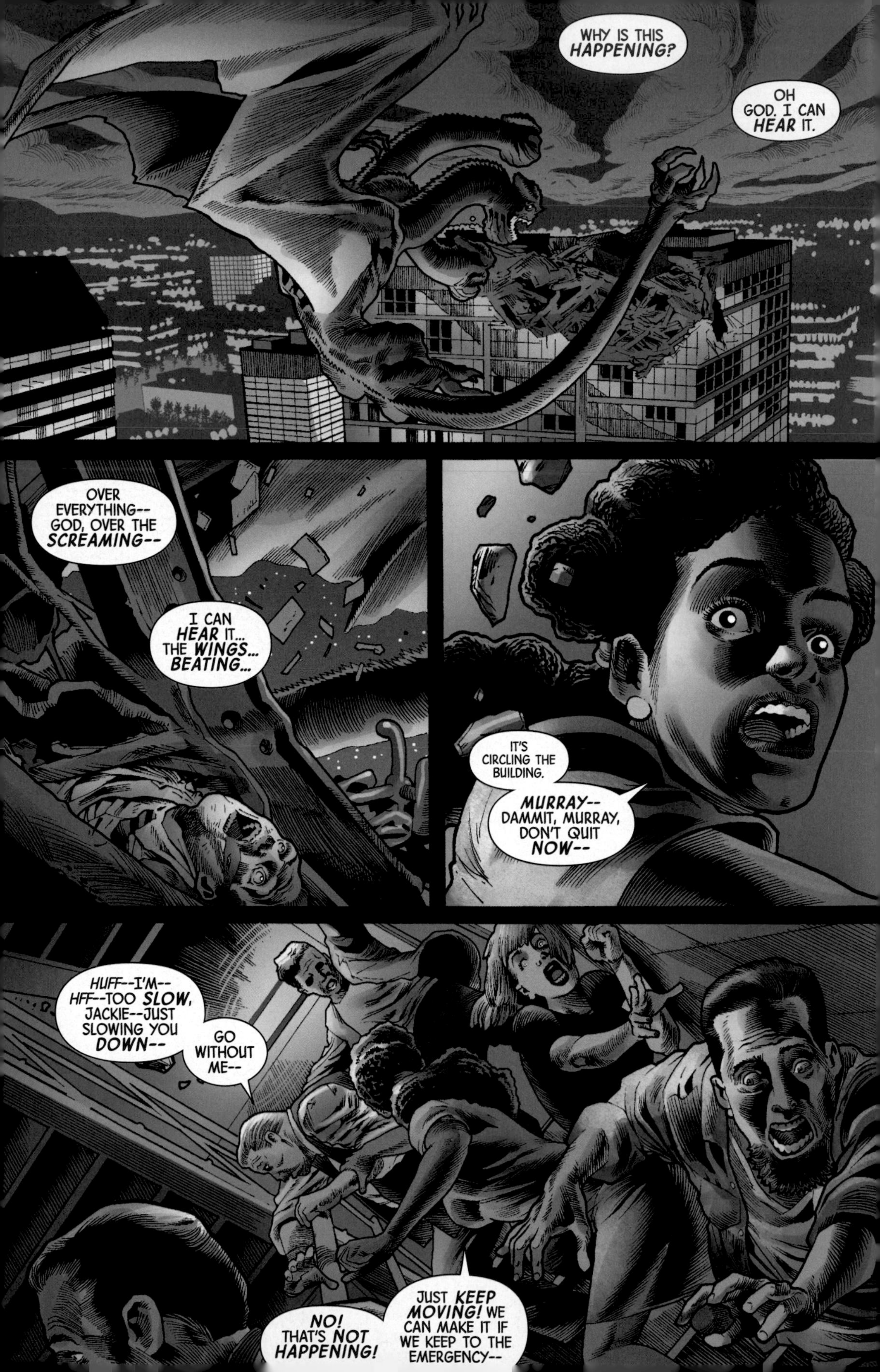
WHY IS THIS HAPPENING?
OH GOD. I CAN HEAR IT.
OVER EVERYTHING-- GOD, OVER THE SCREAMING--
I CAN HEAR IT... THE WINGS... BEATING...
IT'S CIRCLING THE BUILDING.
MURRAY-- DAMMIT, MURRAY, DON'T QUIT NOW--
HUFF--I'M-- HFF--TOO SLOW, JACKIE--JUST SLOWING YOU DOWN--
GO WITHOUT ME--
NO! THAT'S NOT HAPPENING!
JUST KEEP MOVING! WE CAN MAKE IT IF WE KEEP TO THE EMERGENCY--

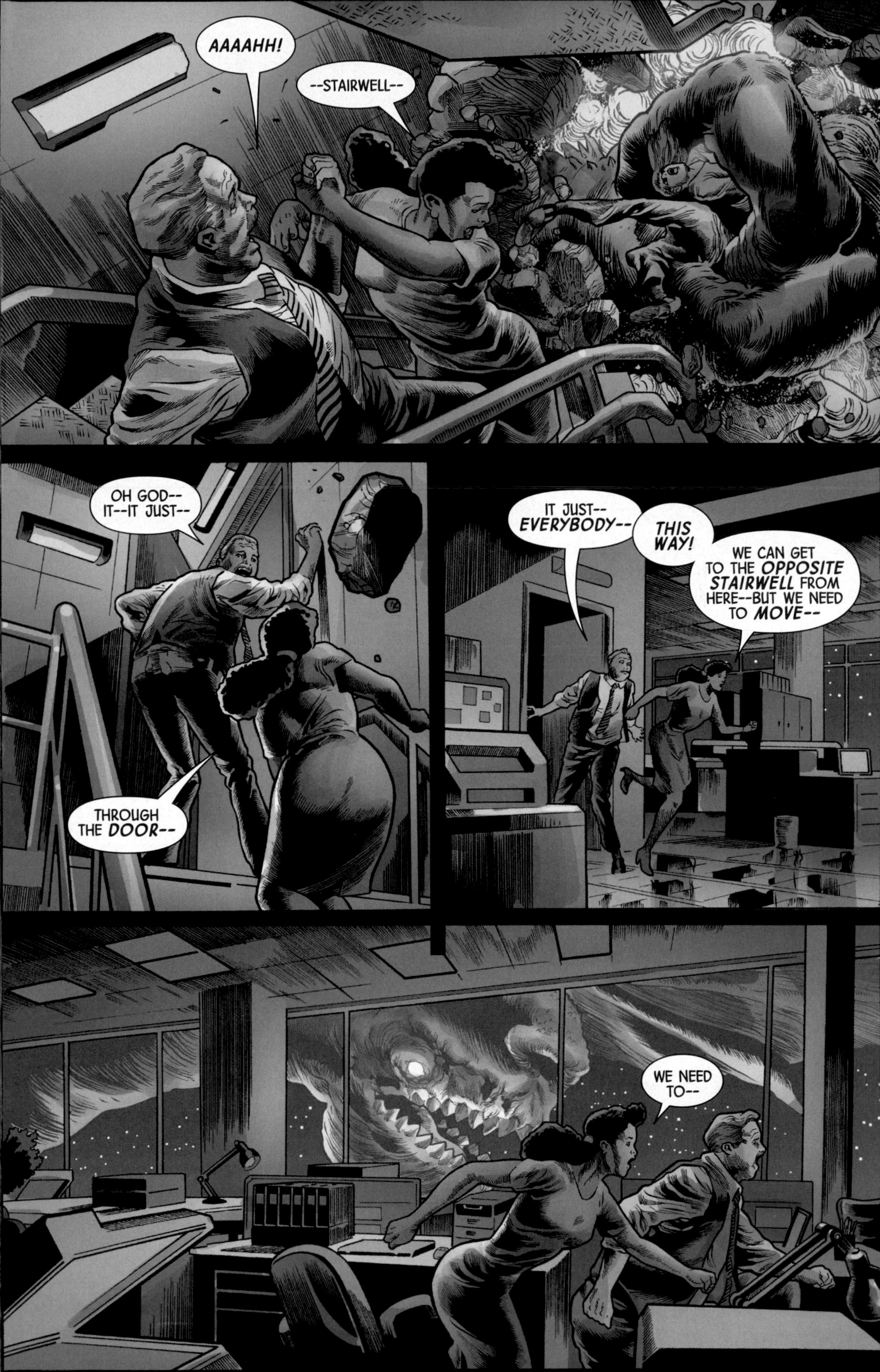
AAAAHH!
--STAIRWELL--
OH GOD-- IT--IT JUST--
THROUGH THE DOOR--
IT JUST-- EVERYBODY--
THIS WAY!
WE CAN GET TO THE OPPOSITE STAIRWELL FROM HERE--BUT WE NEED TO MOVE--
WE NEED TO--

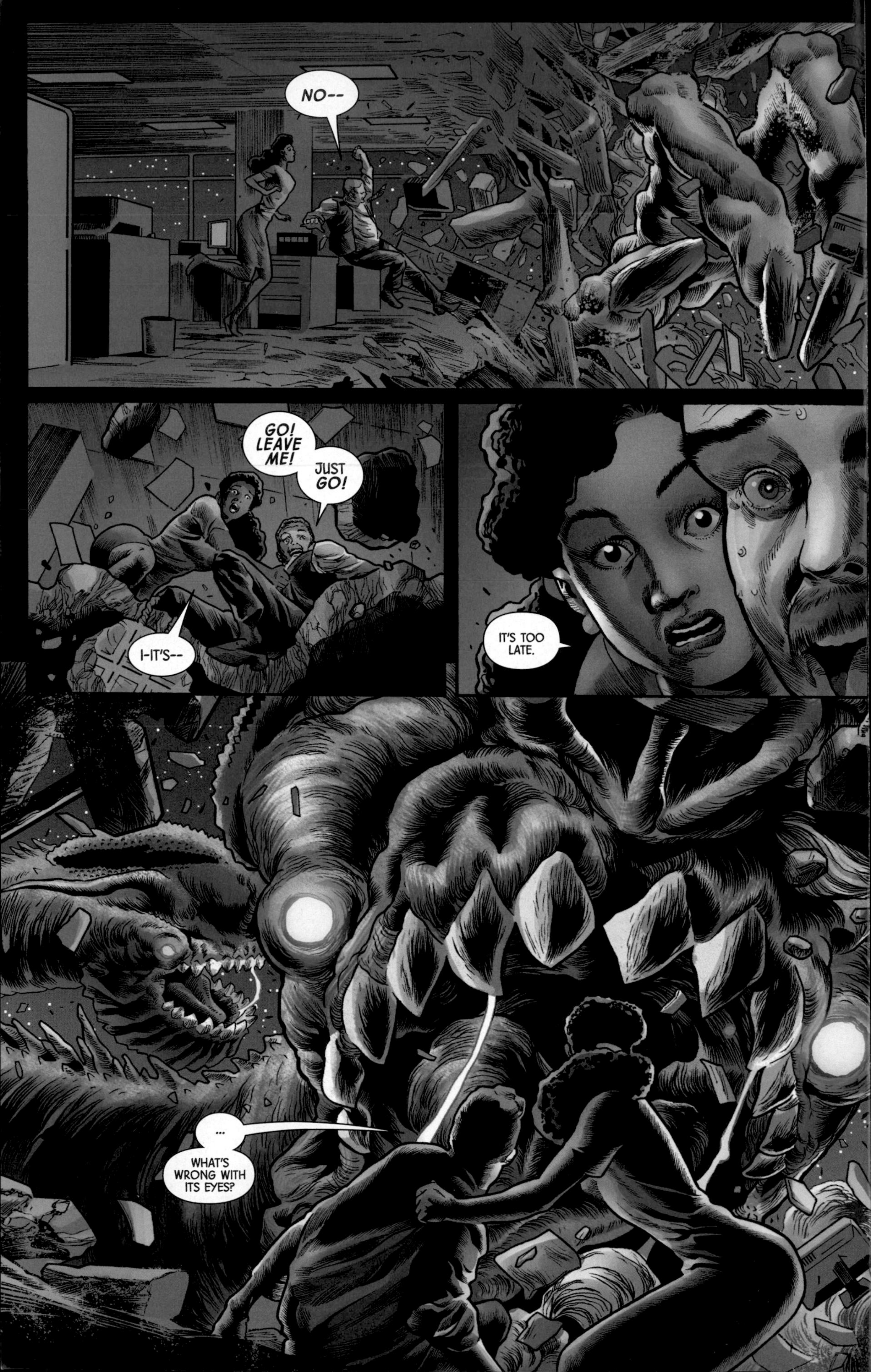
NO--
GO! LEAVE ME!
JUST GO!
I-IT'S--
IT'S TOO LATE.
...
WHAT'S WRONG WITH ITS EYES?

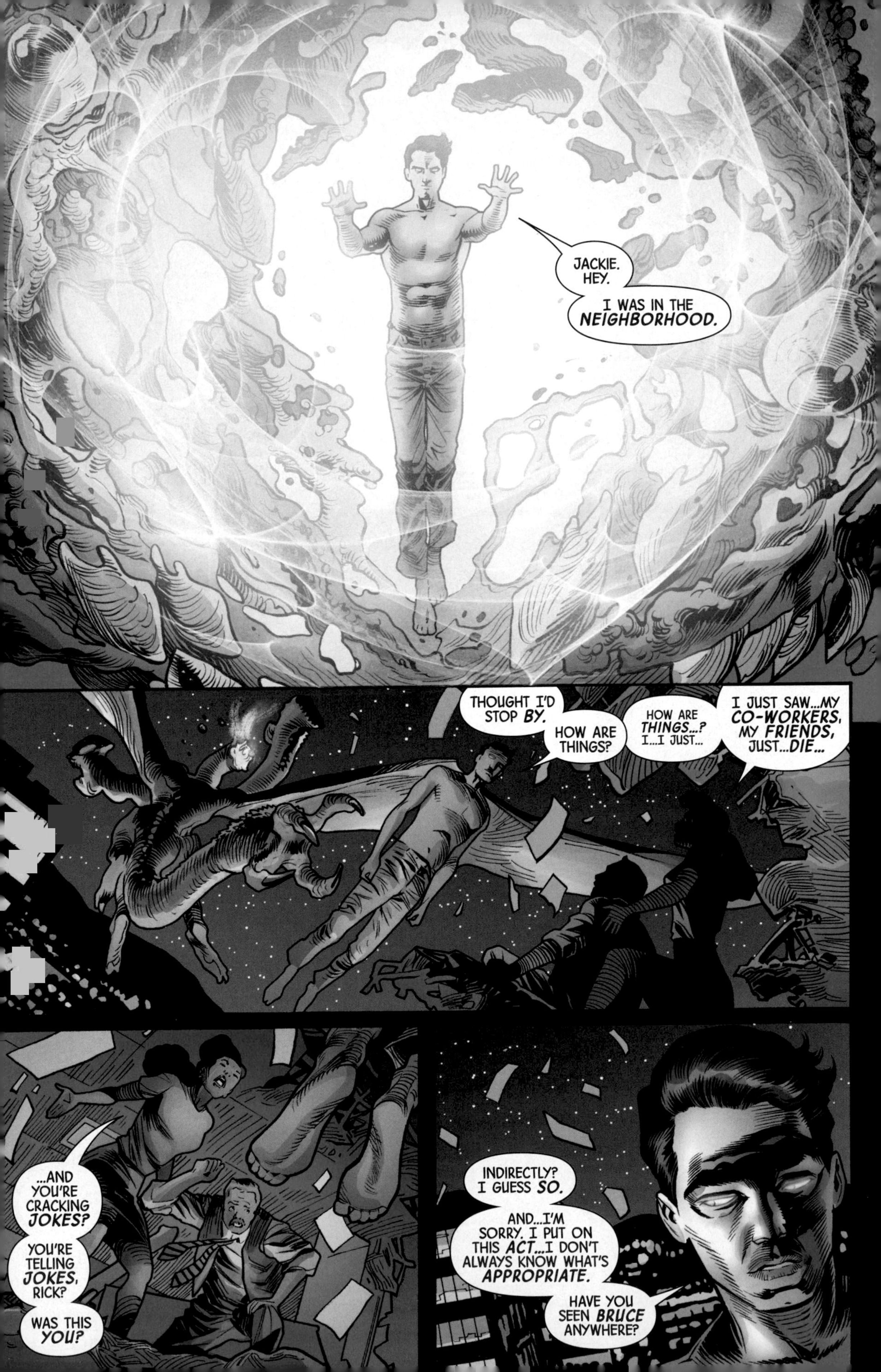
JACKIE. HEY.
I WAS IN THE NEIGHBORHOOD.
THOUGHT I'D STOP BY.
HOW ARE THINGS?
HOW ARE THINGS...? I...I JUST...
I JUST SAW...MY CO-WORKERS, MY FRIENDS, JUST...DIE...
...AND YOU'RE CRACKING JOKES?
YOU'RE TELLING JOKES, RICK?
WAS THIS YOU?
INDIRECTLY? I GUESS SO.
AND...I'M SORRY. I PUT ON THIS ACT...I DON'T ALWAYS KNOW WHAT'S APPROPRIATE.
HAVE YOU SEEN BRUCE ANYWHERE?

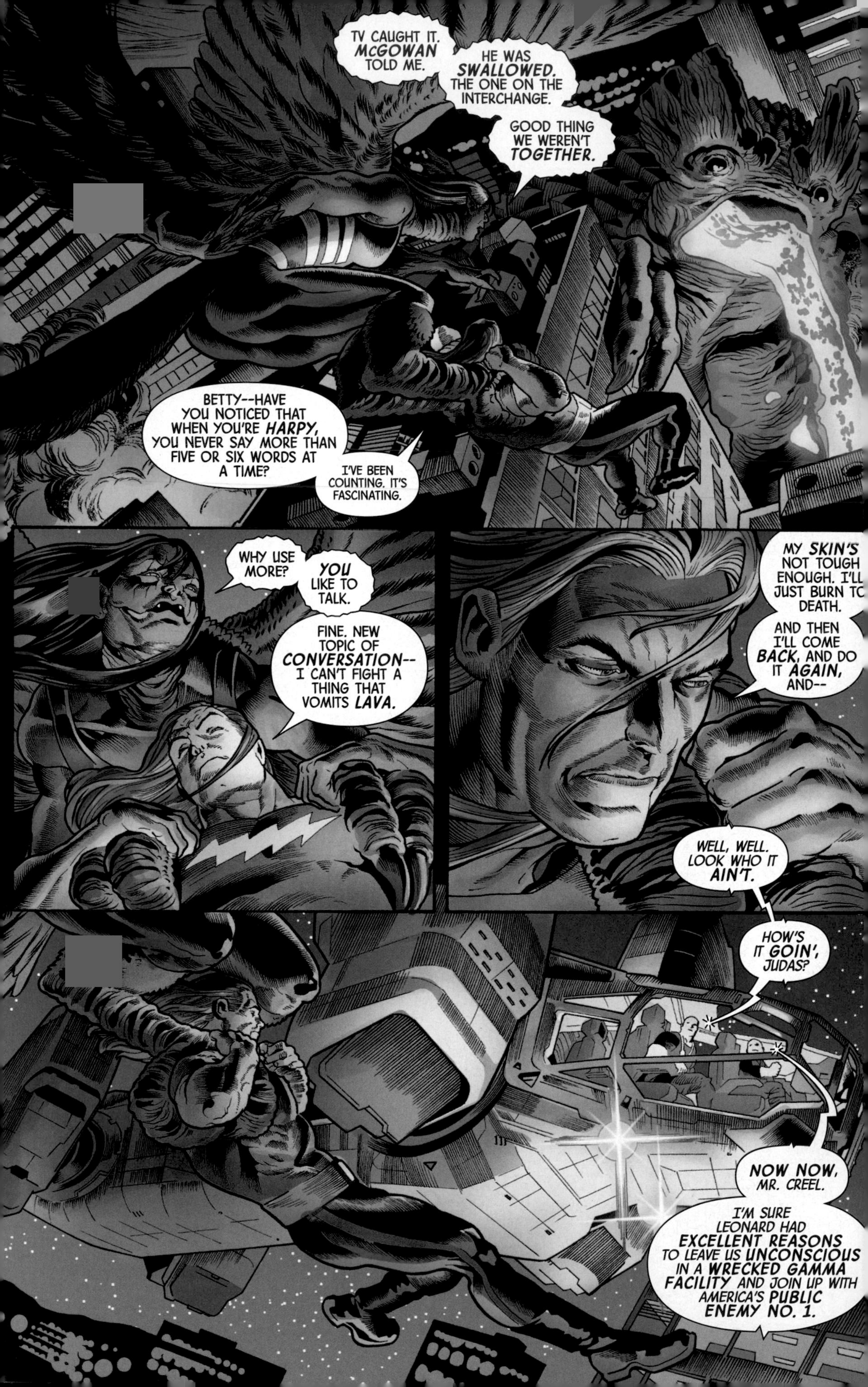
TV CAUGHT IT. McGOWAN TOLD ME.
HE WAS SWALLOWED. THE ONE ON THE INTERCHANGE.
GOOD THING WE WEREN'T TOGETHER.
BETTY--HAVE YOU NOTICED THAT WHEN YOU'RE HARPY, YOU NEVER SAY MORE THAN FIVE OR SIX WORDS AT A TIME?
I'VE BEEN COUNTING. IT'S FASCINATING.
WHY USE MORE?
YOU LIKE TO TALK.
FINE. NEW TOPIC OF CONVERSATION-- I CAN'T FIGHT A THING THAT VOMITS LAVA.
MY SKIN'S NOT TOUGH ENOUGH. I'LL JUST BURN TO DEATH.
AND THEN I'LL COME BACK, AND DO IT AGAIN, AND--
WELL, WELL. LOOK WHO IT AIN'T.
HOW'S IT GOIN', JUDAS?
NOW NOW, MR. CREEL.
I'M SURE LEONARD HAD EXCELLENT REASONS TO LEAVE US UNCONSCIOUS IN A WRECKED GAMMA FACILITY AND JOIN UP WITH AMERICA'S PUBLIC ENEMY NO. 1.

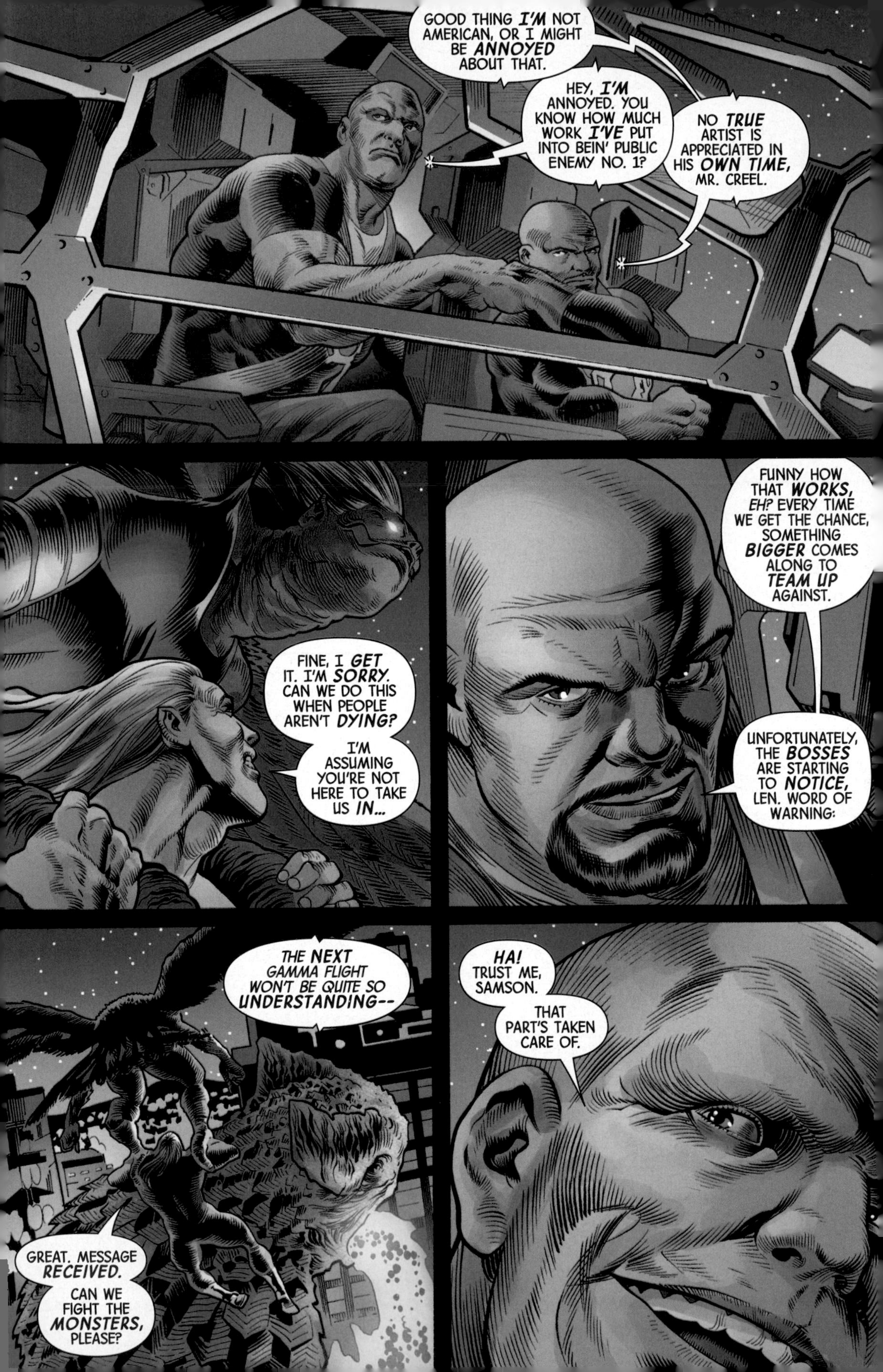
GOOD THING I'M NOT AMERICAN, OR I MIGHT BE ANNOYED ABOUT THAT.
HEY, I'M ANNOYED. YOU KNOW HOW MUCH WORK I'VE PUT INTO BEIN' PUBLIC ENEMY NO. 1?
NO TRUE ARTIST IS APPRECIATED IN HIS OWN TIME, MR. CREEL.
FINE, I GET IT. I'M SORRY. CAN WE DO THIS WHEN PEOPLE AREN'T DYING?
I'M ASSUMING YOU'RE NOT HERE TO TAKE US IN...
FUNNY HOW THAT WORKS, EH? EVERY TIME WE GET THE CHANCE, SOMETHING BIGGER COMES ALONG TO TEAM UP AGAINST.
UNFORTUNATELY, THE BOSSES ARE STARTING TO NOTICE, LEN. WORD OF WARNING:
THE NEXT GAMMA FLIGHT WON'T BE QUITE SO UNDERSTANDING--
GREAT. MESSAGE RECEIVED.
CAN WE FIGHT THE MONSTERS, PLEASE?
HA! TRUST ME, SAMSON.
THAT PART'S TAKEN CARE OF.

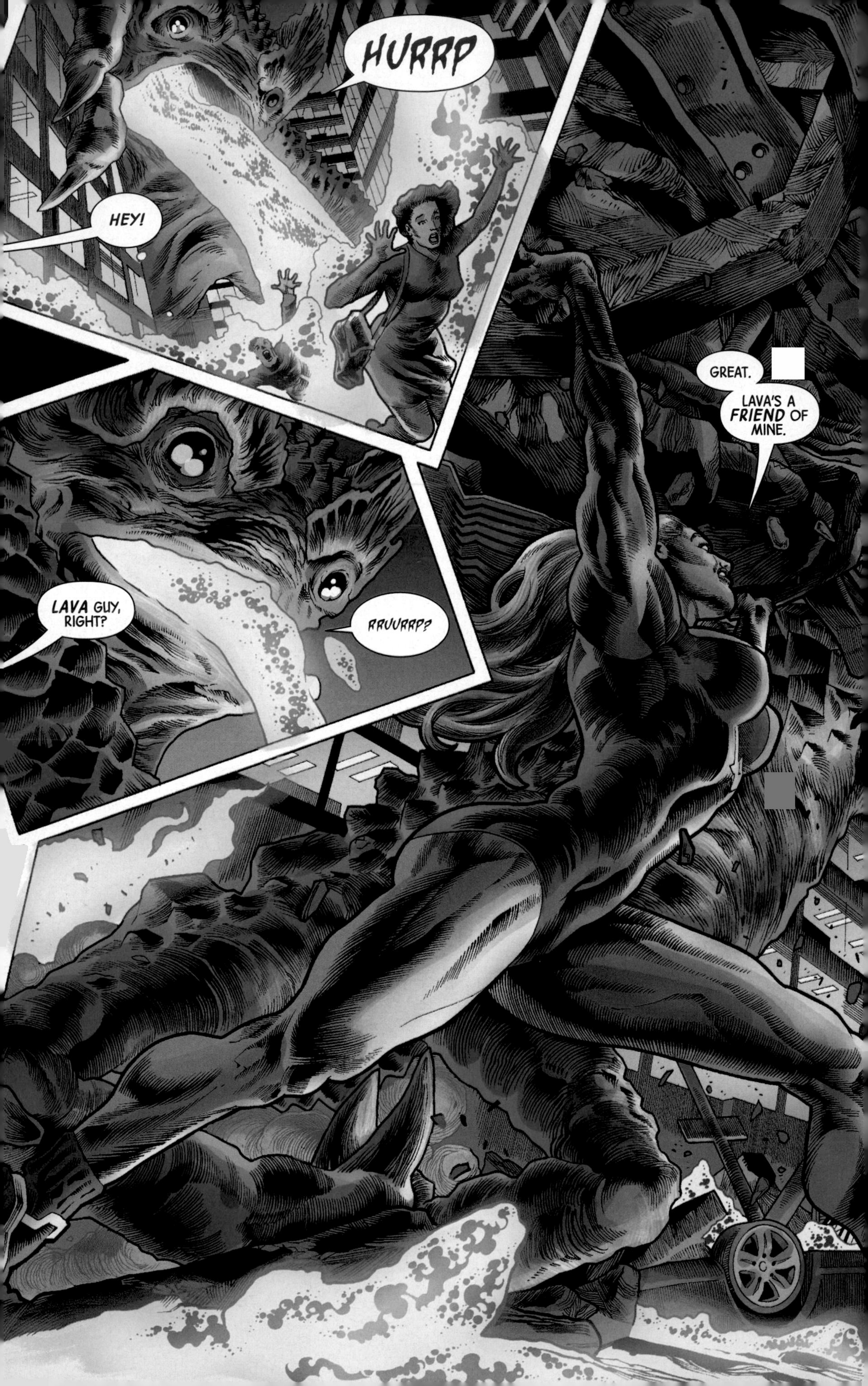
HURRP
HEY!
LAVA GUY, RIGHT?
RRUURRP?
GREAT.
LAVA'S A FRIEND OF MINE.

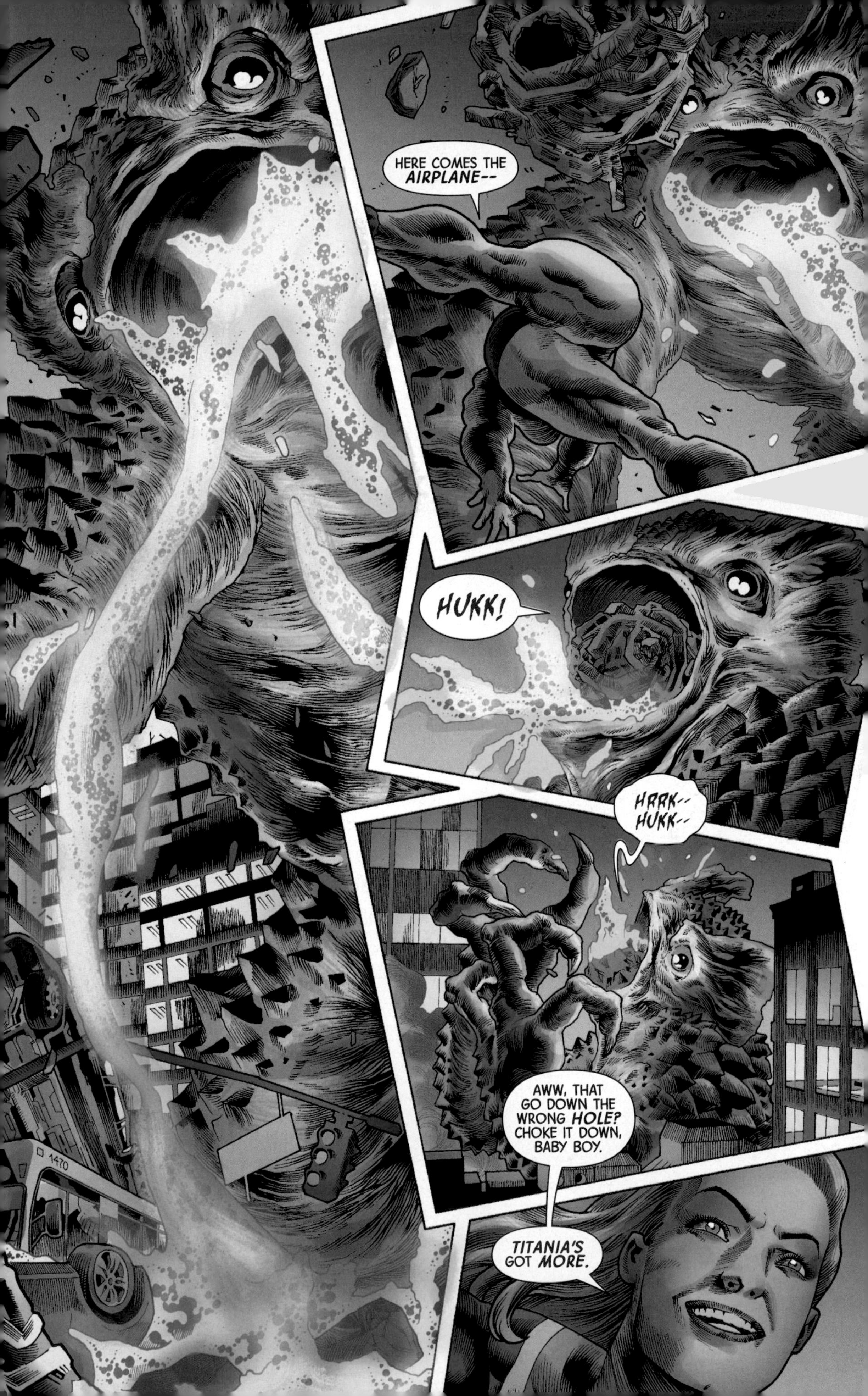
HERE COMES THE AIRPLANE--
HUKK!
HRRK-- HUKK--
AWW, THAT GO DOWN THE WRONG HOLE? CHOKE IT DOWN, BABY BOY.
TITANIA'S GOT MORE.

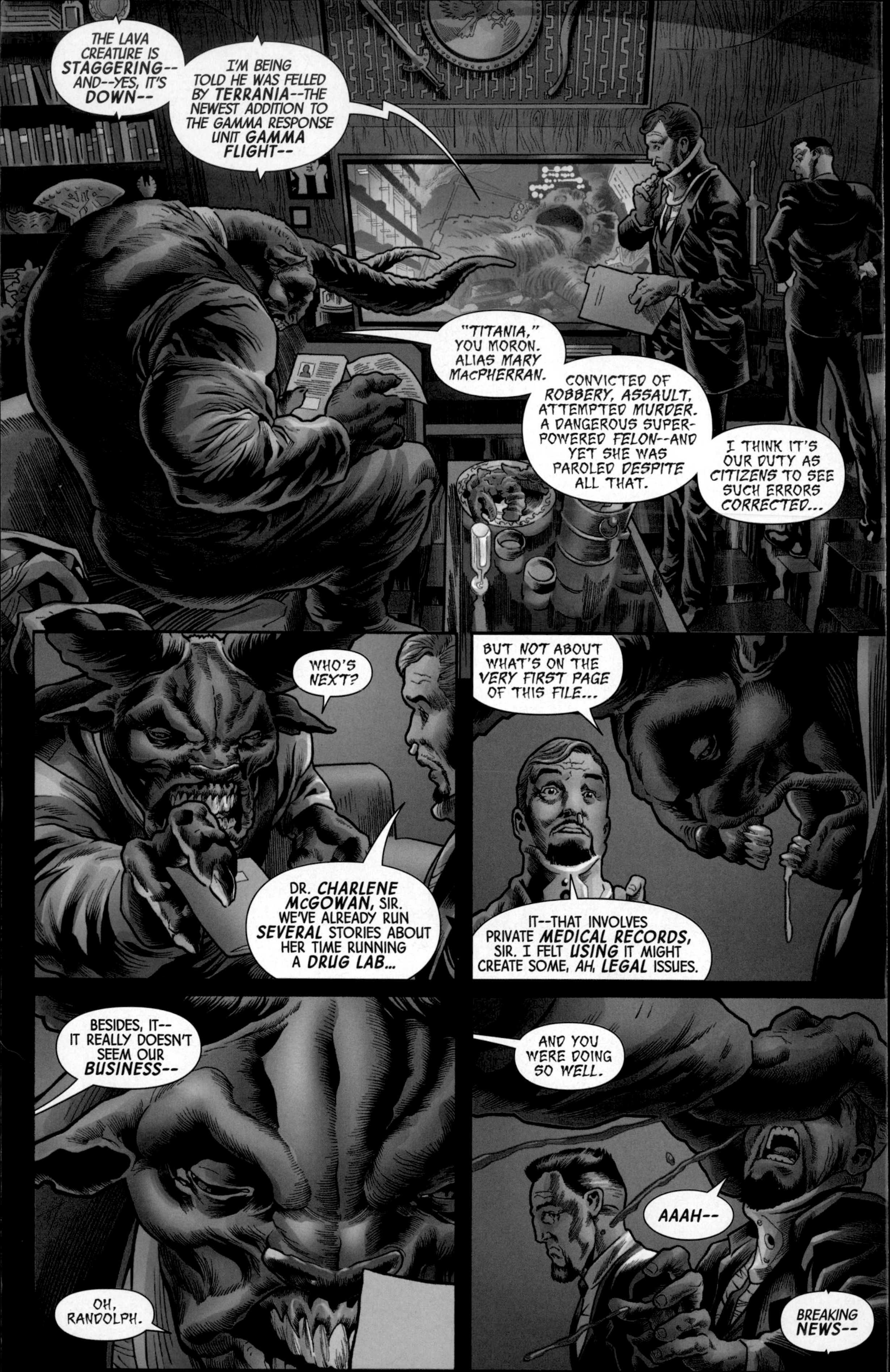
THE LAVA CREATURE IS STAGGERING-- AND--YES, IT'S DOWN--
I'M BEING TOLD HE WAS FELLED BY TERRANIA--THE NEWEST ADDITION TO THE GAMMA RESPONSE UNIT GAMMA FLIGHT--
"TITANIA," YOU MORON. ALIAS MARY MACPHERRAN.
CONVICTED OF ROBBERY, ASSAULT, ATTEMPTED MURDER. A DANGEROUS SUPER-POWERED FELON--AND YET SHE WAS PAROLED DESPITE ALL THAT.
I THINK IT'S OUR DUTY AS CITIZENS TO SEE SUCH ERRORS CORRECTED...
WHO'S NEXT?
DR. CHARLENE McGOWAN, SIR. WE'VE ALREADY RUN SEVERAL STORIES ABOUT HER TIME RUNNING A DRUG LAB...
BUT NOT ABOUT WHAT'S ON THE VERY FIRST PAGE OF THIS FILE...
IT--THAT INVOLVES PRIVATE MEDICAL RECORDS, SIR. I FELT USING IT MIGHT CREATE SOME, AH, LEGAL ISSUES.
BESIDES, IT-- IT REALLY DOESN'T SEEM OUR BUSINESS--
OH, RANDOLPH.
AND YOU WERE DOING SO WELL.
AAAH--
BREAKING NEWS--

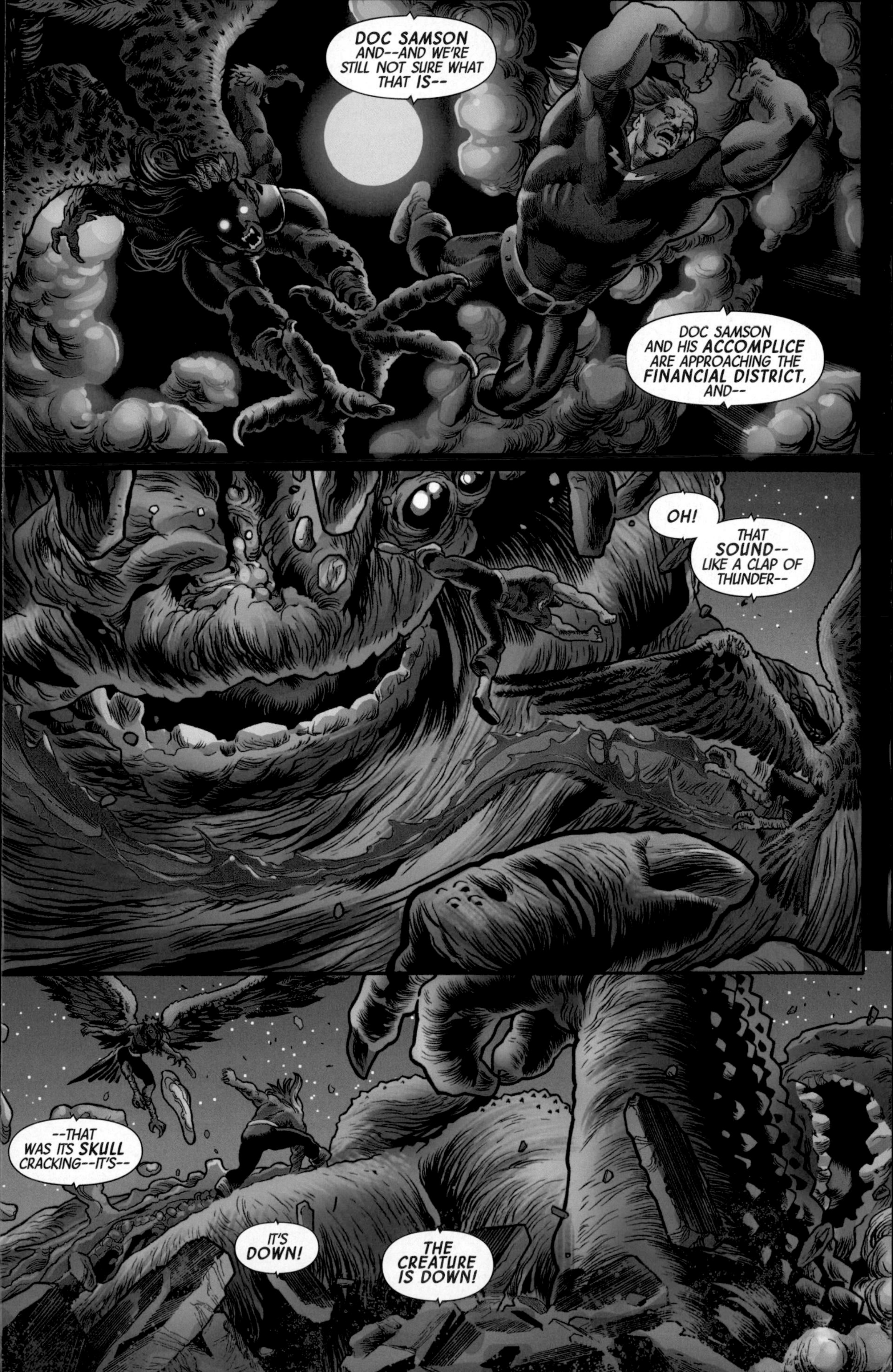
DOC SAMSON AND--AND WE'RE STILL NOT SURE WHAT THAT IS--
DOC SAMSON AND HIS ACCOMPLICE ARE APPROACHING THE FINANCIAL DISTRICT, AND--
OH!
THAT SOUND-- LIKE A CLAP OF THUNDER--
--THAT WAS ITS SKULL CRACKING--IT'S--
IT'S DOWN!
THE CREATURE IS DOWN!

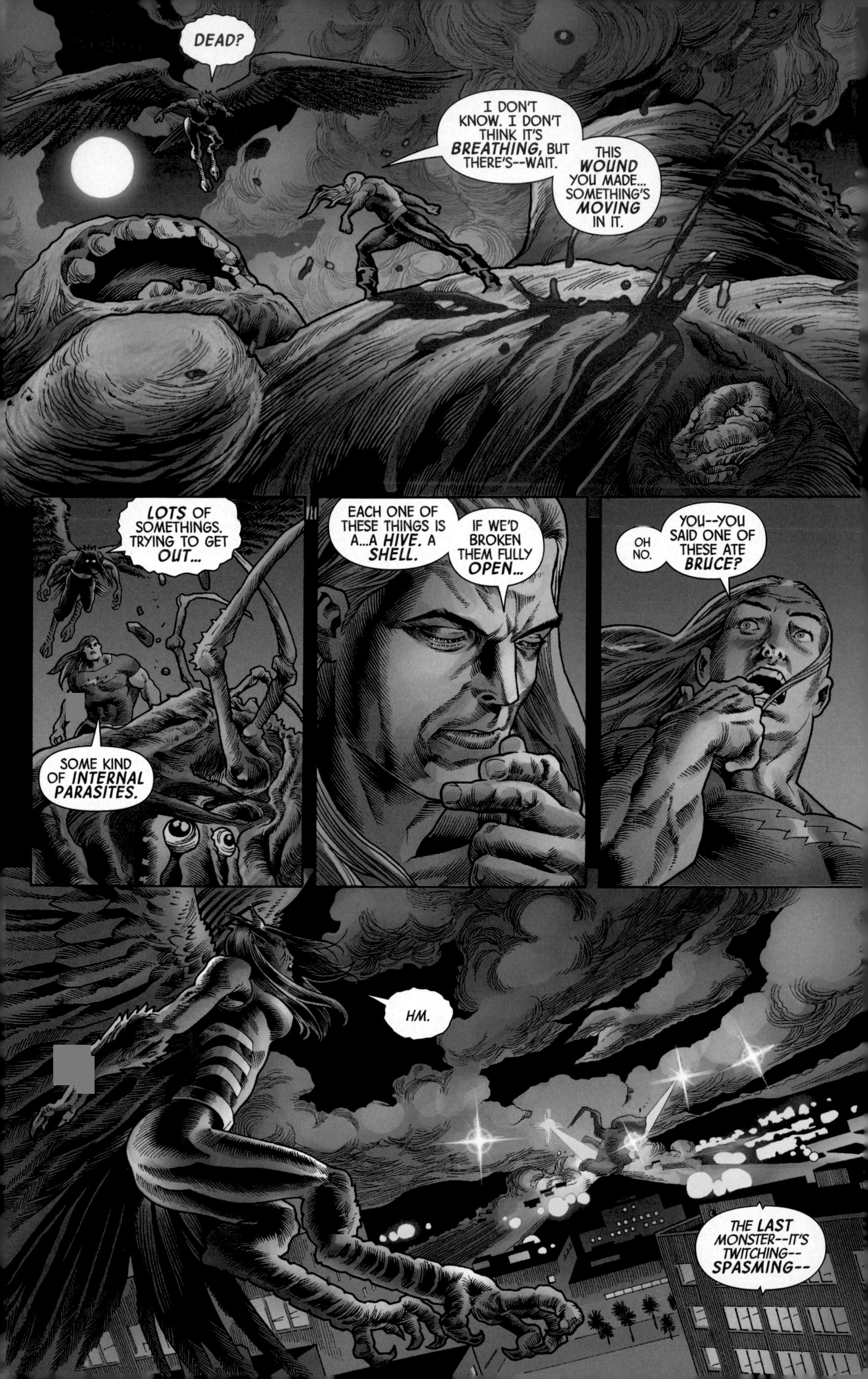
DEAD?
I DON'T KNOW. I DON'T THINK IT'S BREATHING, BUT THERE'S--WAIT.
THIS WOUND YOU MADE... SOMETHING'S MOVING IN IT.
LOTS OF SOMETHINGS. TRYING TO GET OUT...
SOME KIND OF INTERNAL PARASITES.
EACH ONE OF THESE THINGS IS A...A HIVE. A SHELL.
IF WE'D BROKEN THEM FULLY OPEN...
OH NO.
YOU--YOU SAID ONE OF THESE ATE BRUCE?
HM.
THE LAST MONSTER--IT'S TWITCHING--SPASMING--

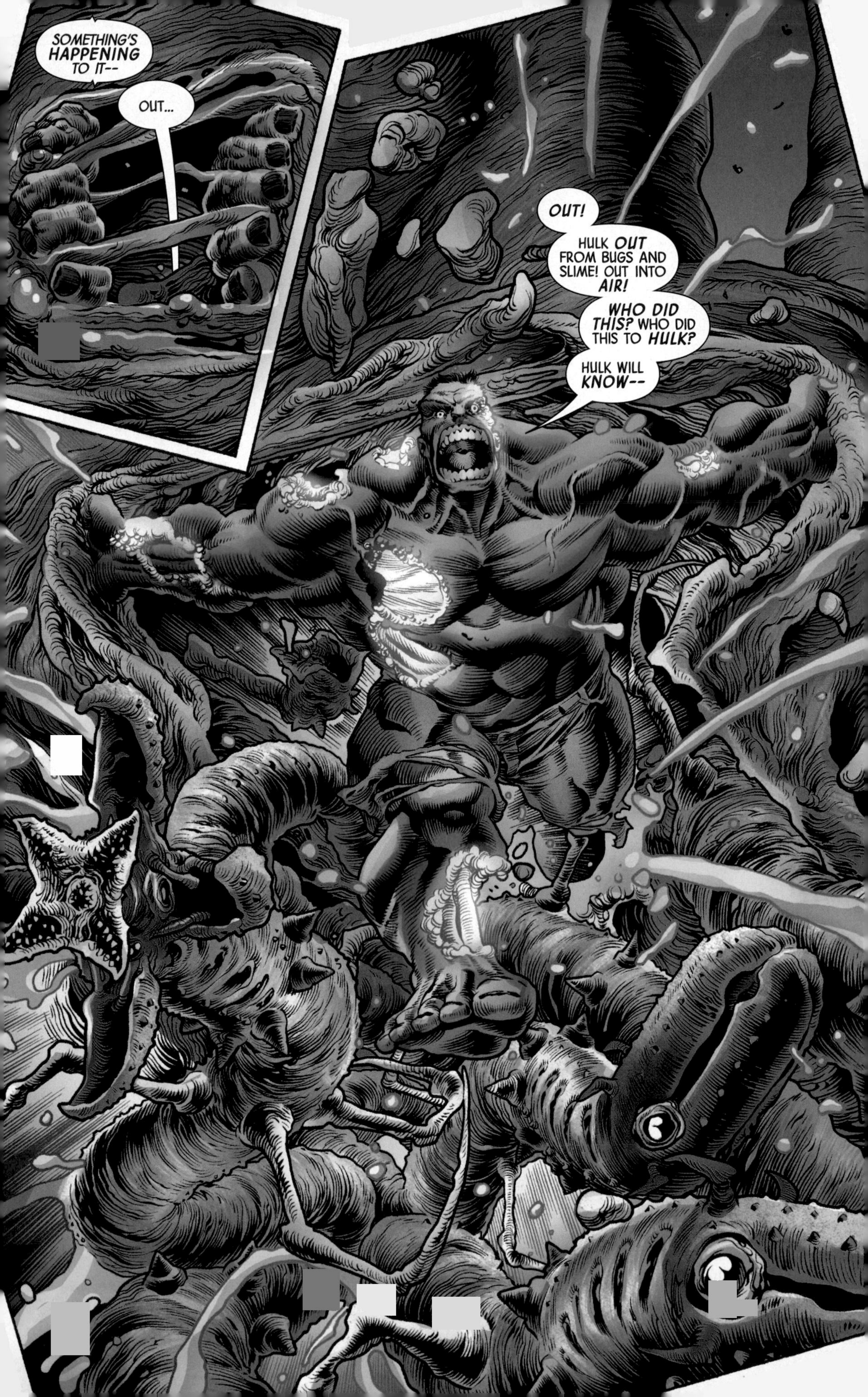
SOMETHING'S HAPPENING TO IT--
OUT...
OUT!
HULK OUT FROM BUGS AND SLIME! OUT INTO AIR!
WHO DID THIS? WHO DID THIS TO HULK?
HULK WILL KNOW--

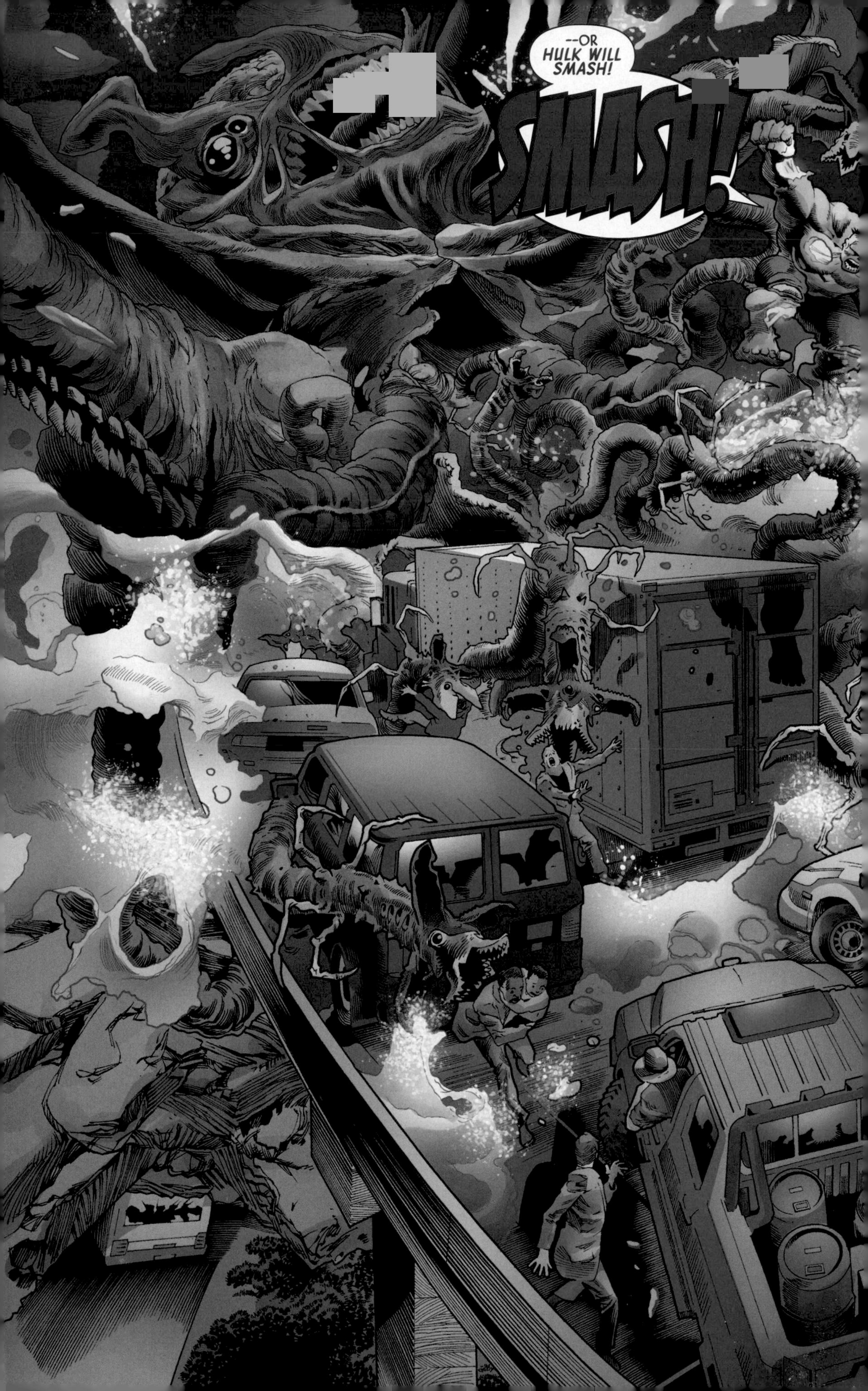
--OR HULK WILL SMASH!
SMASH!

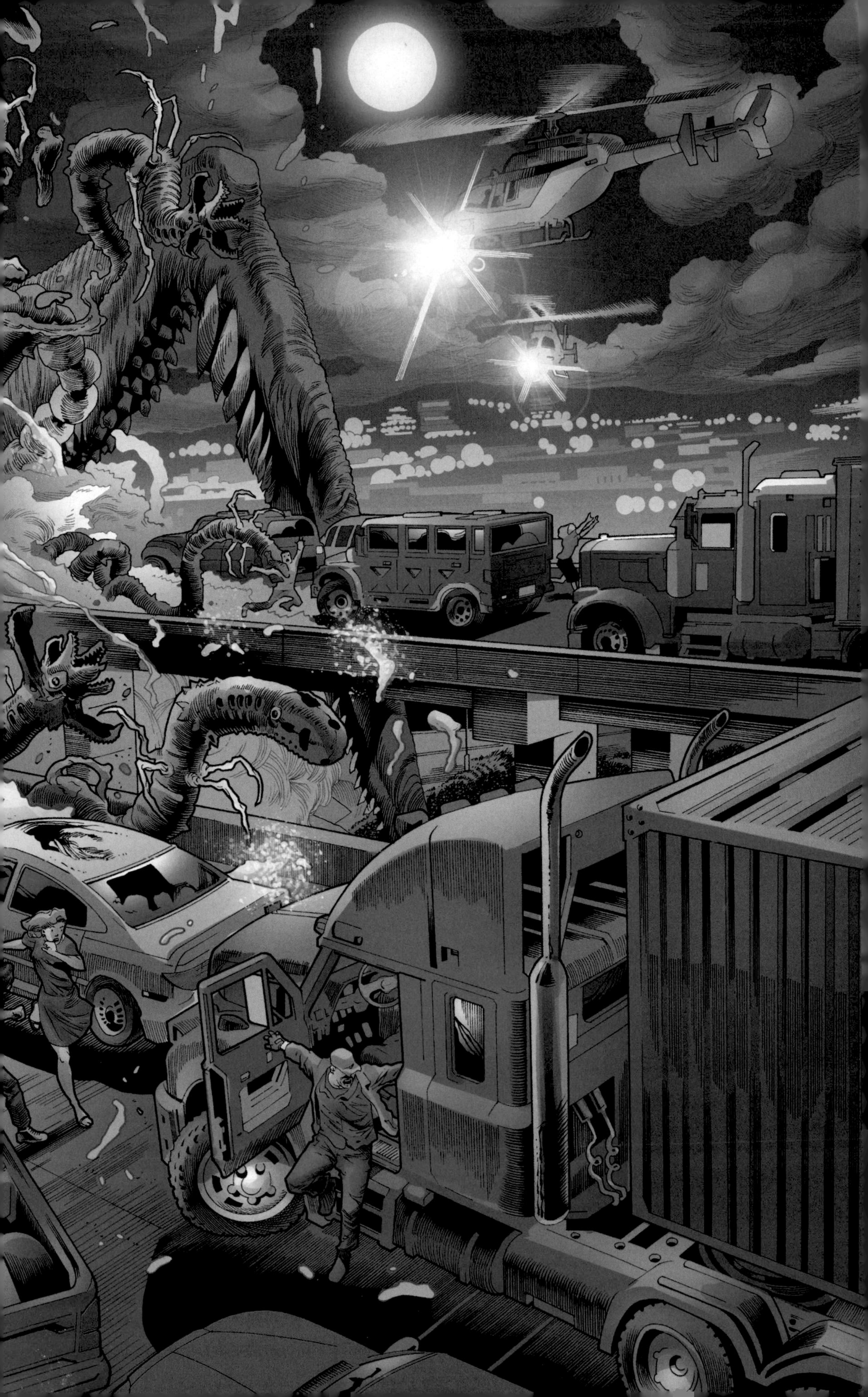

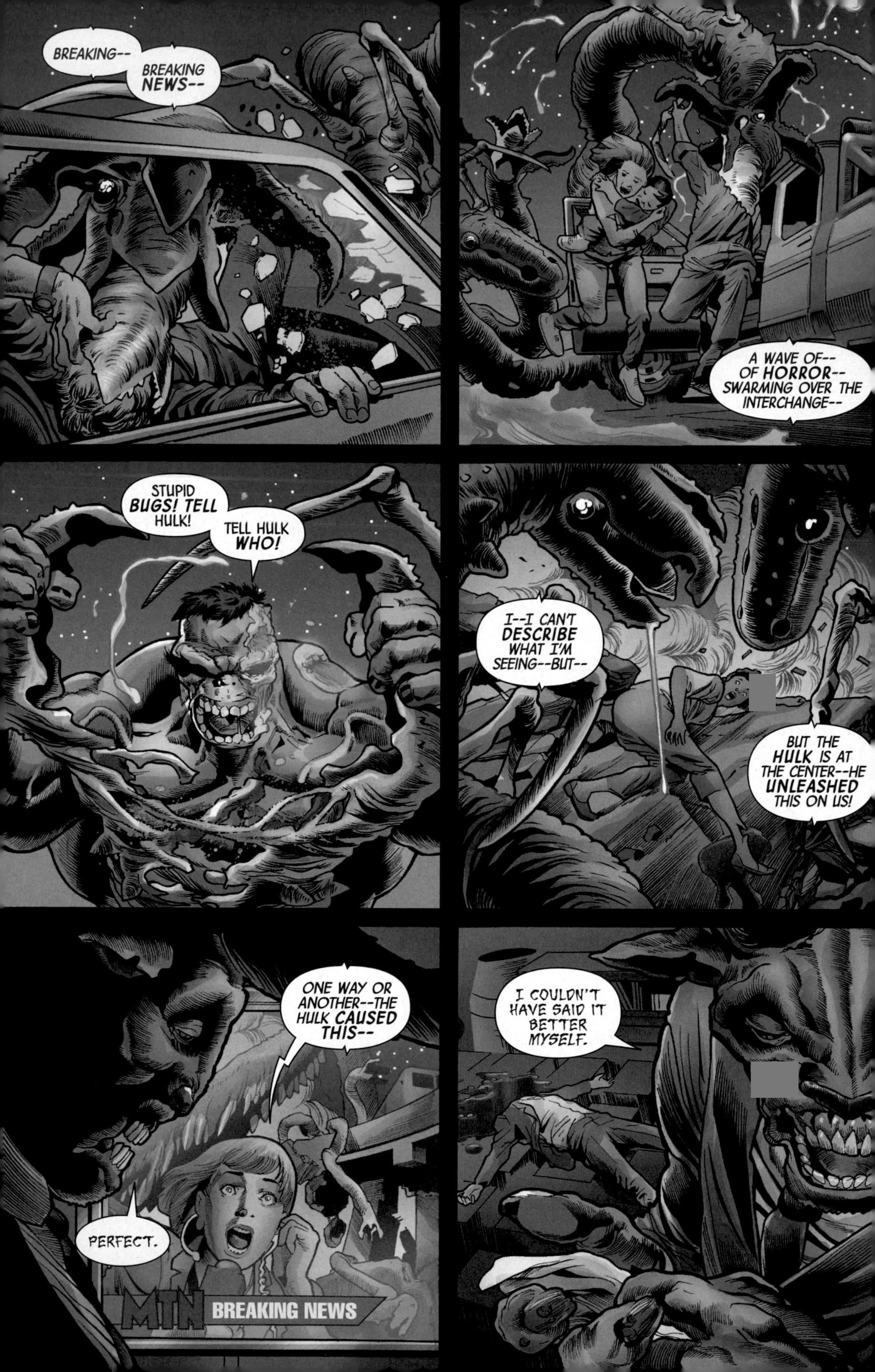
BREAKING--
BREAKING NEWS--
A WAVE OF-- OF HORROR-- SWARMING OVER THE INTERCHANGE--
STUPID BUGS! TELL HULK!
TELL HULK WHO!
I--I CAN'T DESCRIBE WHAT I'M SEEING--BUT--
BUT THE HULK IS AT THE CENTER--HE UNLEASHED THIS ON US!
ONE WAY OR ANOTHER--THE HULK CAUSED THIS--
PERFECT.
MTN BREAKING NEWS
I COULDN'T HAVE SAID IT BETTER MYSELF.

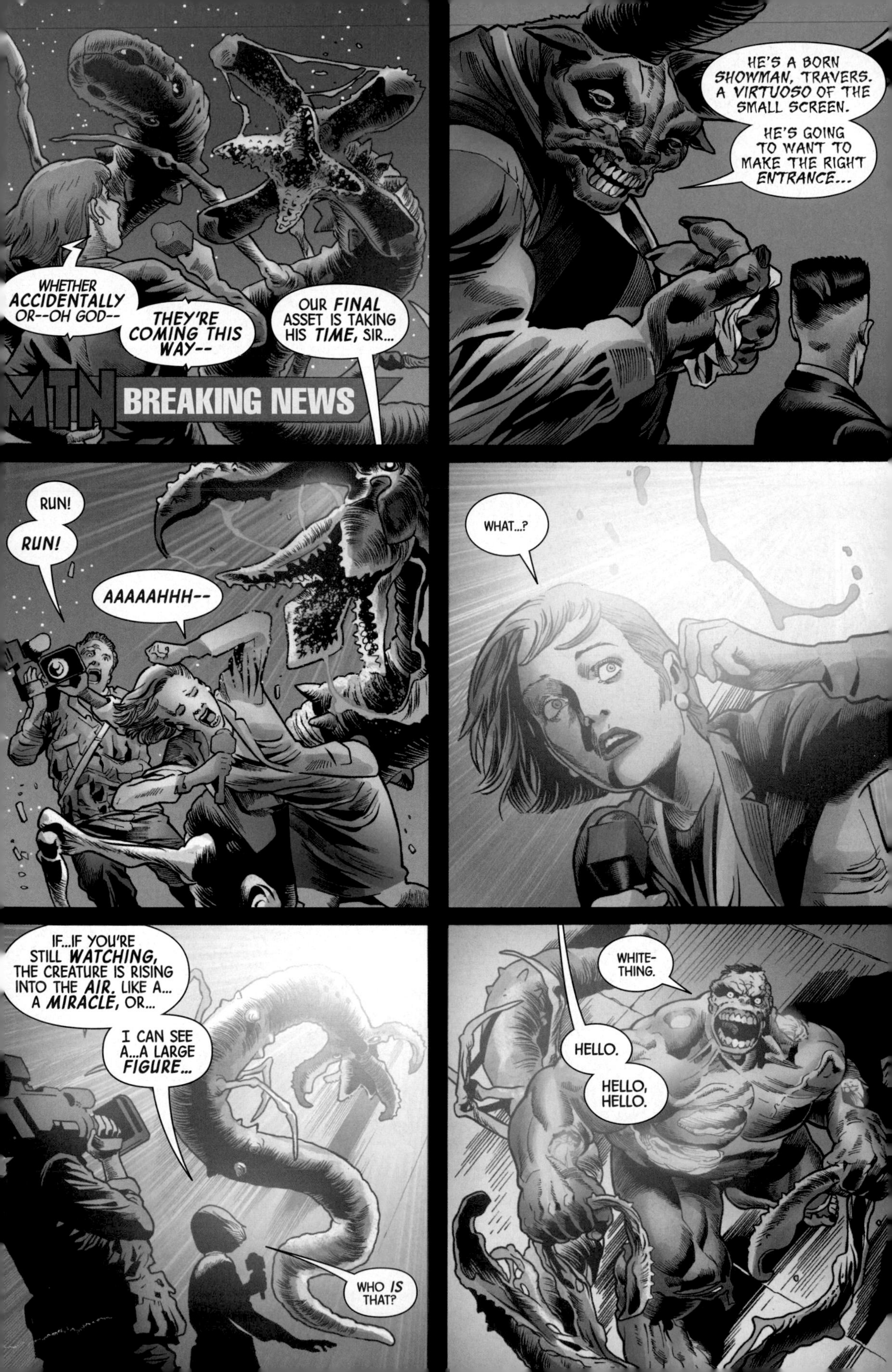
WHETHER ACCIDENTALLY OR--OH GOD--
THEY'RE COMING THIS WAY--
OUR FINAL ASSET IS TAKING HIS TIME, SIR...
MTN BREAKING NEWS
HE'S A BORN SHOWMAN, TRAVERS. A VIRTUOSO OF THE SMALL SCREEN.
HE'S GOING TO WANT TO MAKE THE RIGHT ENTRANCE...
RUN!
RUN!
AAAAAHHH--
WHAT...?
IF...IF YOU'RE STILL WATCHING, THE CREATURE IS RISING INTO THE AIR. LIKE A... A MIRACLE, OR...
I CAN SEE A...A LARGE FIGURE...
WHO IS THAT?
WHITE-THING.
HELLO.
HELLO, HELLO.

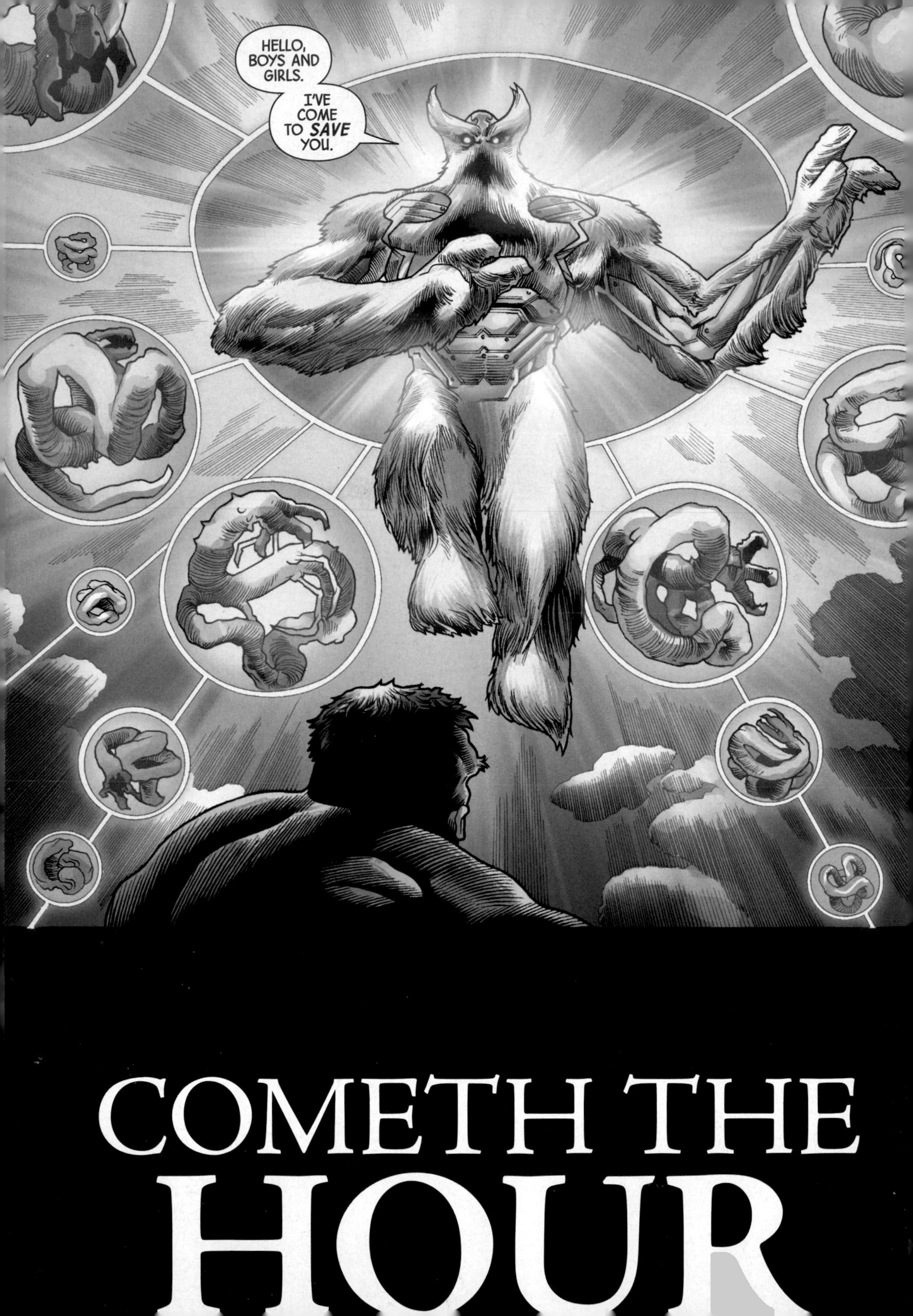
HELLO, BOYS AND GIRLS.
I'VE COME TO SAVE YOU.

COMETH THE HOUR